Praise for
Happy Campers

"HAPPY CAMPERS shines a light on nine positive practices used in quality summer camps and offers readers dozens (and dozens!) of ways to use these strategies to help kids and families thrive year-round...I highly recommend it for *anyone* living or working with young people!"
—Signe Whitson, author and international educator

"Concrete simple strategies to help kids become well-adjusted adults who continue strong relationships with their parents."
—Catherine Pearlman, PhD, LCSW, and author of *Ignore It!:
How Selectively Looking the Other Way Can Decrease Behavioral
Problems and Increase Parenting Satisfaction*

"I've been a parenting and happiness expert for more than fifteen years, and I can honestly say that HAPPY CAMPERS is one of the best distillations and applications of research-backed practices for parenting happy, self-motivated, kind, and resilient kids I've seen yet."
—Christine Carter, PhD, author of *Raising Happiness*
and *The Sweet Spot*

"[HAPPY CAMPERS] will help parents understand that the magic of the immense growth many kids experience at camp is not simply magic but a set of practices and approaches explained in clear and pragmatic frameworks throughout this book."
—Devorah Heitner, author of *Screenwise: Helping
Kids Thrive and Survive in Their Digital World*

"Monke...translates the simple joys of childhood into great parenting and happy families. A great book for remembering the fun of being a kid—and carrying that fun forward into your family life!"
—Karen Lock Kolp, MEd, child development expert, parent
coach, and podcaster at weturnedoutokay.com

"You know you want your kids to be resilient problem-solvers, kind and thoughtful, willing to try new things, and able to make the most of opportunities. But how do you help them get there? Audrey Monke's HAPPY CAMPERS offers practical strategies parents can start putting into effect today that will help kids learn to thrive tomorrow and beyond."   —K. J. Dell'Antonia, author of *How to Be a Happier Parent*

"I've long wished life could be like summer camp. In this readable and practical book, Audrey Monke shows how to bring a little bit of that camp magic home to your family."

—Laura Vanderkam, author of *Off the Clock* and *Juliet's School of Possibilities*

"This book is such a compelling invitation to be more intentional, and in such a fun way, to support the friendships and self-esteem of our kids when they need it most."

—Shasta Nelson, author of *Frientimacy: How to Deepen Friendships for Lifelong Health and Happiness*

"Inspiring and irresistibly practical! HAPPY CAMPERS is a post-millennial parenting treasure—brimming with dozens of essential, achievable, and transformative parenting strategies…that will guide your family to great joy and fun together."

—Tom Rosenberg, president and CEO of the American Camp Association

"A remarkably powerful parenting guide…Audrey has worked with thousands of kids and their parents. She has seen what produces capable and content kids—and what produces the opposite. In HAPPY CAMPERS, she shares a wealth of knowledge and truly practical advice. The unexpected benefit is that her advice actually makes being a parent more enjoyable as well as more effective!"

—Steve Baskin, owner/director of Camp Champions, *Psychology Today* writer, and TEDx speaker

"Children are transformed by camp, and parents can learn so much from Audrey's thoughtful counsel on how to translate camp to home—how to encourage positive transformation all year-round. HAPPY CAMPERS is a must read."   —Harriet Lowe, editor in chief of *Camping Magazine*

Happy Campers

9 Summer Camp Secrets
for Raising Kids Who
Become Thriving Adults

Audrey Monke

Foreword by Tina Payne Bryson, PhD

CENTER
STREET

New York   Nashville

Copyright © 2019 by Audrey Monke
Foreword copyright © 2019 by Tina Payne Bryson

Cover design by Edward Crawford
Cover illustration by Getty Images
Cover copyright © 2019 by Hachette Book Group, Inc.

Center Street
Hachette Book Group
1290 Avenue of the Americas, New York, NY 10104
centerstreet.com
twitter.com/centerstreet

First edition: May 2019

Center Street is a division of Hachette Book Group, Inc. The Center Street name and logo are trademarks of Hachette Book Group, Inc.

The publisher is not responsible for websites (or their content) that are not owned by the publisher.

The Hachette Speakers Bureau provides a wide range of authors for speaking events. To find out more, go to www.HachetteSpeakersBureau.com or call (866) 376-6591.

Library of Congress Cataloging-in-Publication Data
Names: Monke, Audrey, author.
Title: Happy Campers : 9 Summer Camp Secrets for Raising Kids Who Become Thriving Adults / Audrey Monke ; Foreword by Tina Payne Bryson, PhD.
Description: First edition. | New York : Center Street, [2019] | Includes bibliographical references.
Identifiers: LCCN 2018053043| ISBN 9781546081791 (hardcover) | ISBN 9781546081784 (ebook)
Subjects: LCSH: Camps—Psychological aspects. | Child rearing. | Child psychology. | Parent and child.
Classification: LCC GV192 .M66 2019 | DDC 796.54/2—dc23
LC record available at https://lccn.loc.gov/2018053043

ISBN: 978-1-5460-8179-1 (hardcover), 978-1-5460-8178-4 (ebook)

Printed in the United States of America

LSC-C

10 9 8 7 6 5 4 3 2 1

For Gretchen, Meredith, Charlotte, John, and Owen,
my favorite happy campers.

Contents

Foreword

I never expected that I'd become such a big fan of the camping experience. I didn't grow up going to camp, and I didn't know kids who went. I'm a mom to three boys, and I didn't intend to let any of them be away from me for any extended period of time during their childhood. It took some research, a big leap of faith, and some self-soothing skills before I could even seriously consider it. It helped, too, to have several conversations with a trusted, respected, dear friend who had grown up going to camp in the north woods of Minnesota each summer, and who eventually went on to be a counselor and even a camp director. As he talked about how his summers at camp had impacted who he became as a man and father, my resistance shifted to openness. The final nudge I needed to move from openness to investment came from this same friend, as he revealed that when he faces setbacks, heartbreak, or other adversity in his life, he has a deep knowing that he can handle anything because of the strength he *grew* by weathering the challenges of his wilderness trips at camp.

So I let my boys go—initially for two weeks at a time. It felt excruciating that first summer. But each summer as they came home, I easily observed the rapid and dramatic benefits of camp in them, as they showed more independence, confidence, flexibility, resilience, character, grit, and responsibility. And even as part of me hated letting them go, it thrilled me to know that they were in nature, that they were playing, that they were away from screens, and that they were having the time of their lives, even though they occasionally felt homesick or faced some challenges. What's more, I came to see that it wasn't just these experiences or environment that made a difference, but it was also the relationships and connections that the staff made with my children by encouraging them, amplifying positive moments, supporting them as they struggled, and evoking the curiosity and courage that changed them.

Fairly quickly, then, I moved from being an anxious mom—my son's camp director that first summer can attest to that—to a cheerleader for the camping experience. I began to write and speak about the importance of camp, and I met more and more of the amazing camp directors all over the United States and the world.

One of those people was Audrey Monke, and when I met her, I knew she was someone special. It's a rare thing to find someone who is not only a ninja when it comes to successfully and positively working with kids through any kind of issue that comes up, but who also knows the science of child development and child-rearing, *and* who can be authentic and practical when advising parents. Audrey sees challenges with kids as welcome opportunities. She is gifted—grounded, creative, and informed—and she approaches these struggles as invitations to build skills so that kids come out stronger and more resilient on the other side. She helps her staff and parents find the caregiver's sweet spot—where kids are supported enough to tolerate the challenge in front of them, but still empowered to become competent, confident, and resilient problem-solvers who valuably contribute to the world.

In writing this book, Audrey offers powerful and practical advice, which she has gleaned from working with thousands of kids and by guiding numerous counselors in developing relationships with, and encouraging growth in, the children they serve.

The abilities kids need to be successful are often things that parents recognize automatically. But sometimes we need help to recognize what we're doing right and to see the impact of our investment. Audrey helps illuminate the building blocks of development that happen in our everyday interactions, and in the "Bringing Camp Home" section at the end of each chapter, she helps us become more intentional by giving us strategies to make our family time transformative, as development unfolds.

What Audrey is doing here is *so* important. As a child development specialist with expertise in mental health and interpersonal neurobiology, I've spent a lot of time considering how camp experiences influence brain development, particularly the middle prefrontal cortex (the MPFC, which is right behind the forehead and eye sockets and is the frontmost part of the frontal lobe). The MPFC gives us the ability to do all kinds of crucial things: regulate our body and emotions, have insight into ourselves and others, feel empathy, communicate in an attuned way, bounce back after failure, adapt to new situations, make thoughtful choices, and overcome fear. That's pretty much what's needed for a successful life with good emotional and mental health, meaningful relationships, and the conscientiousness to make things happen in the world. And the good news is that since it is the last part of the brain to finish development, it's the most open to the influence of experiences and relationships throughout childhood and adolescence and even young adulthood. So parenting and life experiences don't just influence kids' *minds*—or character, or help them feel more confident—they actually change the structure of their *brains*.

When I say that experience changes the brain, I mean the actual activation and wiring of the brain. Particularly when experiences are emotional, novel, and challenging, they literally alter the architecture of the brain. Like a muscle, when it's used, it grows and strengthens. So when kids have camp experiences that require them to overcome fear, be flexible, handle their emotions (especially away from their parents), be persistent to master something, build relationships, and so on, it builds this important part of the brain, the MPFC.

What's more, when the *structure* of the brain changes, so does the *function* of the brain. This means that camp is one place that can play a role in how our kids function in the world, and ultimately who they become as adults, even on a neuronal level.

The way I like to say it is that bunks are good for brains. Quality camps—those that are intentional about all facets of the camper experience and how they choose and train their counselors—inherently provide the kinds of experiences that activate and build this *character* part of the brain. That's why we can see significant changes in kids who have camp as part of their lives. When kids have experiences that challenge them emotionally, when they're given opportunities to make friends that are outside their typical circles, when they have to keep working at a skill to achieve mastery—these kinds of experiences change the connections in the brain regarding kids' capacity for persistence, how they see themselves, and how healthy they can be, both emotionally and relationally. This is the magic and the science of camp experiences.

Whether your kids go to camp or not, *Happy Campers* is a guidebook to bring some of that magic and science of camp home. As parents, the way we create family rituals and traditions and the way we create a rhythm of daily life for and with our children are experiences that impact how their brains get wired, what kinds of skills are built and become automatic, and ultimately who they become.

Audrey distills decades of wisdom that we can readily use to make changes in ourselves, in the way we interact, and in our home environments, so that we bring out the best in our kids and help them build skills at the same time. She humbly calls her strategies "positive psychological interventions for children," and they are that, but they are more. With each chapter focusing on a social or an emotional skill area, character trait, or parenting practice, her recommendations offer a path to cultivate the most important life skills kids need, like self-advocacy, resilience, optimism, problem-solving, endurance, kindness, social intelligence, empathy, and independence—all of which are essential for success, mental health, and a happy life.

Our need to be connected to each other has been wired into our brains since the earliest of days. Our brain and nervous systems are automatically, instinctually primed to value, seek, and find reward in our connections to others because, at the most primitive level, it increases our odds of survival. And even though there are so many distractions and obstacles to connection in our modern lives, it turns out that this primitive need is as essential as it ever was. In fact, across many decades of research from many fields, we see that it is the quality and degree of relationships we have that significantly impact our well-being, including our mental health, our physical health, and even our happiness. We also know from decades and decades of research that the quality of the relationships with our first loves, our parents or caregivers, is one of the most important influences on who we become and how we turn out. These relational experiences have a dramatic influence on how our brains get wired and what becomes automatic in how we function in the world and in our relationships.

Certainly, there are many factors outside of parents' influence. Genetics, environment, peers, life events, experiences, and many other variables impact development and how the brain wires as development unfolds. But the science is also very clear that parents matter. The quality of the relationships we have with our children—what we *do* and how we *are* with our children—matters very much. So when we devote ourselves to connecting in more effective, fun, and deeper ways with our children, we not only become the recipients of the tremendous joy of having strong relationships with our children, but we are investing in their development as well. This book helps us do just that.

Parents are now privy to many gems of wisdom from Audrey's many years of intentionally fostering the best outcomes for kids at camp. In a time when our lives are often structured in ways that hinder connection within our families, I'm thrilled that *Happy Campers*— full of practical and powerful tools that can be immediately put into practice—lights a path to help parents nurture a culture of connection in our homes so that we can all keep working together to help our children become their best selves.

Tina Payne Bryson, PhD, LCSW

Introduction

What Parents Can Learn from Summer Camp

My time at camp has changed me in ways I never could have expected. I have grown into a completely different and happier person. I have become so much more confident in myself and have learned to always be true to what I believe in. I have learned how to make genuine connections and have face-to-face conversations with people I have never met before. I'm so much more easygoing and positive because of my time at camp. Camp has taught me how to be the best version of myself every day.

—*Sydney*

As a mother of five and the longtime owner of Gold Arrow Camp in California's Sierra National Forest, I have spent the past three decades researching and implementing specific strategies to create a warm, supportive culture for children. My goal is for campers' lives to be enriched because of the positive relationships they form as well as the life skills and character traits they develop. While doing this important work at camp, my husband and I simultaneously created a nurturing, growth-focused family culture for our own kids. Many of the strategies I learned and implemented at camp were easily transferable to my own parenting.

I am passionate about learning what is required to help kids thrive and grow into flourishing adults, and I have been researching and learning about positive psychology for many years. My deep curiosity about how summer camp and family life can promote positive growth in children led me back to the classroom to complete a master's degree in psychology. My research focused on the impact of camp experiences on campers' well-being (the positive psychology term for *happiness*) and social skills.

During the summer of 2014, I collected data from 167 families—campers and their parents—at six participating summer camps.[1] Of the campers surveyed in my research, 80 percent reported that their camp experiences made them feel "a little" or "a lot" happier.[2] Campers, as well as their parents, also reported statistically significant improvements in their social skills. I finally had the data to prove what I have observed and known to be true for years: kids really are happier at camp. *Happy camper* is not just a glib idiom, but a real description of the affective changes children experience at summer camp.

Thousands of grateful parents have sent me letters, marveling at the impact camp had on their children, and I've witnessed the positive changes in campers' outlook and demeanor myself. The wonderful benefits of camp that children and parents report affirm the good work we do. Sadly, our kids' need for the transformational camp experience is a troublesome commentary on the difficult social environment they must navigate when they are not at camp.

Our kids have been born into an anxious, high-pressure world. Overscheduling, high-stakes academics, lack of free-play time, and other cultural factors are having a negative impact on them. In 2017, 11 percent of youth ages twelve to seventeen reported suffering from at least one major depressive episode (MDE) in the past year. MDE is characterized by pervasive feelings of sadness associated with suicidal thoughts.[3] Anxiety disorders affect 25.1 percent of youth ages thirteen to eighteen and, when left untreated, often lead to substance abuse problems.[4] Suicide is the second-leading cause of death for five- to twenty-four-year olds.[5] Ever-rising statistics about depression, anxiety, addiction, and suicide can cause even the calmest and most level-headed parent among us to worry about our children's future.

Among the factors being blamed for adolescents' increasing mental, emotional, and physical health problems are increased screen use, lack of sleep, poor nutrition, poverty, and the overparenting style that has become increasingly common, especially in economically privileged families.[6] The evidence is mounting that we need to make changes in order to help our kids thrive both during their youth and in adulthood.

It's no wonder that—with screens safely stored at home, less focus on competition and more focus on collaboration, and lots of fresh air and outdoor fun—campers feel that camp is a haven, a safe place to relax and be themselves. Without the pressures of academics, athletics, social media, and their parents', teachers', and coaches' expectations, kids—many for the first time—experience living in the moment, enjoying each other's company, challenging themselves, and figuring out who they truly are and what they really like. Many campers feel healed, restored, or changed by their camp experience and don't want to leave. Parents, too, feel relieved to give their children the gift of a few weeks of bliss in the midst of their pressured, stressful lives.

I have watched many kids struggle with leaving camp because they treasure their time at a place where they feel happier and more relaxed. Witnessing their heart-wrenching sobs as they cling to their counselors and cabinmates before boarding the buses home, I've felt sad for them and also a bit guilty. I've talked with my good friends and fellow camp directors Sara Kuljis (Yosemite Sierra Summer Camp) and Maria Horner (Catalina Island Camps) about this phenomenon, as well as with colleagues I meet at camp conferences and workshops all over the country. We all feel some of the same ambivalence. On one hand, we are thrilled to have created a positive environment where kids thrive, discover a different way to live, and treasure their time with us. But we also feel a sense of responsibility to help our camp families maintain the positive momentum for our campers, who spend most of their year away from us. As we watch our campers head back into the real world, we worry that the culture they are reentering won't do much to sustain the positive changes they have experienced at camp.

Many camp directors share the same concerns about the changes we've witnessed over the past decades in the campers we serve, the

Millennial and Gen Z counselors who come to work for us each summer, and the anxious parents frequently on the other end of our phone lines. Camp director Brooke Cheley Klebe (Cheley Colorado Camps) says, "I find myself talking with many parents who need to update me on mental health challenges their preteens and teens are facing. Not feeling anxious is starting to seem like the exception, not the rule." Just as schools are experiencing new and unique challenges, summer camps are also experiencing a worrisome rise in the frequency and severity of our campers' mental, social, and emotional issues.

I want the kids we work with during the summer to thrive all the time, not just during the two weeks they're at camp. This book is my way of spreading the research-based wisdom and methods behind the *magic* of camp. The overarching reason for the transformational changes campers experience at summer camp is not, in fact, the fresh air and the fun. It is the culture, and that culture is intentionally created through very specific, planned practices. The nine secrets of summer camp that I share in this book can help you create a happier, more connected family culture. When we provide kids with this kind of environment, they thrive. The research (mine and the experts on whose shoulders I stand) proves that we can improve our kids' lives by changing their environment.

My experience using these secrets isn't limited to my job at summer camp. I have used these camp techniques in my own home, so I have seen that they're applicable not just around campfires in the mountains, but also at home while living our day-to-day, ordinary family life. I am honored to share these ideas with you in the sincere hope that you can create the positivity and happiness of summer camp at home and have your own *happy campers*. By implementing these ideas, you can create a family culture where your kids feel connected, capable, confident, and loved in that most important and sacred of all places: home.

Happy Campers

The "Magic" of Summer Camp

Dear Sunshine,

   I don't know the child who was returned to me on Saturday. It definitely wasn't the child I dropped off two weeks earlier. The only logical explanation is that your camp is magic. Magic transformed my scared, sad boy into a confident, smiling, laughing young man. My son had a hard year in school. He was stressed, worried, and anxious. He came out of his two weeks loving the mountains, loving activities he never would have tried in a million years, and, most importantly, believing in himself. He has never been a kid who in almost nine years of life has ever believed in himself despite everything we've tried, and you changed that. Magic!

With gratitude,
Lindsey

Parents often share the positive changes and increased maturity they notice in their children when they arrive home from camp. Years later, those who were regular campers and their families continue to testify about the lifelong, positive impact camp had on their children's social skills, character development, and emotional well-being. Kids often meet their best friends at camp, gain newfound confidence in their own abilities, discover lifelong recreational passions, and even pursue careers based on interests and strengths developed at camp. Campers describe experiencing their first feelings of belonging and acceptance and of discovering their true selves while at summer camp. I've had the privilege of watching two generations of campers return as camp counselors and even as camp parents. Our loyal, longtime campers consider their time at camp the most important and pivotal part of their childhood. Many call camp a "second home" and often use the word *magic* to describe what it feels like to be part of the camp community.

Those of us who have dedicated our careers to working at summer camps know that no one actually has a magic wand. The transformations that happen at camp are the direct result of the research-based, intentional strategies we've implemented to create this positive environment for nurturing optimal growth. Of course, it's super-fun for children to live in a tent, enjoy the beautiful outdoors, learn adventurous recreational skills, and gather around a nightly campfire roasting marshmallows, but there are important principles behind the work we do. While teaching a child to water-ski or rock climb, we know they're gaining far more important skills, like the courage to try something new and the perseverance to do it over and over, despite failure.

As parents, we can look at the skills we teach our children in the same way. When we have our child help with a regular daily household chore, like washing dishes, they are learning more than just kitchen hygiene. They're gaining a sense of responsibility, a work ethic, and an understanding of how each family member contributes to running the household. When we think about our parenting choices, it's important to remember that our end-goal is helping our kids develop life-changing skills and character traits that will help them thrive as adults. With this framework, it's clear that washing dishes is not just about having a clean kitchen.

Young people require much more than intellectual growth and physical health to become happy, successful adults, and yet much of our time as parents is focused on their academic, athletic, and other endeavors. This is why summer camps work so well to produce profound changes in a such a short time; the camp environment fosters connection and is one of the only places where the culture is focused primarily on kids' social and emotional development.

Just like children practice important social skills at summer camp, at home kids can gain those same important relationship skills. When we sit around the family dinner table, sharing our ideas and dreams or talking about our highs and lows from the day, our children are developing important social skills like better listening, learning to ask questions, offering compliments, and sharing appropriately. Regular opportunities to practice engaging translate into our children being better able to navigate social interactions at school and in other settings.

The close connections children feel to parents and siblings have a profound and positive impact on the way they successfully navigate relationships outside the family. Knowing that social skills, positive relationships, and character traits like kindness, grit, and optimism are so closely linked to our children's present and future happiness and well-being, in *Happy Campers* I share the tools I've developed at camp to foster these and other important traits so that you can provide the same guidance to your kids at home. Camp experiences, I have determined, can be accurately viewed as a positive psychological intervention for children, contributing both to their social skills development and their overall wellness.[1] In this book, I'll show you how to create that intervention in your own home, where the benefits last not just two weeks but a lifetime. Magic!

They Call Me "Sunshine"

My time at camp has made me realize the version of myself I've
always wanted to be. Camp made me feel like I was spending my
time in a way that I was going to remember. Camp reminded me I
have the power to live my best life. Camp has inspired me to take
my aspirations and happiness into my own hands.

—Chloe

The transformative power of summer camp is, for me, very personal,
because I experienced it myself. In the 1980s, while my Stanford University classmates dressed in suits and pursued internships at Oracle
and Coca-Cola, I spent my final three summers of college working
as a camp counselor at Gold Arrow Camp. During those summers
while I drove a ski boat, taught kids to water-ski, and led cabin group
games and discussions around the campfire, I learned several things
that would shape my future. First, I realized I did not have the same
career ambitions as most of my classmates. In fact, although I couldn't
pinpoint exactly what I wanted to do postcollege, I knew what I
did not want—a job that required me to work in a cubicle or wear a
pencil skirt and heels. Second, I discovered that although I had long
thought of becoming a classroom teacher, the kind of teaching I really
loved did not happen in the confines of a classroom. Back then, the
career of "life coach" hadn't been invented, but looking back, I loved
being a life coach for my campers. I relished the chance to talk with
kids about their dreams and struggles, and I appreciated having ample,
unrushed time in the outdoors to get to know them and hear their
stories.

I knew the life skills I could teach and the positive influence

I could have were exactly what I was created to do. Before *passion* had become a buzzword, I had found mine. My sense, from my very first summer as a camp counselor, was that I was teaching children so much more than how to water-ski. Overcoming fears and experiencing multiple failures were, for many of my campers, their first lessons in perseverance. I was hooked. Their accomplishments felt like my own.

Another positive outcome from my summer camp counseling experiences came from the sense of community I felt. I had never been in a setting where the values were so in line with my own. Being outdoors and chatting around the campfire with my campers and fellow counselors, I felt a sense of belonging. I enjoyed being with people who were unconcerned about appearance, accomplishments, or material belongings, which was a big cultural shift from what I had experienced outside of camp. Having been on the academic treadmill of a college-preparatory high school followed by attending a competitive college, with the level of academic pressure and expectation not too dissimilar to what many kids are experiencing today, I had never stepped off the prescribed path long enough to figure out what I was actually interested in. No one had ever asked me or encouraged me to think about my real strengths and interests. I had always felt a bit like a fish out of water at Stanford University, and the difference was even more striking after I had experienced camp. Once I had lived in the supportive, familial, noncompetitive community of camp, and experienced the calming simplicity of living in a tent with a few old T-shirts and some hiking boots, I—like the campers we serve today—spent my school year counting down the days to summer. It turns out I had found what I was meant to do.

I was less than a year out of college with a degree in an unrelated field (International Relations) when I had the chance to purchase the camp where I had gone as a child and worked as a counselor. I had spent the fall substitute teaching and applying to teaching credential programs. Over winter break, the elderly, widowed camp director—who had been ready to retire and sell Gold Arrow Camp for several years—contacted me after a prospective buyer backed out of a purchase. My father, a lifelong business executive with outstanding leadership skills and financial sense, gave me a quick course in writing a business plan and securing a loan, and I was on my way to a great adventure, one that an older, more risk-averse me might not have considered. At a very young age, before I was married or had children of my own, I took on the weighty responsibility of taking care of other people's children—and took on the camp name "Sunshine." It's been an incredible ride.

I love my job and feel both honored and humbled by the trust parents place in my staff and me when they send their precious seven-year-old to spend two weeks with us at camp. Being part of that same child's growth and development over the years and being able to witness many of them successfully move into the leadership role of camp counselor, are the greatest rewards of what I do. I have taken my role and responsibility seriously, and I continually strive to create and enhance the camp culture that has garnered so many loyal camp families over the years.

During my years at Gold Arrow, I met and married my husband, Steve, and became a mother to my own five kids. My own parenting has influenced my belief that many of the simple practices used by camp counselors can be replicated at home to help parents create a more loving, supportive environment where kids thrive. Steve Jobs once said, "We're here to put a dent in the universe. Otherwise, why else even be here?" My work with our campers, the mentoring I've done with counselors, my many counseling conversations with parents, and being a loving mom to my own kids have been of significant value. I measure my success one child and one parent at a time. If a camper learns to be a little kinder or more grateful, or overcomes homesickness, anxiety, or a social fear to thrive at camp, or if a parent discovers a way to have a closer connection with their child because of something I've shared, then I have successfully made my dent.

Strategies for Bringing the Magic of Camp Home

The strategies presented in this book will, if implemented consistently, help you create a more positive and connected family culture where your children will feel accepted for who they are and have the best chance at becoming *happy campers*—thriving, positive individuals who feel a sense of purpose and belonging.

Each chapter of this book covers one social or emotional skill area, character trait, or parenting practice, including the research backing its importance. This research is interesting, but necessary only if you need convincing of the significance of a particular skill, trait, or parenting practice—or if you need ammunition with which to convince your co-parent of the importance of developing certain character traits or skills in your child or yourselves.

To make *Happy Campers* a useful parenting tool that encourages, inspires, and doesn't leave you overwhelmed, in the back of each chapter I've included the "Bringing Camp Home" section, which you can flip to when you have only a few minutes. There you'll find specific activities and discussions to foster the character trait or skill you are interested in developing in your kids. The activities range from simple things you can implement alone, to more detailed suggestions for how to create new family habits or encourage a culture shift around a particular trait.

Here is an overview of the types of activities, discussions, and suggestions included in each "Bringing Camp Home" section:

One Simple Thing

This is intervention on the most basic level and involves making only a small tweak to your own behavior. The simple suggestions here don't require "buy-in" from your parenting partner or your kids. You don't even need to talk about it with anyone. This is something you can try on your own and conduct a personal experiment. *Does your simple behavior change have any impact on the rest of your family? What changes do you notice in them from your own small shift?*

The Sticky Note Solution

I believe in saving my parental energy and have found that sticky notes are often extremely effective in getting my kids to do something I'd like them to do. This, again, will be a simple strategy requiring nothing more than a sticky note pad, a pen, and one minute.

Make It Fun

At camp, we try to incorporate fun into much of our day. Here is where I'll share ways to bring some of that fun home.

Around the Campfire

I am a huge believer in the value of daily family sharing, usually at dinnertime. While it may feel awkward at first, kids really do end up enjoying this time when each family member shares a topic or question. I find that around the dinner table is the best time for this, but it can also be part of your bedtime routine.

Family Meeting Topic

One concept that you may not be familiar with is the family meeting. Just like successful companies have regular check-in meetings and strategic planning sessions, your family can benefit from regular formal communication. In case having a family meeting is a new concept for you, in each chapter I share a topic suggestion to cover at your family meeting. I also give some ideas and guidelines for family meetings in the "Resources" section at the back of the book.

Diving Deeper

This is where I'll share a more detailed approach to addressing under-lying issues to create a change in family culture. This can be especially helpful if you think your kids need some more serious redirection in a particular area.

As you read on, think about what you value most and which area of family life you are most wanting to enhance to create a happier, more connected family. New habits and activities take time to develop and are best incorporated one at a time. Different activities and ideas will work better for different families. Whether you read the book all at once or in smaller doses, I encourage you to focus on just one chapter or *secret* at a time, starting with what is most important to you. Focus-ing on creating close relationships with your kids is a great place to begin.

Camp Secret #1

Connection Comes First

There is no doubt in my mind that I am the person I am today because of camp. The lessons I have learned at camp about being optimistic, positive, friendly, and outgoing have helped me through many hard times and have helped me to achieve successes that I never thought possible. I learned that with everything I do, "it's about the process, not the end result." That lesson I have applied to my life and every experience I am in. Leaving camp this summer, it was very hard to close this chapter of my life and experience the transformation from child and camper to adult, but as I look back I honestly know that camp was the highlight of my childhood and a major part of my life. I cannot thank you enough for eight amazing summers filled with pure happiness and for creating a second home for me where I can truly be myself.

—Stevie

Some of the most touching testimonials I've received about camp include the words *home* or *family*. Many campers think of their few weeks at camp as their annual time to get back in touch with themselves and their close friends. As young adults, they are often drawn back to camp to serve as counselors because of their desire to pass along these values to the next generation. When adults reminisce about their camp days, they often say things like, "I met my best friend at camp; we're still friends thirty years later." The relationships and connections campers experience are not just a small part of the program we offer, but the basis for the entire experience; the story about camp is a story about connections. If our campers don't feel accepted, included, and valued, nothing else we teach or do at camp matters. We could have the snazziest cabins, the most delicious food, and the coolest zip lines and Jet Skis, but if we aren't helping kids form connections, we aren't doing what matters most.

I believe the exact same thing is true in our families. Creating a close and connected family culture that promotes positive, lifelong relationships is the most important thing we can do for our children. Warm and supportive parent-child relationships, a sense of being loved, and help and support from family members serve as protective factors and increase children's resilience and their ability to face many of life's inevitable challenges.[1] This doesn't happen just because you live under the same roof, and it doesn't happen by filling your home with cool stuff or your calendar with lavish vacations. Just like at camp, connections are the result of intentionally chosen, day-to-day family habits that create feelings of warmth and belonging.

Social Connections Predict Happiness and Success

> Very little that is positive is solitary. When was the last time you laughed uproariously? The last time you felt indescribable joy? The last time you sensed profound meaning and purpose? The last time you felt enormously proud of an accomplishment? Even without knowing the particulars of these high points of your life, I know their form: all of them took place around other people.
>
> —Martin Seligman, Flourish[2]

To understand why it's important to take connections so seriously, we need look no further than the multiple studies, including the landmark eighty-year Harvard Men's Study, that have shown how social connections are the greatest predictor of all aspects of lifelong success, including health, academics, and career.[3] This study, along with much recent research in the field of positive psychology, has provided countless examples of why our social connections are so important.

One such researcher and a founder of the positive psychology movement, Martin Seligman, wrote the book *Flourish: A Visionary New Understanding of Happiness and Well-Being*. In it he explores PERMA, the acronym he uses to define his theory and five measurable elements that lead to well-being. According to Seligman, in addition to positive emotion (P), engagement (E), meaning (M), and accomplishment (A), a key element of well-being is positive relationships (R). When I first read *Flourish*, I kept having "ah-ha" moments. Finally—I'd found the science behind why kids flourish at camp, which led me to how this science could be applied for kids who will flourish at home. Below I explore PERMA as a framework to show you how.

P: Positive Emotion

Positive emotion is exactly what it sounds like: feeling happy and having positive thoughts about yourself, the people around you, or your surroundings. At camp, positive emotions are the norm, not the exception. We're singing; we're dancing; we're doing skits that don't make sense but that cause us to laugh so hard our stomachs hurt. Whether we're telling jokes and stories around the campfire or just entertaining ourselves by talking and hanging out together, positive emotion is literally swirling around camp.

Creating positive emotions at home requires that we make sure to do activities that elicit positive feelings. Anything we can do with our families that makes us laugh, smile, or feel good increases the positive emotion in each of us as individuals. A few years ago, when I was deeply sucked into Pinterest, during nightly sessions of pinning I started a board called "Funny." While most of the things I put on there were not funny to my kids, what was funny to them was watching me laugh so hard until I cried. Whatever we can do to bring some laughter and fun to our homes, the better we all feel.

E: Engagement

Seligman describes engagement as being interested in and connected to what you are doing. When you're engaged in your hobby or book or job, you're fired up about learning something new and energized by the activity. At camp, kids are constantly exposed to new experiences and challenges—both recreational and social—that get them interested and excited to learn. They're pushed to get outside their comfort zones and really engage. For some kids, their stay at camp is the first time they've slept away from home and their parents, and they are engaged in learning to live with a group of new people. For others, the camp dance is the first time they've ever danced with other kids, so they're being engaged socially in new ways.

With our families at home, one way to increase engagement is to try a new activity or visit a new place together. Perhaps there's a craft you make as a family, or everyone could go for a hike or a bike ride. Each time we expose our kids to something new that they haven't done before, we present them with the opportunity to engage with something potentially fascinating to them. This can lead to their continued interest in trying new things and finding the engagement that makes them excited to wake up in the morning.

R: Relationships

As Seligman and other researchers found, and most of us intuitively know, "other people are the best antidote to the *downs* of life and the single most reliable *up*." We all know that positive relationships are one of the main contributors to our happiness in life, so it's no surprise that relationships are an important pillar of Seligman's theory of what it takes to achieve well-being. Our life's relationships—with our parents, our siblings, our friends, our spouses, and our coworkers—are key to our happiness. At camp, everyone comes to see their old friends, make new friends, and just spend quality time connecting with others and building positive relationships. These relationships at camp are positive, grow strong quickly, and help kids flourish because they do not come with all the competition and baggage that kids have in some of their relationships elsewhere: Two bright students who are close friends are also competing for the valedictorian spot. Or, two athletes who have grown up together are competing for the same position on a soccer team, and so on. The stress that's part of relationships in the real world may challenge our kids' ability to connect.

That's why our family relationships are so important. For our kids, family relationships are their first opportunity to experience the positive connections that teach them how to learn and relate to others, even amidst challenge. The love and caring they experience from parents and older siblings teach kids skills they will use their entire lives in friendships and romantic relationships. At home is where our kids first experience the positive relationships that are key to their well-being.

M: Meaning

To flourish in life, we need to feel that there is meaning to our existence, that we matter and have value in this world. According to Seligman, meaning comes from "belonging to and serving something that you believe is bigger than the self." Being a member of a cabin group at camp helps kids gain an understanding of how they are valued by others. For some kids, camp is the first place where they understand what it means to be a valued and an accepted member of an outside community. Unlike at school, where some kids can feel *invisible* and go through a day without connecting with others, camp forces integration. Through the experience of being an integral part of their cabin group, kids discover their character strengths through recognition from peers and counselors.

While at camp, kids also have the opportunity to feel part of something bigger than themselves—a camp community that goes back nearly a century, where we still get to follow the same traditions our predecessors did. While learning about friendship, gratitude, and kindness, and practicing those skills, kids learn that they can positively impact others. They learn that they have purpose and that there is meaning in life.

At home, we can help our kids find meaning in their roles in our family by making sure they know they are a necessary and important part of making our household and family function well. Something as simple as asking them to help cook dinner or clean up afterward presents the opportunity for kids to increase their feeling of connection and meaning in the family.

A: Achievement

People flourish when pursuing goals and challenging themselves toward the mastery of a skill. While having a one-time achievement is wonderful, much of the benefit comes from the good feelings we get while striving toward the achievement. Many people report that it was a lot of fun working their way up and accomplishing small steps on the way to a goal. In fact, many people feel disappointed once a goal has been achieved and realize the truth in the saying, "Life is a journey, not a destination." My husband, an accomplished runner and triathlete, has often shared about his postrace blues. After all the hours of training and working toward a specific time or milestone in a race, once the race is over he has a feeling of being let down, *even* after achieving his desired goal. Working toward the goal is what he enjoys most, so he signs up for another event!

Every day at camp, kids have the opportunity to try new things, master new skills, and both give to and receive encouragement from others who are there to do the same. Some kids arrive at camp with a specific goal: a bull's-eye at archery or getting up on a slalom water ski. But others simply practice and work toward improving or challenge themselves to try something that frightens them—like completing the ropes course. And all of their progress and achievements made in the supportive company of friends add to kids' flourishing at camp.

At home, we can encourage our kids to set goals by modeling that we, too, are setting and reaching goals. My pursuit of a master's degree, and the hours of reading, research, and study, showed my kids firsthand what it looks like to set and work toward a goal. Our kids learn much more from how they see us living than anything we tell them to do. If we want our kids to set and reach big goals, we need to demonstrate how that's done and show them how we encourage other family members to dream big.

Speaking of goals and how connection fuels a successful life, we now look to Harvard researcher Shawn Achor's book *The Happiness Advantage*. In it he describes his study of 1,600 undergraduates that determined "social support [is] a far greater predictor of happiness than any other factor, more than GPA, family income, SAT scores, age, gender, or race." Further, for those who remain unconvinced that happiness is a valid goal, Achor relays the finding that "the happier you are, the more advantages you accrue in nearly every domain of life."[4] For our kids, feeling connected—and the associated appreciation and belonging—is vital to their well-being and their future success. The research therefore validates putting as much—if not more—effort into having kids who feel connected and have close relationships with other people than having kids who excel at academics or athletics. Which college our kid goes to is less likely to determine their eventual "success" than the quality of their relationships.

REALationships

Quality of relationships is so important. There is one concept counselors at Gold Arrow focus on throughout each summer. The concept is reinforced with a word we created: *REALationship.* In order to help our campers distinguish between the many "friends"—online and in person—they have already encountered, instead of "relationship" we say, "realationship," with emphasis on the *real.* Many of our campers come to us from lives drenched in social media and face competitive pressure academically, in sports, and sometimes between siblings in their own family. Some children believe, whether accurately or not, that their parents' and others' love and acceptance of them is based on their appearance or individual achievements. The most important thing their time at camp can do is fuel their spirit with strong friendships and acceptance for who they are.

Just like our counselors' most important priority is to form positive, close relationships with each of their campers, parents, too, need to prioritize forming REALationships with each child. This close connection is more important than any other aspect of parenting. Forming a positive, nurturing relationship with your child will help ensure your child's future success and happiness in all areas of life.

A (Acceptance) + B (Belonging) = C (Connection)

Forming close connections with children can be remembered using the acronym "ABC": Acceptance + Belonging = Connection. The most basic element of any REALationship is spending time getting to know each other. At my camp, starting with their very first interaction and continuing throughout the camp session, we strive to go beyond simply learning our campers' names and surface information about their family, like where they're from, and what hobbies and sports they like. The goal, once a comfort level has been achieved, is to learn about each camper's inner strengths and what makes them tick. Camp counselors learn these deeper character traits through asking a lot of questions, listening well to their answers, modeling and encouraging vulnerability, and expressing sincere interest in each camper.

Parents, too, can practice these same techniques at home—asking questions, listening well, and sharing personal stories—to form closer bonds with children. While it may feel awkward at first, you can start a family habit of having conversations similar to the ones camp counselors lead. More ideas for conversation-starting questions you can ask your kids are in this chapter's "Around the Campfire" activity and in "Questions for Connection" in the "Resources" section at the end of this book.

At Yosemite Sierra, counselors build close connections with campers with a nightly "tuck-in." Whether the camper is eight or seventeen, starting on the first night of camp and continuing throughout the two-week session, the counselor comes over to each camper's bunk, shares a kindness or an affirmation with them, checks on how they're doing, and wishes them a good sleep. On the first night, added messages include, "I'm so glad you're in my group. I've been waiting for you," as well as comments about any information counselors were made aware of ahead of time. While it may feel strange on the first day of camp when they've just met, campers quickly come to expect their nightly tuck-in. They also quickly come to love the nurturing from their counselor. Kids of every age enjoy this kind of nightly connection with parents at home.

My daughter, at age eleven, returned from a sleepover at a friend's house and told me she was surprised that her friend's mother didn't come to say good night to them or tuck her friend in. It was my daughter's first experience of not having an adult say good night, as she had become accustomed to the practice of a nighttime connection both at home and at camp. No matter their age, kids enjoy being tucked in, whether that means an actual bedside chat or a simple hug good night. Often, when our kids most need those nightly chats (pre-adolescence and the teen years), that's when parents start to believe they are too old to be tucked in and stop the regular nighttime visits. For as long as possible, stop by your kid's room, give them a quick back rub or hug, and see if they have anything to share. Many important conversations and sharing happen in the comfort of a dark room right before sleep.

In our busy family lives, we can easily fall into unhealthy patterns that ignore some of our own and our children's basic needs to be seen, heard, and loved. By focusing on connecting daily, you can help your child feel the acceptance (A) and belonging (B) they need in order to feel the connection (C) that is vital to their well-being. This formula produces close friendships in just two weeks of camp, friendships that campers say are the closest relationships they've ever experienced. Parents, too, can create these same feelings at home.

A (Acceptance): "Be You"

Campers often say that while at camp they feel accepted just the way they are, without judgment. In the words of one camper, "Camp is my getaway. I can be myself. I come back every year because it's the one place I feel safe."

After hearing this same message from many different campers over the years, I have come to understand more clearly that many campers don't feel as accepted for who they are when they're not at camp. Taking a look at the lives my own kids lead outside of camp, it's easy for me to see how hard it is to "be you" in a world that pressures kids to fit in. With much of their social lives being lived online and not face-to-face, kids spend a lot of time presenting themselves and their lives as far from "real" as one can get. Being genuine, or even being in touch with who they really are, can become challenging. Finding people who accept them just the way they are, and embracing their own unique personality and strengths, is the furthest thing from our kids' minds when they walk into middle school or post and chat online. Instead, many are so desperate to fit in, to be popular, and to be liked, that they often go to extremes to *not* be themselves.

At home, our children need to feel accepted for who they are instead of feeling compared to others or pressured to pursue interests that are more valued by parents or our culture at large. When parents recognize and encourage their unique strengths and interests, children feel accepted. Parents can encourage children to be themselves by showing their own quirky traits and expressing positive feelings about people who are doing unique things. At camp, being goofy or what would be considered uncool in the real world becomes the norm, because counselors model for campers that it's okay to just relax and be themselves. New campers quickly learn that they will be treated with kindness and respect, accepted and embraced for who they are, regardless of their quirks. At camp we embrace and celebrate individuality, and we model this in our interactions with fellow counselors and our campers. By embracing and celebrating your child's individuality, you, too, can create this same culture of acceptance at home.

What can parents learn from camp counselors to foster feelings of acceptance? Perhaps the most important lesson is what to focus on in conversations with kids. Summer camp is, naturally, not a place where kids get asked much about school. Instead, counselors focus on asking kids questions about what they like, their goals, and their dreams. Encouraging kids to share stories about themselves is one way counselors get to know their campers better. Camp sessions always start with icebreakers, either as a whole camp, in small groups, or some combination of both. Normally relegated to kindergarten classrooms, "Show and Tell" has made a resurgence at Cape Cod Sea Camps (CCSC). As a get-to-know-you activity, campers and staff share an item that is meaningful to them and explain why. "The objects they share tell you so much about the kids," says director Daniella Garran. In the very first day of camp, counselors at CCSC know something special and unique about each of their campers based on the items they share and the stories they tell.

In describing the traditional first night activities at Yosemite Sierra, Sara Kuljis describes all 200 campers and staff members (120 campers, 80 staff) gathering in a meadow for a series of large and small group icebreaker games. The culminating game, called "The Biggest Fan," is a huge game of "Ro Sham Bo," with a twist. Once someone loses in a match, they become a fan of the person they lost to. By the end of the game, two huge groups of fans are cheering on the final two competitors. According to Kuljis, the game creates in kids the feeling of being each other's fans and encouraging each other that carries over into camp. She says they use the game with all different populations, including inner city groups that attend camp for a week, and all of the kids enjoy the game and feel more connected to each other after playing.

Creating a "camper code," or what campers at Cheley Colorado Camps call a "Code of Living," is an important part of the beginning of each camp session and can provide inspiration for families seeking to live together with more kindness and respect. "The campers create a list of five to eight character traits that would be important in their community, traits that they like in their friends. We reference the Code of Living throughout the summer to keep it alive and ingrained in our community," says Jeff Cheley, owner and director of the camp.

This type of counselor-guided discussion is a common way to start a camp session. Counselors assert that put-downs, negative comments, teasing, or shaming, even done in jest, will not be part of camp life. Counselors also let campers know that the cabin group is like a family and each of them brings different qualities to the group that will add to the experience. Counselors lead a brainstorming discussion of ways campers will support one another. The campers themselves usually come up with ideas like building each other up, encouraging one another, and focusing on positive qualities. These are then introduced as the group norms, written down, and reviewed as needed. Campers who need extra practice at being kind and accepting are given specific coaching by counselors in one-on-one meetings. Even with teenage boys, who are accustomed to disrespecting each other for fun, and teenage girls, who have grown accustomed to social aggression through backstabbing, gossiping, or leaving people out, counselors are able to model and insist upon a new way of interacting with one another, one that is far from the cultural norm in middle and high school.

B (Belonging): "You Are Valued and Needed Here"

Right from the start of camp, counselors are intentional about doing specific activities that create a sense of belonging. Parents, too, regardless of our children's ages, can use these same types of activities to foster greater feelings of belonging at home. Games and discussions that help people get to know each other, often called "team building," are a way of life at camp, done throughout the day during walks between activities, while waiting for programs to start, and around the campfire. Counselors select partners for paired activities like canoeing and charge campers with a "get to know you" task to complete during the activity. For example, the campers might be asked to find three things they have in common. At the end of the activity, they share with the rest of the group what they learned about each other. Cabin group cheers, stories, made-up words, and inside jokes also bring kids closer to their group and make them feel like they belong.

Another way to intentionally create feelings of belonging at home is by leading children through a daily reminiscing of events similar to the discussion counselors lead around the campfire. Around the dinner table or at campfire, children enjoy talking and laughing about shared and individual experiences from their day. Each shared camp or family experience children discuss—even seemingly negative ones like being stuck on the shore of the lake for an hour or having a car break down on vacation—serve as another connection point that helps kids feel a sense of belonging to their group or family.

Group memories, recollected in sharing time, create a deep sense of belonging and are one of the reasons campers say their camp friends are their closest ones despite spending only a few weeks a year with them. Don Whipple, director of Mountain Camp, describes a daily activity they do to connect with each other called "Roses, Thorns, and Leaves." Each camper shares their "rose" or highpoint of the day; their "thorn," which was their most challenging moment; and their "leaf," which is what they're looking forward to tomorrow. Parents can elicit these same feelings of belonging at home by intentionally creating times to reflect on individual and family memories. Photos and family videos also create a great starting point for reflecting on shared experiences.

Chores, and the accompanying sense of being an integral and important member of their cabin group, are a way of a life at camp. Working together at cabin cleanup, campfire building, outdoor cooking, setting up their campsite on backpacking trips, clearing and cleaning their dining table, and much more all offer opportunities for campers to feel a sense of belonging and being needed. Kids rarely sit idly by, watching counselors do daily chores. Instead, kids are working side by side, learning the skills they'll need in order to be able to do these things for themselves, without help, soon. Not only do campers develop good cleaning skills, but they also gain a key understanding of how important each of them is to the successful functioning of their group. Being needed fosters feelings of belonging. Kids benefit from feeling needed at home as much as at summer camp, and shared household chores—despite being a cause of complaint—make children feel that they are an important and valued member of the family.

C (Connection): Unplug and Connect Face-to-Face

> I get to come out here and not have my phone—it sounds weird for a teenager to say that, I know—but it's just fun to be able to not have it, not have to worry about it, not have to stress about it.
>
> *Jack*

One of the reasons kids feel such a sense of connection at camp is, ironically, that they are disconnected from technology. Most traditional camps continue to embrace being "unplugged" as a fundamental part of the camp experience. Campers leave their devices at home. No television or Netflix, no texting, no posting, no Snapchat streaks to keep up with. No wondering who has the latest iPhone model. Nor are there worries about low batteries. No screens at all. Just them, face-to-face with other kids, living in the moment without worrying about recording the moment for others to see.

Besides helping them get to know and accept each other, a side benefit of being unplugged for a few weeks is the brain space that gets opened up for reflection. Moments watching the sun set over the lake or the stars shoot across the sky, five-minute quiet times on backpacking trips and hikes, and hours spent doing crafts like friendship bracelets, crocheting, and painting offer opportunities for reflection campers do not normally experience when they are constantly on their screens or rushing from one activity to the next. These moments sometimes give campers clarity about how they'd like to change the way they spend their time, and often lead to decisions about sports or activities they no longer want to participate in, as well as new goals and activities they wish to pursue.

On pickup day from camp, I was chatting with parents (who happened to be former campers and staff themselves) when their son told them, "I've decided not to play baseball this year." He explained that it was taking up too much of his time, and he had other activities he wanted to pursue. Serving as a place where kids can take some time to both get in better touch with who they really are and feel accepted for being themselves is one result of the intentional decision to prohibit screens at camp. It's also the result of scheduling times for reflection and introspection during organized group events. Allowing unscheduled, unstructured downtimes when campers can think about and pursue their own interests is a priority at camp.

Kids growing up in this media and screen-saturated time are a living experiment. We don't know how all this screen use is going to impact their future lives, but we've already seen clues. Generational researcher Jean Twenge has found a direct cause-and-effect relationship between the rise in smartphone use and the rise in adolescent anxiety, depression, and suicide.[5] My oldest three children were already close to adulthood when the smartphone and social media craze hit. They were flip phone users until age eighteen. But my youngest kids (born in 2001 and 2003) are experiencing growing up in a different era. They don't remember a time before smartphones were ubiquitous, and they've been playing on devices since they were young. They are what Twenge calls "iGen," and others refer to as "Gen Z." Following the Millennials, they are having their own unique experience of childhood, one that is dominated by screen use by their parents and everyone around them.

It's no surprise that it's now the norm to see a group of kids sitting at Starbucks together or hanging around after school, all looking down at their phones. They've been watching adults and are mimicking what they've seen. While I'm driving my boys and their friends around, they are on their devices the majority of the time. They are often talking about and connecting over what they're doing and seeing on each other's phones, but they are still looking mostly at the screens instead of each other. Until kids are specifically asked to put their devices away, they generally won't voluntarily do so. What most adults are modeling is constant checking of phones during any moment of pause or boredom, so that's what kids are learning to do, too.

A side note here is that when I only have my two teenage sons with me (without any friends), my front passenger seat is a designated "no phone" zone. My reason for this no-device (and no-headphones) rule in the front seat is that before my kids were teens, I saw so many kids sitting with their headphones on in the front seat of their parent's car, not talking or interacting with their parent, and I didn't want that to happen with my own kids. If I'm a passenger with a friend, I interact and talk with my friend. That's the polite, respectful thing to do. So, if my kids are passengers in my car, it's more polite for them to talk with me (or not talk with me) and be in charge of the music or the map. I also put whoever is in the front seat in charge of my phone to answer any texts, etc. They're also free to stare out the window, a pastime mostly lost to this generation. Plus, my kids often end up talking while we drive around, and we have some of our best conversations in the car.

Another side benefit to my no-phone, shotgun-seat rule is that there are rarely squabbles about who sits in the front seat, and it's not always the oldest in that spot, because there are benefits to both the front and the back seat in my car. I know some parents who enforce a "no screens" rule in their car, preferring their kids use the time for conversation or just the all-important staring out the window that dominated our own childhoods.

Researchers, I am certain, will continue to find that all this screen use is not good for our kids—or for us. In a November 2016 article, the American College of Pediatricians encouraged "parents to become media literate and limit all screen time for their children. Parents, too, must limit their own screen time, especially the use of smartphones, to improve their interaction and engagement with their children."[6] I, of course, focus on the "interaction and engagement with their children" piece of this advice. The screen problem is not just our children's. It is ours as well. I know, from my own research at camp, that kids feel closer connections, and more happiness, while they're at camp. While there are many factors that contribute to these positive outcomes, I believe that being disconnected from screens is one of the most important variables.

Closer connections come through intentional time spent together, fully present with the person we are with, preferably doing fun and enjoyable things not associated with a screen.

In their book, *The Danish Way of Parenting: What the Happiest People in the World Know About Raising Confident, Capable Kids*, Jessica Alexander and Iben Sandahl share about the Danish tradition of *hygge* (pronounced "hooga"). Hygge, they say, involves, "cozying around together [...] lighting candles, playing games, eating nice meals, having cake and tea, and just generally being in each other's company in a cozy atmosphere." This Danish tradition seemed foreign to American-born Alexander (who married a Dane), who was accustomed to the more limited, around-the-holidays-only family gatherings more prevalent in the United States.

When I interviewed Alexander, I told her that hygge reminded me of our nightly campfires where campers gather to relax, chat, roast marshmallows, and pop popcorn. She remembered her own camp days fondly and agreed that campfires were a good example of hygge. It makes perfect sense that this Danish tradition of hygge—relaxed time just hanging out together and enjoying each other's company (usually with some food involved)—really is one of the reasons why Danish people consistently rank as the happiest. They are masters at connecting.[7]

Bringing Camp Home: Creating Closer Family Connections

Connection is why we're here. It gives purpose and meaning to our lives.

—Brené Brown, The Gifts of Imperfect
Parenting

All of this unplugging and hygge time to connect is far easier to accomplish at summer camp, gathered around our nightly campfire, than it is at home. But as parents, there are simple steps we can take, based on ideas from camp, to create more connected families. Family, after all, is the place where our kids learn about relationships and experience their first connections. Here are some camp practices you can bring home to foster closer connections:

One Simple Thing

Part of our camp counselors' job description includes checking in with each camper, every day. We call these check-in meetings "One-on-Ones." In the camp setting, counselors ask campers specific questions to elicit how campers are feeling. These are individual conversations, out of earshot of other kids, that last anywhere from two to five minutes. The result? Each camper feels seen, heard, and validated each day, and the counselor knows what's going on with each of their campers and knows how to best support them. At Yosemite Sierra, the tuck-in is their daily check-in with campers, and at CCSC they have a nightly health check to note how kids are feeling physically, but also to find out how they're doing in general. Counselors at CCSC will often ask campers to share a word that describes their day. One of Garran's favorite camper descriptive words? "Fantabulous."

I've often marveled how, in our busy, go-go-go family life, a day can go by without any real one-on-one conversation with our kids that addresses more than what time soccer practice ends. As a simple way to deepen your connection with your kids, try having just one daily one-on-one chat with each of them:

- Turn off or put away your phone (and have them put theirs away, too).
- Give your child your full attention (eye contact, body turned toward them, not thinking about other things).
- Ask them a few open-ended questions. "What was the best part of your day?" is an easy place to start.

Your one-on-one chats can be anytime. You can make it a daily ritual over an after-school snack, while sharing a hot drink, or while tucking them in at bedtime, but that small, concerted daily investment of time will lead to a closer connection between you and your kids.

The Sticky Note Solution

What is something you appreciate about your kid? Let them know that you notice and appreciate them by leaving an encouraging sticky note on their pillow or bathroom mirror. The note can say something like, "Your great sense of humor makes my days happier," or "Thank you for doing the dishes without being asked. I appreciate how you help our home run smoothly." Our kids frequently hear about what they're doing wrong and how they're falling short. Getting a positive message about a way they make your day better or how they are contributing to the family builds them up.

Make It Fun

In their landmark book *The Whole-Brain Child*, which has changed the way many parents understand children's behavior based on a better understanding of neurology, psychiatrist Daniel J. Siegel and psychotherapist Tina Payne Bryson reiterate the importance of providing kids with opportunities to feel connected within the family. Their Whole-Brain Strategy #11 is, "Increase the Family Fun Factor: Making a Point to Enjoy Each Other."[8] They explain that it is through play that parents can best prepare kids to connect with others. Here are some ideas I've developed for doing just that:

• Watch a family video or slide show, or look through a family album together, because remembering shared experiences creates connection. Talk about the experiences. What does everyone remember most? What was the best part? The worst? One famous Monke family home video includes my then two-year-old daughter exclaiming with glee after taking the wrapping off of a gift, "A new box!" We've rewatched that video many times, laughing about her excitement over packaging.

• 100 Memories: Over the final few weeks of each year, my family creates a list of one hundred memories from the previous twelve months. We usually start the list over dinner on a legal pad, and we keep the pad handy so that everyone can keep adding to the list. We generally start with the big events of the year. If someone graduated, got their driver's license, or had some other big accomplishment, that goes on the list. But funny and other smaller, memorable things also end up on the list, especially as we get into the higher numbers. Brainstorming together is a fun experience in itself, and the remembering of our shared experiences makes us all feel closer. As my kids are getting older, with three of the five home only for occasional vacations,

I am more and more thankful for this annual practice, which not only reminds us of our collective and individual important and memorable events of the year, but also serves as a family history to help us remember the experiences we've shared.

• Shared Outdoor Activities (even ones not everyone likes): My husband and I are both runners, so from an early age, we took our kids along to local races where they'd often do the kids' runs while we'd do the adult 5K or 10K. As the kids got older, some became a bit more resistant to getting up early to go to the events. But we stuck with it and still did several races every year. Consistently, the races ended up being fun times together followed by breakfast out. Although there were some complaints at the time, all of our kids look back fondly on our early mornings at the races together. And our adult daughters regularly participate in half marathons and other running events now (sometimes alongside Mom or Dad). More recently, to appease the desires of our two youngest (now teenage boys) and to utilize some of our camp equipment in the "off-season," we've turned to wakeboarding as a family shared activity, and we get out on the lake together as often as we can.

Around the Campfire

When introducing your first "around the campfire" family discussion, you can say something like, "I've been reading about how it can be fun to have some daily family sharing. Let's try it tonight." And then introduce the sharing. To make it a habit, stick with the same sharing topic for a while. A great starting activity (and one that many families use) is "Highs and Lows." Each person shares their high of the day (a good thing that happened) and a low from the day (something that didn't go well). The only rule is that everyone else listens attentively as they look at the person who's sharing. If your kids are over age nine, they may balk at the suggestion of family sharing. Press on. Even if you have a tween or teen who claims to dislike it or shares nonconsequential items, keep going. The opportunity to have everyone listening to them will eventually grow on them. You may even find, after time, that they will remind *you* about sharing if you forget to get it started.

A great sharing conversation can also begin with asking everyone to share the answer to a question. We've had a box of Table Topics on our table for years, and those have been fun questions to ponder.[9] Taking some time each day as a family, during dinner or at bedtime, to ask a "Question for Connection" (see the "Resources" section) or another question, and listen intently to each other's answers, is a great way to continue fostering closer connections in your family. These simple questions can sometimes elicit unexpected responses and can go a long way toward helping us know what makes our kids tick as well as showing them our interest and support. Many of the questions will also help kids know you better and learn some of the stories that made you the adult you are.

I've marveled at some of the things my children have mistakenly assumed about me that aren't true. My son once commented about me spending all my time in the library during college. He assumed this vision of me based on his experience seeing my voracious reading habit and my diligence in my master's program. I had the opportunity to share that the diligent student I was as a forty-seven-year-old adult was very different from my college self, and it led to a good conversation about how I didn't know what I was most interested in learning about during my college years and therefore was more enthused by football games and other social events than by my studies. Sometimes, I learned, our kids think that we were always the way we are now. It's reassuring for them to learn that we took some time to develop into who we are now and that they, too, will take some time to grow into their best adult selves. By learning about each other through asking questions and sharing stories, we gain a deeper understanding that leads to greater acceptance as well as closer connections.

Family Meeting Topic: Screen Time

If you have younger kids, I advise starting at a very young age to limit screen time and not allow devices to be the go-to thing when bored in line, at a restaurant, and so on. It is much easier to give them more screen time when they get older than to take time away. Have a family meeting to set the rules around screen usage. Following are examples of screen rules some families (including my own) have established during kids' early screen years:

- All devices are used and charged at home (not bedrooms) and shut down at least one hour before bedtime.
- At-home, non-homework-related tech use is limited to thirty minutes on weekdays, two hours on weekends. The weekend hours will include any TV time. Keeping track of time is your own responsibility, and you lose screen time for not keeping track or going over.
- Use one screen at a time.
- If you want to get an extra hour of screen time, read a book for an hour.
- All schoolwork gets finished before screen time.
- If you respond with a crabby attitude when you're told to put your device away, you lose your next day's screen time.

Now that our kids are older teens, they are allowed more time on their devices, but we've continued to insist that at 9:00 p.m. on school nights, devices are plugged in and stored in the downstairs office, far from their bedrooms. Weekends bring a later screen curfew (11:00 p.m.) and charging in the same location. Dinners and other meals are also screen-free zones in our house.

If you have older kids and you're concerned that you and your kids are spending too much time on screens, a family meeting can be a good way to motivate everyone to change their habits. You can brainstorm together an agreement about screen rules everyone (even parents) can agree to. Begin with having everyone (including parents) answer the following questions, loosely based on a counseling approach developed by clinical psychologists William R. Miller and Stephen Rollnick called "Motivational Interviewing,"[10] which is effective in inspiring people to change when they feel ambivalence about the change:

- What do you enjoy most about being on your phone (or whatever device is your "main" one)?
- What bothers you about being on your phone?
- What are some of the good things that come out of using your phone?
- What are some of the bad things that come from using your phone?
- What are some of the benefits to your relationships that come from using your phone?
- What are some of the problems phone use has caused in any of your relationships?
- How much time are you currently using your phone each day?
- Have you noticed in yourself or heard about any negative impacts of screen use?
- What are some positive changes that might result from us using our phones less?
- What fun activities could we do together instead of being on our phones?
- How do you think less screen time would impact our family?

Depending on how the discussion goes, and how receptive to change each of you are, you can next brainstorm some guidelines you can all agree to follow. If you've had no rules around screens, I would start with making one small change. And if you don't already have these rules in place, I would recommend that no devices be allowed at family dinner or in bedrooms. Yes, this may require purchasing old-fashioned alarm clocks for everyone, but it's a worthwhile investment. Charging devices in a location other than bedrooms is good for everyone's— including adults'—health. Researchers have found that everyone gets a better night's sleep with less screen use within one hour before bed and phones turned off at night, so that notifications don't disturb sleep.

End the meeting with deciding on a follow-up time to see how the new guidelines are going for everyone. Adjust accordingly. Changing habits is extremely hard, but kids may actually feel and be able to articulate some of the benefits of reduced screen time. I know at camp—where our screen rules are clear and easy to enforce (none, ever)—kids often comment to me about how much they're enjoying the break. Brace yourself for some resistance (maybe even from yourself) but stay strong. Your family's closer connections will be worth it.

Diving Deeper

Author Brené Brown says that "love and belonging are a birthright," and that we need to make sure our children know, in no uncertain terms, that they belong in our family and in our home. And that requires, as parents, that we provide firm leadership regarding respect and kindness.

How connected are you all feeling in your family? What adjustments do you want to make? A good place to start is by asking yourself (and your co-parent, if you have one), the following questions:

- Are respect and kindness the norm in our family?
- Does each family member feel accepted and valued for who they are?
- Do kids contribute to the household by doing chores and do they understand they are needed to make the family run smoothly?
- Are there any non-screen-related family "traditions" (e.g., playing ping-pong, a card game, evening walks around the neighborhood with the dog) that we do regularly?

Have a family meeting to create a "Family Contract" and give each family member the chance to talk about how everyone wants to treat each other. I would use some significant event as the reason for this meeting so that it's a natural time of new beginning. A new calendar year, a new school year, and the start of summer are all transition times that may lend themselves to calling a meeting to regroup and talk about your family.

For the contract to be effective, you'll need to start with a blank piece of paper and let everyone give their input. Here are the questions for each family member to answer:

- What are we doing well to get along as a family?
- What are we not doing well?
- How can I change/adjust my own behavior to make our family more kind and respectful? (This is good because each person, including parents, needs to contribute their own idea for how they can contribute.)
- What are guidelines we want to live by as a family?

For younger kids at camp, their answers and ideas often revolve around seemingly small things like "Ask before you sit on my bed." This is age appropriate and just fine. Respect all input and make sure that at least one of each person's ideas gets in the contract. Word the guidelines in the positive.

Most likely, if you've all contributed, you'll have some good, specific guidelines for your family to live by. I would limit the guidelines to no more than five key points. The only imperative things that you need to make sure are in there (in some form) are:

- Respect—We will treat each other with respect. We will address concerns, needs, or problems with empathy and not be dismissive of others' feelings, even if we disagree.
- Kindness—We will build each other up with kind words and actions and not put each other down.

By establishing family practices where close relationships are fostered through intentionally creating feelings of acceptance and belonging, we provide our kids with the foundation on which to build a life full of connection and fulfillment. Our children's ability to form close, positive relationships with others is the best predictor of their future success in all areas of life. Therefore, experiencing close connections at home is vitally important for our kids and well worth our time and focus. It is only when our kids feel this close connection with us that they will be open to our guidance and behavior coaching. Psychologist Tina Payne Bryson coined a phrase I use to remember this concept and teach to camp counselors: "connection before correction."[11] A close relationship and connection with our kids always needs to be our first priority. Of course, our kids also need help learning how to behave appropriately. Parenting techniques to elicit our kids' best behavior is what we'll cover next.

Camp Secret #2

Catch Them Doing Something Right

Watching the head counselors and camp directors converse and interact with children was the best teacher training available on the planet. Learning how to teach starts with a great relationship, and communication between the adult and child all begins with a high five, big smiles, and active listening. That's what I learned at camp: "Catch them doing something right." I still say that now to frustrated colleagues dwelling on an undesirable behavior.

—*Matthew (former camp counselor who is now a teacher)*

In the mid-1980s, when I started working at camp, a common practice was to tie a toilet paper roll around the neck of a camper who had a potty mouth. Never mind that this would now go viral as a scandalous news story about child abuse; it simply wasn't an effective way to solve the camper's language problem. In fact, the potty-mouthed kid got even *more* attention thanks to his "necklace." Most of this attention was actually *positive*, as other kids found both the toilet paper roll and his bad language funny. The camper gained notoriety, and the bad language continued. Other kids joined in the fun, wanting their own toilet paper necklaces, so the f-bombs multiplied rather than subsided in camper's language use at camp.

Counselor orientation in those days consisted mostly of painting buildings and learning how to start a lanyard. No specific training was given on how to communicate with campers effectively and respond to their behaviors. College-aged counselors were, for the most part, left to their own creative devices about how to address behavioral issues. Corporal punishment was specifically prohibited, but counselors usually drew on the same ineffective methods their parents, camp counselors, and teachers had used with them in the past: nagging, yelling, and punishing, usually with a time-out. And, like the adults who had used these techniques on them during their childhoods, counselors found that negativity and punishments didn't work to improve camper behavior. They discovered instead that negative camper behaviors increased at approximately the same rate as the decibel of their voices.

Frustrated parents have discovered this same truth. Many of the punitive, negative parenting methods used on us, which frazzled parents still use today on children misbehaving in the supermarket, don't work to produce the lasting positive behavior changes we desire for our kids.

Kids will find a million ways to test the patience of the adults who care for them before they master the self-regulation they'll need to succeed in life, but there are some simple tools you can use to make parenting more fun and less taxing. Because while you can't choose your kid's temperament, baseline self-regulation skills, or undesirable behaviors, one thing you *can* control is how you respond when those inevitable negative behaviors bubble to the surface. Your response can profoundly change your children's behavior and ensure their success both now and in the future.

Why Take a More Positive Approach to Behavior Management?

The word *discipline* has a negative connotation for most people. None of us wants to be disciplined at work, and our children certainly don't want to be disciplined at school or by their parents. However, discipline is not, by its original definition, meant to be a negative experience. Being a disciple once had positive connotations and meant a leader or teacher would provide mentorship. Systematic instruction was given until the disciple no longer needed it. Once the disciple gained the knowledge, skills, and *self-discipline* needed to succeed on his or her own, the discipleship would end. In this context, then, the word *discipline* should have a positive connotation. Parents who appropriately discipline their children are giving them the tools they need to develop sound judgment and self-regulation skills throughout the rest of their lives.

Negative connotations about discipline developed, understandably, from the way it has been practiced historically. Until recently, corporal punishment was the norm in child-rearing, and while parents in many states can still legally spank their children, there is much research that has proven this to be ineffective, along with yelling, nagging, and grounding. These traditional forms of punishment simply fail to change children's behavior. Most often it's because they are administered by an angry parent caught up in their own emotions while trying to manage an emotionally charged kid. In these cases, the punishment winds up harsher than intended and, worse yet, the child learns an unproductive way to deal with anger.

But there's a more effective way to direct children toward better behavior, and it starts with relationship. Kids respond to having a close connection with a trusted adult and are more likely to make good choices in an effort to please a parent. My own parents had a less punitive and more relaxed, relational focus. I *wanted* to make good choices so that I wouldn't disappoint them. Of course, I wasn't always perfect. As a senior in high school, I got caught drinking alcohol. My dad's deep disappointment and calm discussion about the dangers of what I had done were almost too much to bear. I remember thinking that being yelled at or grounded would have been preferable. Instead of being angry with my dad, I was embarrassed by my actions and full of enough guilt to think twice about drinking like that again.

Perhaps the most compelling argument I can offer is that learning positive behavior management techniques will make your life more enjoyable. Parenting this way is much less taxing than yelling and punishing, so your stress level will be lower and your family happiness will be higher. In addition, these tips preserve your close, loving relationship with your children and nurture their ability to self-discipline, which is the ultimate goal of parenting. We want our children to grow into adults who are able to make good choices and decisions.

Parenting Plans for Better Behavior

Depending on your family history, your current interaction patterns with your child, your child's temperament, and your own, practicing positive parenting may require either a slight adjustment or a complete overhaul in your habits. The desired outcome—a child (and future adult) who is able to behave respectfully and appropriately in the family and the community—is well worth the effort involved in adjusting to a more positive parenting style. I am under no illusion that the shift to a more positive behavior management approach, perhaps after generations of a negative style in your own family, will be easy. All parents, regardless of personality disposition and personal experience, can benefit from utilizing these skills. Specific aspects of a more positive style include learning to regulate our own emotions, focusing on our relationship with our child, and practicing simple positive behavior management techniques. A starting point in this style adjustment is learning how to better manage our own emotions in order to help our children learn to regulate theirs.

Keep Calm and Parent On

> When little people are overwhelmed by big emotions, it's our job to share our calm, not join their chaos.
>
> —L. R. Knost

As parents, we are so emotionally invested in our kids, and our kids in us, that we can inadvertently create dysfunctional dynamics that hold them back from being their best selves. With all we've learned about how the brain works, we now understand that *we cannot talk logically to our kids, and they will not be able to hear us or learn anything from us, when either of us is upset or emotions are running high.* As Dr. Daniel Siegel and Tina Payne Bryson, PhD, explain, "If kids are upset or out of control, that's the worst time to try to teach them."[1] In moments of intense emotion, from either our child or us, no problem will ever be solved. In fact, it's more likely that the problem will escalate when emotions are running high. Let everyone calm down before trying to talk about or solve anything. *And let the calmness begin with you.* Not only will you be in a better position to react appropriately to your children, but you will also be modeling for them an important interpersonal skill that will help them in future relationships—how to respond calmly in emotional situations.

When I train counselors, I let them know that a really important ability they need to develop is knowing when they need a short break from their campers to regroup physically and emotionally. When they feel themselves losing patience with children, they need to seek help from another counselor rather than taking their frustrations out on campers. Likewise, we train counselors to look out for each other and tap out anyone who they see starting to lose it with campers. For parents, and for camp counselors and anyone else who works with kids (who can really test our patience!), there are numerous research-based ways to calm down, so find one that works for you and start using it:

1. Take a walk.
2. Find a "chill spot" where you can relax on your own for a few minutes.
3. Take a few deep breaths.
4. Count to ten (or one hundred).
5. Listen to music.
6. Think about one or more things you are grateful for.
7. Laugh.

8. Hug someone.

9. Stretch or do a yoga move.

Then there's this gem from camp director Erica Jameson (Jameson Ranch Camp), who has trained herself to be "underwhelmed" in highly charged situations that many would react to with high emotional intensity (yelling, swearing, and the like). Whether at her camp or with her own kids at home, Jameson has learned not to let the intensity level of a stressful situation or event dictate her response. Rather than overreacting in an already precarious situation and making it even worse, Jameson has learned to stay calm in the midst of chaos. She recognizes that high-stress situations are part of life as a camp director and as a parent. She takes a deep breath and focuses on staying calm and underwhelmed even in situations that seem overwhelming to outside observers. She keeps herself mentally ready to respond calmly rather than react. Jameson *keeps calm and parents on.*

Connection Before Correction

The foundation of positive parenting is forming and maintaining a close relationship with each of our children. This book started with the topic of connection, and it's a theme that runs through all nine parenting lessons. At camp, we use the phrase "connection before correction" to remind counselors that before campers will listen to us, accept our guidance, and follow our example, they need to know that we care about them individually and like them regardless of their behavior. There are two tools camp counselors use that parents can use, as well, to develop and maintain close relationships with our children, even when we are correcting them: empathy and validation. Even in the midst of correction, children need to understand our fundamental desire to connect with and understand them.

Regardless of our child's behavior, if we lead with empathy, we maintain our relationship while still allowing for consequences. In the *Love and Logic* parenting curriculum, Jim and Charles Fay offer examples of leading with empathy and provide wording for how to respond, regardless of the misbehavior or mistake. A simple, concerned "Oh, that is such a bummer" lets your child know that you feel bad about what has happened.[2] Empathy does not mean rescuing your children from facing the consequences of their actions. Instead, it means letting them know you care about them and their feelings.

Along with empathy, kids need validation of their feelings. Kids, especially younger ones, often have unfounded fears. It's tempting to say "There's nothing to be scared of" about a dark bedroom. Instead, if we acknowledge those feelings, it will help children articulate and process them: "It sounds like you are really scared. What's scary for you? Where are you feeling the fear in your body?" We use this technique at camp with homesick campers; instead of trying to talk them into having fun "like everyone else," we get with them in their sadness and validate their feelings.

Positive Behavior Management Strategies

Once you can implement the practices of *not* overreacting out of emotion and prioritizing connection before correction with your child, there are several positive behavior management strategies you can implement.

Identify Strengths

Every Monday morning I get an email with my kids' current grades. Typically, I scan over them for any assignments or subjects with lower grades. I scroll past the As, because those don't grab my attention. Like most parents, it is my natural inclination to look for a missing homework assignment or poor test score. And yet I've learned that focusing on deficits does not motivate kids to do better in school. Why do I skim the good grades and not celebrate them? I should instead revel in my kids' strengths, which in turn will motivate them to do more of what they do best.

One of my favorite quotes is "Comparison is the thief of joy."

When we spend our time wishing we were more like someone else, we're not creating good, joyful feelings in ourselves. Kids do *not* learn how to appreciate their own good qualities when their time and energy are focused on qualities they don't have. As parents, we can positively impact our kids by using the language of strengths, emphasizing qualities that come naturally to them. The VIA Institute on Character defines "Signature Strengths" as "character strengths that are most essential to who we are."[3] When kids are appropriately challenged to use their signature strengths—whether in a hobby or a sport or at school—we provide a path to a state of flow and ease that enables our kids to be their best and truest selves.[4]

Alternatively, if we consistently pester our children about shortcomings and neglect to highlight the strengths they naturally possess, we risk raising kids who dislike themselves, which *does not* promote happiness. I'm not advocating constantly telling our kids how great they are. Instead, I propose we help them learn to celebrate their strengths while also acknowledging their weaknesses; we can flip the conversation and make strengths and "what went right" the focus. We can talk about the gain (how far we've come) rather than the gap (how much further we have to go). By doing these things, our kids can learn to see themselves in a more positive way and not condemn themselves for qualities they lack. By focusing on your child's strengths and what you appreciate in them, you put yourself in a better frame of mind to address undesirable behaviors.

Clearly Articulate Expectations

As adults, we often make a fundamental error when leading kids: We neglect to tell them exactly what we want them to do. Instead, we get angry and frustrated over their undesirable behaviors, without ever having clearly explained what our expectations are.

The set of expectations we must articulate first—those fundamental to the values we wish to instill in our children—are what I refer to as *nonnegotiables*. These will vary with the age of your child; they might revolve around emotional and physical safety and include things like when to go to an adult with a problem, what language is acceptable in your family, and whether or not your family respects laws (drinking age of twenty-one, provisional driver's license, etc.). You need to be clear about the nonnegotiable expectations for your kids so that you can plan how you are going to communicate those important values.

Once the *nonnegotiables* are in place—those behaviors you *must* see in your children—you can turn your attention to *desired behaviors*, those you *want* to see in your children. Such behaviors might include:

- Saying "thank you" upon receiving a gift or favor from someone else.
- Holding Grandma's hand to steady her while walking.
- Telling a positive story from their day at dinner.

Try brainstorming a list of other desired behaviors, a process that will help you better articulate clear expectations to your child. Once you have the list, you can prioritize the ones that are most important to you.

Focus on Privileges, Not Punishments

When we began teaching positive behavior management techniques at camp, counselors often raised their hands and asked questions like "But how can we punish them?" or "What punishment is allowed?" They couldn't believe that other, more positive approaches would work.

Whether we present consequences as punishments or privileges, the outcome is the same for kids. They'll get the same answer, and we'll get the same result. It's just the presentation that needs to be different. Instead of saying, "You are taking too long to get ready for bed, so we will not have time for a whole chapter tonight," which sounds like a punishment, instead we can say, "We'll read an extra chapter if you're in your sleeping bags by 9:00 p.m." It's a subtle difference with the same outcome.

As parents, it's important to remember that we are the keeper of our children's privileges and that, other than the basic rights and care (nurturing, food, shelter, rest, attention, medical care), everything our children get to do and use while under our care is a privilege we provide. Any toy or electronic device is a privilege. Any special event, activity, or family outing is a privilege. Even participating in a club or on a sports team is a privilege. In our consumption culture, many children believe that having the latest iPhone is their right. Unless they are earning the money to buy it and pay the monthly phone bill, it is not.

Start thinking of these statements as formulas you can use for explaining actions that result in privileges:

What you're willing to allow them to do:

- "You can _____ after you _____."
  Here are examples:
  - "You can watch TV after you finish emptying the dishwasher."
  - "You can use your phone after you finish your homework."

What you're willing to do for them:

- "I will _____ once you _____."
  Here are examples:
  - "I will take you out for ice cream once you've finished your science project."
  - "I will reactivate your phone once your grades are at a B average."

At camp, we outline campers' rights so that our counselors clearly understand what things can be viewed as privileges. Usually, privileges are extras, like more time reading or an extra game of "Mafia" around the campfire. Often, we use fun events as motivation for getting somewhere faster or getting cleanup done more quickly: "If our cabin is clean by 8:30 a.m., we'll have time for a round of 'Ninja' before morning assembly."[5]

Privileges that involve time spent doing something they enjoy (like having a story read to them or playing a game) are more motivating and get better results than either punishments or material rewards. I've heard stories of parents overusing material gifts for behavioral incentives. A babysitter who regularly watches a four-year-old after school reported that the little girl gets a stuffed animal every Monday, Wednesday, and Friday for "staying at preschool." Besides the house being overrun with stuffed animals, the reward is not necessary nor meaningful.

Rewards should not be given for actions that are expected normal behaviors. In fact, we do our kids a disservice by rewarding them for activities that should become intrinsically satisfying. Giving our kids rewards for successes that are satisfying on their own decreases the natural feeling of accomplishment and pride that comes from a job well done. Our biggest accomplishments and successes in life come from work we've done because of our intrinsic motivation. By offering material rewards and incentives to our kids (extrinsic motivation), we rob them of the opportunity to gain that wonderful feeling of wanting to do something because we enjoy the challenge and desire to work hard at it.[6] Validation, encouragement, and sincere congratulations and celebration for goals accomplished and jobs well done will better serve our kids than any material rewards.

When our kids become adults, no one will give out stars and bonuses just for doing what they are supposed to do, so we shouldn't create that false expectation when they're young. Time spent doing something enjoyable together, and encouraging notes just because we love them and want them to know we're thinking about them, are far better than material gifts tied to a task or an accomplishment we want our child to develop intrinsic motivation to repeat.

Just Say Yes

There's a popular children's picture book called *No, David!* In it, toddler David goes around wreaking havoc in his home to a constant stream of "No, David!" Poor David can't seem to do anything right, so the word he hears most often is, of course, "No!" Even in the book, all those noes don't succeed in changing David's behavior.

Parenting can sometimes feel like an endless stream of noes:

"Can I have another bowl of ice cream?"
"No."
"Can I jump off the roof into the pool?"
"No."
"Can I stop going to school? It's so boring."
"No."

You get the idea. It's no fun to be the one who has to say no all the time, but it's a common experience for many parents. There are many questions to which the answer really is no, but because our kids' brains respond much better to yeses and positive instructions than to noes and don'ts, we can reframe how we say things to get better results. When we focus on turning as many noes into yeses, we'll elicit better responses from our kids:

"Can I have dessert now?"
"Yes, you can have dessert after you finish wiping the table."
"Can we play cards?"
"Yes, we can play cards as soon as your homework is done."
"Can I have a friend over?"
"Yes, you can have a friend over as soon as your bed is made and your laundry is done."

In instances when what is about to roll off your tongue is a resounding no, think about whether to use the "Yes, as soon as…" or "Yes, after…" formula to make it a yes instead.

Catch Them Doing Something Right

We're fighting biology when we try to shift to a more positive behavior management approach. Our brains are wired to be more aware of negative events and threats to our environment, so it is no surprise that we tend to notice more of what our kids do wrong and less of what they do right. For the kid who's accustomed to spending a lot of time in the corner in time-out or on the bench outside the principal's office, the cycle of "getting in trouble" seems endless. Adults unknowingly contribute to the situation by putting a negative label on the kid and noticing every small infraction, even when the child's behavior is similar to other kids who are not getting in trouble. But there is a way to stop this negative cycle.

People who work with children are often on high alert for catching kids when they are doing something wrong. This negative focus is prevalent in classrooms, on sports fields, and, unfortunately, in our own homes. At camp, we flip this concept on its head when we train our counselors, who are taught the following steps for addressing a misbehaving child:

Step 1: Notice your child's behavior.

Step 2: Take a deep breath and remind yourself that when kids are acting the most unlovable, they need the most love.

Step 3: Remember that this is a good kid who needs help learning how to behave appropriately. This is not a bad, or problem, child.

Step 4: Finally, find something they do right, even if it's a tiny thing, and compliment them right away. Let your first words to them be positive, affirming ones.

For example, a counselor may say, "I noticed you helped your cabin mate carry their luggage to our tent." At home, it may sound like this: "I saw that you put your backpack away right when you walked in the door!" Note that you do not need to be effusive or give a huge amount of thanks or praise. Simply noticing a desired behavior and pointing it out is enough.

Finding something positive to say can be challenging with some kids, but the results are amazing. Our goal is to let our kids know—right from the start—that we will notice good things they do. We need to stay on the lookout to catch kids doing something right so we can encourage more positive behavior!

Positively Managing Negative Behaviors

Identifying positive behaviors can be fun, and the practice may even help mitigate the number of negative behaviors we see in our kids. But as parents we know the negative, undesirable actions are still there, waiting to surface; inevitably, there will be a worm or two in the apple! For those times, I offer some time-tested strategies for dealing with negative behaviors without negatively impacting your relationship or causing emotional family upheaval and arguments: identify the issue, talk less, and wait for "prime time."

You, Me, and The Issue

Many of my favorite counseling and parenting strategies have come through leadership and management trainings, seminars, and books. The same strategies that create positive corporate cultures also work in families. During our leadership training in the 1990s and early 2000s, corporate trainer Debby Winning drew three circles: two above and one centered below. In the circle on the left, she put the word "You." In the circle on the right was the word "Me." And in the circle below, she wrote "The Issue." She drew two arrows: one from "You" to "The Issue," and one from "Me" to the "The Issue."

I'm a visual learner so this image has stuck with me for years and has served as a reminder of how to talk with someone when something is not going well. Whether it be an employee, a camper, or my own kids, before I approach them to talk, I need to figure out the issue. Because the most effective conversations about a negative behavior need to be focused on the behavior itself, not an attack on the person or their character, the first thing to determine is what the actual issue is. Labeling a

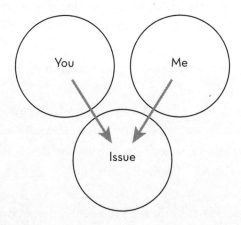

person with a negative adjective or giving vague negative feedback does not change behavior.

At home with our kids, we may lean towards labeling them as "messy" or "lazy" and order them to "wash the dishes!" But instead of name-calling or barking commands, which most of us would never do with an employee at work, we can instead calmly discuss a specific issue with our child:

Parent: "Let's talk about the dirty dishes you left in the sink this
    morning."
Child: (Silence.)
Parent: "Let's figure out how to solve the problem of the dishes
    left in the kitchen sink." (The issue.)
Child: (Silence, possibly with a scowl.)
Parent: "The breakfast dishes in the sink are harder to wash at the
    end of the day when the food has really gotten stuck on there."
Child: "So?"
Parent: "What's a good plan for dealing with your dirty breakfast
    dishes?"
Child: "(Insert sibling's name here) doesn't do her dishes either."
    (Excuse.)

Parent: "Thanks for letting me know. Right now, we're talking about the dishes you left in the kitchen sink." (Redirect back to the issue.)

Child: "I'd rather do another chore." (Trying to side-track conversation.)

Parent: "Okay, we can revisit who does which chores and see about shifting duties around at our next family meeting. Right now, we're going to focus on the issue of the dirty dishes in the sink." (Redirect back to the issue.)

This conversation can continue in a few different directions. Your child could continue to make excuses or try to switch the direction of the conversation. For each excuse or reason they give for not doing the dishes, you can offer acknowledgement or validation that you've heard followed by redirection back to the issue. Eventually, when your child sees that they will not get you side-tracked or veered away from the issue you're discussing, they will succumb and do the dishes (mostly to avoid a long conversation about a topic that they do not want to discuss). Or, you may end up having a solution-focused conversation about different plans that could work to solve the problem. For example, your child may say they want to just rinse the food off the dishes in the morning and load them into the dishwasher after school. Whatever the plan is, if you get your child involved in the solution, they will be more likely to follow through. But the trick is keeping the conversation focused on the one issue you are trying to address and not raising your voice or labeling your child. You aren't talking about the child as a person, you are talking about the issue!

At camp, when our head counselors need to meet with a counselor they supervise about a performance issue, they often come to me with something like "He's grouchy with his campers in the morning." I challenge the head counselor to identify a specific issue they can discuss with the counselor. Once they think about it, they usually come up with something more specific: "The issue I want to talk with you about is how campers are perceiving your tone of voice in the morning. I know you want your campers to get a sense of how much you enjoy being with them, so let's talk about how to solve this issue of their negative perception."

Instead of attacking the counselor as a person, or calling them "grouchy," the supervisor identifies a specific issue that can be discussed and planned around, in this case, *tone of voice*. This makes the conversation more productive and focused on a plan for improvement of a specific behavior. The counselor can't get defensive and say, "I'm not grouchy," because the counselor was never called "grouchy" or any other negative labels, and the issue was identified clearly. The resulting conversation is a productive one about specific things the counselor can do to be perceived more positively by campers in the morning.

With our own kids, it's also more effective to determine and discuss a specific issue rather than labeling them with derogatory adjectives or attacking them as a person. Here are a few common parent complaints about kids and a possible issue to discuss around each:

Complaint	*Possible Issue*
Slow in the morning:	"Let's talk about the morning schedule."
Poor work ethic:	"Let's talk about your D in math."
Not helpful around the house:	"Let's talk about laundry."

Regardless of the issue, the bulk of the conversation is about a plan for improvement in a specific area rather than a sweeping—and possibly hurtful—generalization about our child's character.

The 80-20 Rule

Unless (like my husband) you're blessed to be more of an observer and a great listener (often traits of introverts), you may (like me, more of an extrovert) talk *way* too much during conversations with your kids. What you may also have noticed is that all that talk gets you nowhere—fast.

I've been to a number of leadership trainings over the years, and in many of them, facilitators have introduced the "80-20 Rule" for management conversations: that is, we should be listening 80 percent of the time when talking with our employees and using the remaining 20 percent to ask open-ended questions rather than lecturing or spouting off ideas.[7] I have worked hard to implement this rule in my professional life, and I have applied this same principle into conversations with campers and with my own kids. The best way to ensure we do less talking and more listening with our kids is to use open-ended questions and get comfortable with pauses in the conversation. Some good open-ended questions include:

"How do you plan to fix this."
"What do you think you could do differently next time?"
"How can you solve this problem?"
"What steps are you going to take?"
"What is your whole plan?"

Kids have learned that if they pause long enough after being asked a question, the adult will often tell them what the answer or solution is, saving them from having to think for themselves and solve the problem, so it's almost always best to wait their pauses out. Ask the open-ended question and allow for the silence (which can feel awkward) while they think about their response. Once they realize you are not going to rescue them and solve the problem or issue for them, they will usually offer up some of their own ideas, and you can have a productive conversation to resolve the issue. By having the child take ownership for the plan for improvement, rather than you telling them what they need to do differently, they are more likely to feel the ownership necessary to follow through on their plan for improved behavior.

At camp, we use training videos from psychologist Chris Thurber, which provide simple and practical tips for working with campers. Thurber offers sage advice: Expend as little energy as possible, he says, "no more energy than a Tic-Tac." To direct campers toward desired

behaviors, such as hanging up their wet towels, Thurber suggests powerful, yet subtle, options:

> *A look*—Counselor looks over at the towel.
> *Show (point)*—Counselor points index finger at the towel.
> *Say name quietly*—Counselor says camper's name quietly and
> points to towel.[8]

What counselors learn from watching the video is how little energy
they need to use to correct small behavioral issues. They also learn to
compliment the camper the next time he hangs his towel in the appropriate place—on the line outside. Tired parents can also take a break
from the lectures and instead use the low-energy responses of a look, a
point, or just saying the child's name.

Find "Prime Time"

After all these years of parenting, I know that my teenage sons are
crabby first thing in the morning on school days and right after school.
It's understandable; they're normal teens. In the morning, their sleep
was interrupted by a too-early alarm. At the end of the school day,
they've just finished dealing with social and academic pressures for
seven hours. Liken it to how you feel after a busy day at work full of
constant input and interaction. They need a few moments to decom-
press without having to comment about their day or hear some more
demands made on them and their time.

They need food.

They need some exercise.

What they don't need me is for me to badger them about a school
project or their chores. So, instead of getting into the same struggle
again and again, and then taking it personally that they are being rude
or disrespectful to me, I now expect that our time after school will be
quiet, listening to music and having our own thoughts, unless one of
them initiates a conversation. Anticipating the quicksand of my boys'
after-school moods, I tread cautiously until they've had a snack and

their blood sugar has come back to center. Dinnertime and evenings are our "prime time," where we have our best conversations and interactions. Knowing this, I can relax during the uninspiring mornings and rides home from school.

One advantage you have as a parent is that you know your children and their daily patterns better than anyone else. Look back over the past few days or week: When were the quicksand periods for your child? What time of day have you had your most negative interactions? Your most positive? Perhaps you'll find a pattern. And, knowing the pattern, you'll be able to give your children some space and focus on interacting most during their prime time.

Bringing Camp Home: Practicing Positive Behavior Management

Kids who feel good about themselves behave better, so the best approach to positive behavior management hinges on helping our kids feel better about themselves.

One Simple Thing

In a recent lecture[9] by Tina Payne Bryson, she showed camp directors an amazing way to approach our kids' challenging behaviors. She had us create a two-column list by putting a line down the middle of our papers. On the left side, she had us title the column "Discipline Problems." Under the heading, we wrote things like "cooperation," "listening," "lack of kindness to young sibling," "table manners," and so on. Next, she had us write the heading for the column on the right: "Skills to Build." Those same discipline problems transferred nicely to the skills-building column! Bryson's point was this: Simply by viewing our children's bad behavior from the perspective of a lack of skill, we can reframe the way we see our children's behavior *and* see that our role is to help them build the skills they need.

A simple way to start positively shaping your child's behavior is to brainstorm a list of the skills they need to build. These are behaviors your child has not mastered that you (or someone else) will need to teach them. Make a list of *undesired* behaviors that you are seeing in your child. Then, rewrite that behavior as a skill they need to build. See the examples in this chart to get an idea of how to word your list. In the "Resources" section at the back of the book, I've provided a blank chart to use for your child. You can also download and print a chart at http://happycampersbook.com.

EXAMPLE "SKILLS TO BUILD" LIST

Undesired Behavior	Skill to Build
Being unpleasant to family members	Self-monitoring their mood and developing tools to improve mood
Waiting until the last minute to do school projects	Time management
Forgetting items needed for school	Managing belongings
Interrupting	Waiting their turn to talk

Keep this list private and discuss and share only with your co-parent. This is not a list to go on your refrigerator! As you look at the list, highlight or circle the one or two behaviors that you think are the most troublesome. View this as your list of priority skills to focus on first as you start practicing new, more positive behavior management techniques at home. Ideally, you can use this list as a guidepost to show improvement, however small, over time. It can serve as an encouragement to you that your children can improve their behavior, especially as they start to see themselves in a more positive light.

It's important as well that you start a list of your children's positive behaviors, even if some of them might be a stretch. Remember, *catch them doing something right*. It can be as simple as noticing they brush their teeth well, they put their belongings in the right place, or they set the table for dinner: basic things, but great opportunities to compliment your children and let them know you see their good behaviors. Your list will include positive behaviors you can point out to your children *now*—to show them you see the good they do and accept them exactly as they are.

The Sticky Note Solution

Compliments don't always have to be verbal. An encouraging sticky note can go a long way in boosting your child's confidence in their ability to succeed. Showing your child you notice their good behaviors will reinforce those skills and encourage them as they learn new skills. A simple sticky note, tucked in the book they're reading or in their lunch box, acknowledging that you notice what they're doing well and the positive character traits you're seeing in them, goes a long way. Start the note with "I noticed..."

Here are some examples:

"I noticed you got yourself up for school without my help. I appreciate your responsibility."

"I noticed you helped unload the groceries without being asked. I appreciate your helpfulness."

"I noticed you let your sister watch the TV show she likes. That was kind."

You get the idea. All of these things, written on sticky notes as well as said out loud to our children, boost their confidence and help them shape a positive view of themselves.

Make It Fun

In seventh grade, I took my first sewing class. I enjoyed every part of the sewing process—picking out a pattern and fabric, getting all my supplies together, and then completing the project, step by step. My first sewing projects were simple—pillows, pincushions, small ornaments. But as I continued to grow my skills, I took on more complicated projects, including collared shirts with button holes, pajama gifts for my entire family, and costumes. Some weekends, I would spend both days working on one of my sewing projects, losing track of time and forgetting to do anything else.

As soon as I heard the term *flow* in my study of positive psychology, I knew exactly what it meant, because I had experienced it myself during my sewing binges as a middle schooler and now, as an adult, while doing creative projects like journaling, creating a photo book, or writing an article or a blog post. Another childhood practice that got me into flow (and still does) is reading. Just like when I was a child, I can still get caught up in a great novel, lose track of time, and need to finish it before I can resume my normal day-to-day activities. Flow happens when we're in a state of heightened focus and immersion. It can come to us while doing creative tasks, doing meaningful work we enjoy, or when we're playing. We're in a state of flow when we're so engaged in an activity that we lose track of time.

The concept of flow was delved into by psychologist Mihaly Csik-szentmihalyi. He describes a state that comes naturally to young children immersed in play but often gets squashed right out of most of us by middle school due to our culture and lifestyle.[10]

Flow is the good stuff of life and we all need to seek more. In our busy family lifestyle, flow can go by the wayside. Since learning of the concept, I'm more aware of the times when I find myself in flow (or, usually, after I've been in flow) and see others—especially kids—in flow. For myself, taking a walk with a friend and chatting, writing, reading a book, going for a run, or doing a photo or craft project are activities that get me in flow. At camp, when young kids are given free-play time outdoors, I witness them in that wonderful state of childhood flow. While gathering sticks and supplies to build a fort, or playing an elaborate pretend game with stuffed animals, they are smiling, engaged, and relaxed. They can play for hours, completely losing track of time. Older campers get into the flow state while talking and laughing together, intently working on a friendship bracelet, singing, dancing, or playing the guitar or other instrument. We all have the capacity to get into flow, but we need to learn for ourselves, and help our kids figure out, what their flow activities are!

Looking at your family—both individually and as a group—what activities get you in that state of flow? Is there an activity that you enjoy doing that you haven't prioritized recently? If there's a craft, hobby, or musical instrument that gets you in a state of flow, consider spending more time doing that activity again. Maybe your kids will want to join you, or maybe they won't. But even if your kids get to see you—an adult—in flow, they will learn that childhood doesn't have to be the end of that wonderful state. Think about the last time your family was in a state of flow together—just enjoying being together and having fun, not wanting to stop whatever you were doing. What activity were you doing? Prioritize doing that same activity again and consider making it a weekly ritual that everyone can look forward to.

Around the Campfire

A *family strengths* activity can help parents learn to look at themselves and their children more positively. At camp, we do an activity where campers share about one of their strengths and tell a story of how they've used that strength.[11] Examples of some of the strengths campers identify in themselves are kindness, bravery, love, appreciation for beauty, curiosity, and zest. Counselors encourage kids to think about how they can use that strength more, both at camp and at home. It is remarkable to witness what happens when kids think and talk about a strength, often for the first time identifying it in themselves, and then learn how they can use that strength in different settings. When given a name to a part of themselves they recognize and intuitively know, kids gain a vocabulary to talk about themselves more positively.

You can do this activity around your own dinner table as well. Family members can each identify one or more strengths in themselves (I use the "VIA Character Strengths" list provided in the "Resources" section, but you can use any list of character strengths), without showing others. Next, each family member can use sticky notes to write down one or two strengths they see in each other person in their family. Comparing what we think our strengths are to what strengths others see in us is a fun and enlightening activity.

Thinking and talking about what went well each day is also a great way to start the process of focusing on strengths. During dinner conversation, ask "What went well today?" and have each family member share a success. Oftentimes, strengths come out as you listen to what each person shares.

Family Meeting Topic: Values

A discussion of values and any nonnegotiable rules that go along with those values is an important conversation to have as a family. Before the family meeting, it's important that you brainstorm important behaviors:

• Present those expectations clearly to kids (a written, posted document is helpful).

• Lead a discussion about why particular values or behaviors are important to you. Ask your kids, "Why do you think this is important to us?" Let the kids do much of the talking until you are sure that they not only understand your expectation but, more important, the value and reasons behind the expectation.

In my family, one of the topics we've discussed with our kids, once they're in high school and being exposed to alcohol consumption, are the dangers of binge drinking. Our expectation is that our kids will not binge-drink—even when they are legally of age to consume alcohol, and we've discussed both the health and safety reasons behind our expectation. We've openly discussed with our kids the tragic death of our family friend "Gordy" Bailey from alcohol poisoning and how his death has impacted his parents, sister, and friends.[12] They know both our expectations that we have around their alcohol decisions as well as the reasons we feel strongly about these expectations. Ultimately, they will make their own choices, but be sure your kids know your values and expectations.

- Make sure your kids are very clear on your expectations. Ask them, "What questions do you have about this?"
- Revisit expectations as needed. For younger kids, expectations can include things like:
    - We always wear our seat belts in cars because we value safety.
    - We ask Mom or Dad before going online.
    - We tell our parents if we are concerned about ourselves or a friend being hurt in any way.
    - We all help with kitchen clean up after dinner because we value teamwork.
    - We say "please" and "thank you" to show our respect to others.
    - When we are annoyed or angry, we calm down before speaking.

As our kids get older, the rules begin to revolve around more mature topics, with a continued focus on interpersonal values, as well:

- We do not touch our phones while driving.
- We do not use any illegal drugs.
- Phones and computers are charged and used in public rooms at home.
- We take turns making dinner and cleaning up after dinner.
- We support and encourage each other.
- We fulfill our family responsibilities to make our home run smoothly.
- We let a parent or another adult know if we are concerned for our own or someone else's safety.

I'm certain you can come up with your own set of values and expectations, based on what's most important to you, that apply to your family. Figure out the handful of rules (no more than five) that are your nonnegotiables (at least for the time being, based on your kids' current ages). Talk about your expectations with your kids and the why behind the expectation. Make sure your kids understand *why* you want them to do family errands now that they drive. If this is a new concept for them, explain that these rules are meant to keep them safe both physically and emotionally. It's best to present one set of expectations at a time.

For other expectations—the ones about how you're going to relate to one another in your family—make it a family meeting and have your kids help come up with the guidelines, just like we do at our opening night campfires. This could end up being something like your family motto. Let the kids contribute their ideas for how they want to see your family relating and living together. For younger kids, they may include less consequential things—like our younger campers do—about rules for sitting on each other's beds and asking before borrowing items. That's okay. It's good for them to feel empowered to help shape the family culture in which they live. The important thing is for both parents and kids to be clear about the expectations.

Diving Deeper

Evaluating your parenting without getting defensive is difficult, but it's an important step. In order to provide the positive guidance our children need, we need to look at our own leadership and communication skills and how we are using them in our families.

Openly sharing both our successes and mistakes is part of our camp's culture. Biweekly evaluation meetings start with the counselor sharing with their supervisor three things that are going well in their cabin group or activity as well as three things that are not going well. Defensiveness is rare, because counselors get accustomed to putting self-observations in the context of areas for improvement; conversations thus move quickly to goals and plans to hone counseling skills.

I have seen as a parent the benefits of using this same approach. Instead of harping on each other's shortcomings or blaming the other parent for a child's behavioral problems, my husband and I have regular meetings to discuss what's working and what isn't. In recent years, some of our conclusions have revealed that it's better for him to handle certain aspects of parenting and for me to focus on others. In these meetings (without the children present), each parent can share their successes and concerns. Instead of blaming each other, each parent can focus on their own parenting through the following questions:

- What's going well in our family this week?
- What's been my strength or high point as a parent?
- Where am I struggling or what's been hardest for me?

The discussion can then move to focusing on ideas and action plans for each parent to try, rather than criticizing and blaming. If you can establish a regular, nondefensive time to evaluate what's going on in your family and with your parenting, and to discuss the challenges and issues your family is facing, not only will it help your relationship with your partner, but it will also make for a more peaceful, happy family life.

Applying even just one of the positive parenting practices outlined in this chapter will reduce the stress you experience during these busy family years. Perhaps your new, more positive parenting focus will also help you complain less and foster more optimism in yourself and in your kids. That's what we'll explore next.

Camp Secret #3

Positive Practices Produce Optimistic Kids

At camp, I'm always filled with such high energy and such an overwhelming sense of positivity. It is the environment there and the community that give me all of that energy, that fuel me to just go on and be so creative and so energetic and so full of life, every day, day after day, and I get that from the other people I'm interacting with.

—Henry

My dad, whom we all now call "Poppi," looks out the window each morning and says, "What a beautiful day!" He sits down to each family meal with the exclamation, "Well, isn't this nice?" He has told me, numerous times, that my meat loaf is the best he's ever had. Even while suffering from Parkinson's disease, which has robbed him of the physical strength to do many rigorous outdoor activities he's always loved, his optimism continues to shine through as he focuses on enjoying life's simple pleasures, like a beautiful sunset and a delicious home-cooked meal. My dad was the one who, when I had the crazy idea of buying a summer camp, encouraged me to write up a business plan and dream big. I see now that having a parent who modeled positivity and optimism shaped so much of who I am today. My dad's example demonstrates what research has revealed—our optimism and positive approach to life allow us to take risks and be resilient in facing life's inevitable setbacks and challenges.

Why is optimism a quality that's so important to nurture in ourselves and our children? What does it matter if we and our kids are negative, complain and see our glass as "half empty?" It matters because if our children view themselves as victims of life's dissatisfactions and frustrations, they feel helpless to change their circumstances. Children and adolescents who are pessimistic about life and dwell on their short-comings aren't able to set goals and take actions that lead to thriving adulthood. According to Paul Tough, author of *How Children Succeed*, "Optimists…look for specific, limited, short-term explanations for bad events, and as a result, in the face of a setback, they're more likely to pick themselves up and try again."[1] We need to care about whether our camps, schools, and families are positive, and whether our kids are learning to be optimistic, because a more optimistic outlook predicts success in many areas including health, happiness, and relationships.

At camp, being upbeat and optimistic, even in the face of challeng-ing circumstances, is what successful camp counselors model. The big thunderstorm that suddenly comes up while out on the lake becomes a fun, story-filled adventure. The need to reapply sunscreen multiple times a day becomes a game we call "Screen It Like You Mean It," where kids compete to rub their sunscreen in the fastest. By making mundane tasks fun, and keeping a positive outlook about challenging circumstances, the best camp counselors model an optimism that rubs off on their campers.

Feeling more optimistic leads to positive emotions that actually help our kids grow important emotional and physical resources. Bar-bara Fredrickson, a psychologist and researcher who developed the Broaden-and-Build Theory of Positive Emotions, explains the breadth of these benefits: "These resources can be *cognitive*, like the ability to mindfully attend to the present moment; *psychological*, like the ability to maintain a sense of mastery over environmental challenges; *social*, like the ability to give and receive emotional support; or *physical*, like the ability to ward off the common cold." It's a worthwhile endeavor to help our kids become more positive and optimistic in the way they see and approach life. We do this by intentionally developing a culture at home the exact same way culture happens at camp: by putting in place positive practices.

The Positive Practice of Compliments

Compliments are one of many optimism-producing habits practiced at many camps. At Camp Champions in Central Texas, owner Steve Baskin describes a nightly ritual that includes sharing their "heroes of the day." When talking about their heroes, campers share compliments about cabin mates and camp staff who had a positive impact on their day. Baskin reports that since introducing this practice they've seen "increased cooperation, positivity, and joy from the campers."[2]

The pattern is the same at many camps and can be adopted for home. At camp, counselors model positive words and prompt campers to think about and say positive things to and about each other. At home, this may look like a parent remembering to compliment a co-parent who prepared a nice meal, or a child who set the dinner table without being reminded. As a result, a culture develops where everyone has the habit of complimenting one another.

At my camp, an effective compliment practice called WOWs started more than a decade ago. WOWs are positive messages written daily by campers and staff, who keep special WOW notepads on hand (or use whatever scrap of paper or napkin is nearby) to record kind, helpful, or brave things they've seen others do. A few positive words of encouragement or a compliment that takes less than a minute to write are all someone needs to WOW a camp friend. Over each two-week camp session, we collect WOWs by the hundreds on a special bulletin board located (conveniently) at the entrance to our dining hall. We read a few WOWs aloud at our daily assembly, and then deliver the remaining notes to recipients in their mail. Positive words and compliments are so easy to say or jot down in a quick note, and yet most people do not naturally speak or write them without being prompted.

The practice of giving compliments creates a positivity that permeates camp experiences. Veteran campers frequently express how it translated into a more optimistic and hopeful outlook. Lily, a five-year camper, says, "Camp has made me a more positive person," and

Hope, a ten-year camper and current counselor, says, "Camp has taught me how I can affect others in a positive way and be my best possible 'me.'" These young women are both expressing the deeper, internal change that resulted from being in an intentionally positive community where they've practiced and experienced habits that retrain their brains to be more optimistic.

The Bumpy Road to Purposeful Positivity

You may know some families who seem like they are naturally positive, and perhaps you assume that positivity is something that "just happens," but it can be intentionally created. I know this, because I lived it. WOWs, along with many of the other positive communication and leadership techniques we now use, are relatively new practices to my camp. In the 1980s and even into the '90s, my camp wasn't always so permeated with positivity, which was pretty much left to chance. Camp was by default an upbeat, fun environment. After all, we were doing fun activities together, singing songs, spending lots of time outdoors learning recreational activities, and generally having a good time together. Most counselors were fairly upbeat by nature—fun individuals who naturally led their groups with a positive style. After all, the kinds of people who are interested in working at camp, in the outdoors, and with kids, tend to be fun and happy people.

When we began to pay closer attention, however, we discovered that not every single one of our one hundred counselors was naturally positive. A counselor who pointed out what was going wrong, used a negative tone of voice, yelled, or complained a lot, predicted a cabin group that did the same. I began to see clearly that campers in groups mirrored the outlook and demeanor of their counselors. Our most negative counselors ended up with negative campers who didn't have as much fun at camp. While there were always counselors who made the mundane things like brushing teeth and putting on sunscreen into fun, playful activities, there were those who sounded more like military drill sergeants. I cringed that such behavior could happen at my camp and was frustrated by the negative impact of these few individuals who poisoned the fun in their group or activity.

In response, we tried to figure out clever, elaborate interview questions and scenarios to determine this underlying personality trait in counselors and weed them out before summer began. We asked them to share stories of times they'd overcome challenges in previous jobs and we listened to their tone and demeanor as they recounted their "bad" days and "mean" bosses at previous jobs. We asked for examples of how they had responded in a situation where they had a conflict with a coworker. In addition to lengthy, multiple interviews, we incorporated personality testing, including a Grit Survey, to determine if they had what it took to be a positive counselor.

When a few negative folks still ended up on our staff, we tried to encourage the grouchy counselors to be more positive by telling them to "stop complaining" or to "be more positive." We tried pointing out to them the impact we saw them having on their group and coworkers. We used a vast array of human resource and leadership techniques we'd learned at conferences, from books, and in classes. And we changed our feedback process and evaluation forms multiple times.

What we learned was that in most cases, these negative people didn't perceive themselves as negative or see the impact they were having on others. Instead, they viewed *outside forces* as the source of their negativity. They thought it was their supervisor, or their circumstances, or their challenging campers that were causing their negative behaviors, and that their negative attitude was out of their own control. Most weren't breaking any specific employee rule we had trained them on. They were just not fun to be around. People didn't want to work with them, and campers didn't want to be with them. Each summer, we would have two or three of these counselors who took up a lot of our time and energy. We'd shift them from place to place, trying to find a spot where they would do the least damage with their pessimism. Usually, we limped along and were thankful as we sent them off at the end of camp, never to be invited to return again with their toxic negativity.

Unfortunately, regardless of the sophistication of our screening, a few new negative counselors continued to arrive each summer.

What Positive People Say and Do

Looking back, the answer to this challenge should have been much more obvious. We could never guarantee that every counselor would naturally be fun and positive based solely on their outstanding interview, their favorable references, or even their personality assessment. In fact, some people are quite skilled at seeming positive for a one-hour interview or answering personality surveys with a positive bent. We discovered that in addition to carefully screening counselors for positive personality traits, we also needed to train our counselors in exactly what to say and do to be positive. Our counselor training became extremely specific about the behaviors that were expected of counselors. We began giving feedback, not on overarching perceptions about their personality but instead about specific behaviors and practices we witnessed firsthand and that they could adjust. Gone were the days of using words like *negative*, *grouchy*, or *complaining*. Instead, we began training our counselors with the specific practices to use in order to consistently create a positive environment, regardless of their personality tendencies or previous negative practices.

Below are variations of methods our counselors use to boost positivity in our campers. I've practiced these techniques at home with my own kids, and I believe these steps can create a more positive environment and help you raise more optimistic kids in your own family.

- Smile while talking with your kids.
- Try waking up before your children so that you're ready to greet them in the morning with a cheery demeanor—you might even throw in a happy wake-up chant or song like our counselors do!
- At the end of the day, share something positive that happened to you and encourage children to share something positive, too.

- Make lemonade out of lemons: When faced with unfortunate circumstances, try to point out the positive.
- Make the mundane, everyday things like sunscreen application, hand washing, and teeth brushing fun by creating songs, chants, or games.
- Use the word *challenge* when talking about problems.

I'm often astounded by what campers recount as their best or most memorable moment from camp. Beaching their canoe and huddling together on the lake shore singing songs while a sudden afternoon thunderstorm passes through becomes a positive memory, despite getting soaking wet, because the counselors changed what could have been a bad experience and created fun and adventure. At home, we, too, can focus on creating fun and adventure even out of the difficulties and challenges that inevitably come up for us and for our kids. As we try to maintain a positive perspective, even amidst day-to-day struggles, we're teaching our kids how to be optimists, which is so important for their future success and happiness.

Taking Fun Seriously

Beyond trying to remain positive as we face challenges, like we do at camp, at home we should focus on fun! In our extremely busy lives, fun sometimes gets forgotten or left until after all the work is done. This is a big mistake. Play and activities that elicit positive emotions are what kids (and adults) describe as "having fun." These activities often include singing, dancing, active games, and chanting, and are part of daily life at most camps. If your family hasn't been having fun together, taking up these kinds of activities may initially feel awkward. But if parents take the lead and model playful fun first, kids will eventually join in.

At camp, my counselors are taught the importance of actively modeling fun activities and are encouraged to keep the "in-between" times like walking between activities or waiting in line more fun by knowing several easy, equipment-free games that can be played any-where. Riddles also provide a fun diversion that can make downtime more fun. I'll share some of our time-tested ideas for creating some fun family activities in the "Bringing Camp Home" section at the end of this chapter.

Recent findings about "mirror neurons" explain why it's so impor-tant to surround our kids (and ourselves!) with as many positive people and engage in as many positive—and *fun*—activities as possible. In recent years, neuropsychologists have studied the impact of people's emotions on one another. Using brain-scanning technology, they have been able to see how people's emotions affect others around them. It now makes sense to me why even kids whose parents describe them as negative or disengaged get "caught up" in the positive energy at camp and can experience a shift in their demeanor and outlook. Simply by being near people who are experiencing and expressing positive emo-tions, we become more positive ourselves. This explains the phenom-enon of "happiness pockets." If you work, live, or go to school with positive people, you are much more likely to experience more positive emotions.[3] That's why it's a great idea to make sure our homes are hap-piness pockets for our kids. When we're intentional about engaging in activities that allow us to laugh with our children, we're creating an environment where optimism will flourish.

Practical Skills and Character Growth

Camp professionals like myself have studied ways to maintain positive environments for kids for many years. It's clear from the research that WOWs, fun activities, and other positive practices at camp serve more than one purpose. On the first and most immediate level they make the recipient and the giver feel really good in the moment. If a camper hears their WOW being read aloud, or receives one in their mail-box, they feel special. Noticed. Like what they say and do matters to someone. That feels really good and gives them a brief shot of dopamine and a positive emotion in the moment. When the writer of the WOW sees the joy they can bring a friend and feels a closer connection through the simple act of jotting down a compliment, they, too, get a temporary happiness boost and feel encouraged to do more complimenting. Both the giver and the recipient feel immediate, positive emotions as the result of a simple compliment. These positive emotions that result from verbal praise can be explained scientifically by a dopamine transmission in the striatum, as found in a recent Japanese study.[4] It's not just something people think works; it's proven science.

On a deeper and more lasting level, the positive practices at camp are training campers' brains to be more cognizant of positive incidents and behaviors and to think more positively about situations and people. Martin Seligman, in his groundbreaking study and subsequent book *Learned Optimism*, demonstrated through his research that optimism not only contributes to the quality of life, but also helps relieve depression. According to researcher Shawn Achor, "Training your brain to be positive is not so different from training your muscles at the gym. Recent research on neuroplasticity—the ability of the brain to change even in adulthood—reveals that as you develop new habits, you rewire the brain."[5]

After so many years training our staff in intentional positive practices and helping them understand the why for their positive actions, positivity has permeated the very culture of camp, and over time it can happen at home, too. Like we've done at camp, you can successfully create a place where negativity and complaining have no place to stick. Daily practices like WOWs, having fun, reading uplifting quotes, and spending time outside all contribute to campers' increased positivity and optimism. These simple daily practices encourage more positive thinking, words, and activities and are the secret behind why kids—and counselors—are more positive and optimistic at camp. By expressing positive thoughts about ourselves and our children, we train our minds to be more attuned to the good things going on around us. Using positive words and taking positive actions in turn leads to an increased level of optimism. These positive practices can evolve into a lifelong optimism that changes the behavior and outlook of our kids long beyond their childhood days. And optimism is an important trait we want to develop in our children.

Positive Messages Everywhere

Several years ago, while visiting my daughter at her university, I noticed the monthly newsletter on the back of the bathroom stall door. The university had learned that the stall door was the perfect place to find captive readers. Like everyone else, I read the news and got caught up on the happenings at Santa Clara University, and then I got an idea. We have three hundred campers who are in our bathroom stalls every day, several times a day. What could we put on our doors while we have them captive? As a lifelong collector of inspirational quotes, I knew exactly what to do. I asked our graphic designer, Joline, to design our first set of bathroom posters, and they are now an annual tradition. Each summer, we select ten new positive, inspirational quotes and spread them throughout the bathrooms at camp.

Campers often offer the quotes, word for word, as something they learned at camp. A few of my personal favorite camp bathroom stall inspirations from recent years include this one from Mother Teresa, "Let us always meet each other with a smile, for the smile is the beginning of love," as well as this one from the legendary University of California, Los Angeles basketball coach John Wooden, "You cannot live a perfect day without doing something for someone who will never be able to repay you." Why not create some positive messages in your home to help remind your family about the positive practices that will enrich each of your lives? Repetition and reminders in the form of signs, notes, and postings are a great way to reinforce important lessons. If you have a favorite quote, tell your kids about it and post it in a prominent location. I guarantee your kids will remember it.

Going Outside Is a Positivity Practice

In his 2005 book, *Last Child in the Woods*, Richard Louv coined the term "Nature Deficit Disorder" as a way to describe the "human costs of alienation from nature." Louv recognized that children are spending less time outdoors and that this is resulting in a wide range of behavioral problems. The website he founded, the Children and Nature Network, shares research and resources about the emotional and mental benefits children receive from being outdoors.[6] There are many compelling reasons to get outside; several of them relate to feeling better and more positive, such as providing stress relief, promoting better sleep, boosting brain health, and decreasing anxiety and depression. This is why being in the outdoors and getting more connected with nature are central to our camp positivity practices.

At camp, even though we live in big tents and are mostly outside anyway, we like to get even deeper into nature by going on backpacking trips. Many kids are initially hesitant to put a pack on their back and go for a hike, but they invariably report that their backpacking trip was among their favorite and most memorable times at camp. The exercise of the hike, which boosts their endorphins, combined with all the other benefits of being in nature, lead to feelings of overall well-being that many kids have not experienced in other settings.

Prioritizing outside time for your family can lead to more family happiness and connection. Depending on where your family lives, spending more time outside may require some creativity as well as a change in family habits (think "unplugged Saturdays"). Even in big cities, parks and trails provide a great way to spend time outside. Something as simple as a daily (or nightly) walk around your neighborhood or playtime at a local park are great ways that families can create an outside habit. If feasible, walking or riding bikes to and from school or other activities provides a daily opportunity to be outside in fresh air.

Tennis, golf, and other sports that allow for varying degrees of skill are also fun outdoor family activities. In the past few years, we've discovered tennis as a fun activity that we can do with our teenage boys. Our local public high school has open courts on the weekends, and we often stop by for an hour of tennis after church. Sports that allow for various levels of expertise can be fun to do as a family, especially as our children become more talented athletically than we are!

Yosemite National Park is less than two hours from where I live (near Fresno, California). While visitors come from all over the world to visit the natural beauty of Yosemite, Sequoia, and Kings Canyon National Parks, many people who live right here in our area have never visited. In many cases, depending on where you live, a relatively short drive can get you out of the summer heat or winter fog and into a beautiful natural setting. Visiting mountains, beaches, and other open spaces requires some planning and travel, but it is worthwhile and can create lifelong positive memories for your children. What are the closest nature settings to you? Research what's available nearby and make a new family tradition of driving to take a hike or play in the snow once a month (or more)!

Bringing Camp Home: Raising Optimists

Optimism is the faith that leads to achievement; nothing can be done without hope.

—Helen Keller

Before you try to implement some new positivity practices at home, first take some time to assess your family's positivity quotient to see if you need a positivity intervention. For a few days, monitor what your conversations with your kids and friends are about. What kind of content are you all taking in from the media—news, television shows, music?

One thing I've experienced many times over the years is seeing how much kids emulate their parents. Parents who tend to complain or focus on the one thing that went wrong rather than the many things that went right tend to have kids who mirror the same negative style. I remember getting to the bus stop at the end of a two-week session and having a parent walk up to me—before greeting his child—to ask if I was the person to complain to. I said an enthusiastic "Yes!" (because I've learned from leadership training that positive leaders receive problems and challenges with enthusiasm, knowing that that's how we become better). He then proceeded to tell me that he hadn't received the text update about the bus arrival time (which had been a text to say that we were on time). I remember thinking to myself, *Wow, your kid just had a fantastic two weeks at camp, and instead of going over to your child to say hi and see how camp was, you're complaining to me about a text you didn't receive?* My heart broke that the camper would be going from daily WOWs to that kind of approach to life.

I've also had parents say to me at pickup time, "Well, he hasn't shared any complaints so far," as if the most important question they asked their camper about camp was what they didn't like. I've also experienced, on a few occasions, kids who embellish negative events or even make up events that didn't actually happen in order to garner attention from parents who only seem to react and give attention to the negative. For some kids, it seems, the only way they get their parents' attention is by sharing something bad that happened to them so that their parent can jump into "rescue" mode. When parents focus most of their attention on their kid's complaints about teachers, friends, counselors, and things that went wrong, kids become trained to share mostly negative information. This perpetuates more negativity and trains kids to look for the bad in every situation so that they have something to report.

By assessing for a few days what your conversations with your kids are about, you may see trends you want to turn around. If the conversations are leaning toward the negative, you can think about switching things up. While WOW notepads or a daily morning assembly may not be realistic practices to incorporate at home, you can still find a way to WOW each other and train your family's brains to be more sensitive to and focused on the positive. Here are some ideas to try at home to encourage more positivity and optimism.

One Simple Thing

Our kids are really attuned to how we're feeling, even when we don't realize it. "If Mama ain't happy, ain't nobody happy" is, in fact, a true statement. I can feel it when I've sucked the fun out of the room for my family because of my own bad mood. Conversely, parents who model positive emotions and interactions the majority of the time have kids who do the same. It starts with a simple smile. If you naturally aren't a big smiler, that's okay. Start by giving your kids a smile at these times, every day:

- When you greet them in the morning to start the day.
- When you greet them after school or after not seeing them for a while.
- During at least one conversation, when you're looking them in the eyes.
- At bedtime, as you tuck them in to say good night.

Four smiles, just for your kids, that will help them smile on the inside.

The Sticky Note Solution

Pick one of your favorite inspirational quotes and put it on a sticky note on your own or on your kid's bathroom mirror or the refrigerator. Together, you can think about a positive thought each time you see the sticky note. Switch the inspirations out from time to time and encourage your kids to share their own favorite quotes.

Make It Fun

Sing or dance...or both! Find a simple, daily fun thing to do as a family. It can be music blasting while doing the dishes or something else you all have fun doing together. The goal is to create a fun daily habit when everyone's together. It doesn't need to be long, just five or ten minutes, but those minutes can really make everyone feel more positive.

Going outside for a walk after dinner can also give everyone a boost of positive endorphins both from the exercise and the fresh air. Or maybe you have a local park where you can go kick a soccer ball around, just for fun with no pressure or competition. Being outside will boost everyone's mood and bring you closer together.

Around the Campfire

Some kind of positive daily sharing can improve your family's positivity quotient. Martin Seligman (yes, him again—I'm a fan!) did a remarkable study on the impact of a simple gratitude practice. He found that depressed patients improved their outlook significantly in just a few months by writing down three good things from their day. When I learned of the benefits of this simple practice, we switched our family's nightly sharing from "Highs and Lows" of the day to "Three Good Things," focusing our minds on the positive.

When your family members know that sharing three good things is a nightly ritual, they'll start noticing more of the good things that are happening. Even a day that has had some bad stuff happen also has some good stuff. By having a time each day when you and your kids share one or more "highs" or good things from their day, your brains will eventually become more aware of the positive things.

One way to incorporate WOWs at home is creating a time to give each other compliments. Rather than introducing it as a formal activity, I suggest that parents compliment each other in front of kids. "I really like this dinner you made. Thank you for preparing it for us!" In addition, parents can compliment kids in front of each other, especially on character-related traits. For example, a parent can say, "When I was picking you up from school, I noticed you stopped and held the door for other kids. That was polite." Once kids get used to hearing you give compliments, they may start giving them to each other. It may feel awkward at first, but by modeling that you're noticing good things and pointing them out, your kids will eventually follow suit. If your family gets on board with complimenting or WOWing each other, you may want to create a permanent place to WOW each other—perhaps a bulletin board or a small white board in the kitchen.

Family Meeting Topic: Optimism and Pessimism

Lead a discussion about optimism and pessimism by asking your kids to answer these questions:

- How do you feel about someone who looks on the bright side and sees the positive, even in challenging situations?
- What about a negative person who complains a lot? How do you feel about them?
- What kind of people do you prefer to hang out with, optimists or pessimists?
- How do you want to be perceived by your friends?
- What are steps we can take as a family to complain less and be more positive and optimistic? Write down the list you brainstorm and post it to review and revisit!

Diving Deeper

Perhaps you are troubled about the culture of your family being negative and want to take additional steps. If so, here are some resources to help you get back on track:

- *The No Complaining Rule* by Jon Gordon is a powerful book that offers an obvious cure for negativity. It's a quick read, and over just a few evenings it could serve as a family read-aloud book. It's also available in an audio book that you can listen to as you drive.
- Watch the movie *The Pursuit of Happyness* with your family and talk about how the main character, Chris Gardner, positively approaches many difficult situations.
- Go twenty-four hours without complaining (not even once). Hold each other accountable and discuss it afterward. How often did

you have to stop yourself from complaining? How did it feel not to complain?

A positive family culture is not some fake, Pollyanna-esque home where everyone is always smiling and being kind 100 percent of the time. No place—not even summer camp—is always positive. In any family or community, there will be arguments, negative moments, and crises to deal with, but if we stack the deck with positivity, we can create an overall more positive environment, one that better prepares our children to deal with the inevitable interpersonal conflicts and issues that arise in life.

Over the years, I have heard from many former counselors that the practices and ideas they learned at camp have been incredibly useful and positive additions to their classrooms as teachers and in their own families as parents. As parents, we have the power to shift our family culture into one that's more positive and gives our kids a chance to be those flourishing, super-optimistic outliers who make the world a better place.

Optimism is an important character trait that will help our kids navigate the trials of childhood and adolescence. Their positive outlook will also help them stay on course as they experience the inevitable pitfalls on the way to becoming self-reliant, independent young adults.

Camp Secret #4

All Kids Can Be More Independent
(Even Clingy Homebodies!)

From the timid good-byes as they board the camp bus, aware that they are leaving the safe confines of their family and homes, to the ear-to-ear grinning pictures and roaring laughter just a few days later, they learn that they can be happy away from their parents, and that they do not need to rely on their parents to feel good about themselves and thrive.

—Tim

One of the reasons many parents are willing to send their young kids to overnight summer camp—despite wanting to keep their child close to them and being concerned about the separation—is their knowledge that their child will, in order to become a thriving adult, eventually need to leave home, deal with the discomfort of separation, and develop the autonomy needed for a thriving adulthood. The process of separating from parents and developing autonomy can be challenging for kids. It can also be emotionally difficult for parents. I've learned over my many years at camp that in most cases, the first summer camp experience is actually harder on the parents than it is on the kids.

I once got a call from a mom who was really upset. Her daughter had just returned home from her first two-week stay at overnight camp, and the mom was beside herself with confusion and anger. She had demanded to talk with me, the camp director. I picked up the phone thinking I was going to get yelled at about someone her daughter didn't like in her cabin group or a late bus arrival, but I was surprised at what the mom had to say. She reported that her daughter had a fantastic experience at camp, so good, in fact, that she was now "campsick" and sobbing about missing her cabin group and counselors. Her daughter kept repeating that she just wanted to go back to camp. The mother couldn't understand why her daughter was so upset about being home. "I've poured myself into this girl, loved and cared for her for eleven years," this mom wailed, "and you have her for two weeks and she's happier there? That's not fair!" She was calling to thank me—and also to get some support for a tough moment in her parenting journey—the moment she realized that her daughter could thrive without her present.

This mom articulated a feeling that many parents won't admit to having—the emotional pain we feel when our kids start separating from us and forging their own separate, independent identities. While we know intellectually that our kids maturing and separating from us is a natural stage of their development, and something we want for them, it's not easy when it actually happens. When our children start spreading their wings and flying away from us, it can be emotionally painful.

Most of us talk about wanting our kids to become independent, and we may even express dismay about not wanting them still living at home when they're thirty, but when it comes time to watch our kids walk through airport security for their departure to a far-off college, international volunteer opportunity, the military, or a faraway job, we still feel the intense worry, fear, and sadness that is a natural part of parenting. I've done this separation thing several times now, and even though I've had many opportunities to practice over the past decade, I still feel sadness and worry when they leave. As I watch my independent kid walk out of sight, past security, into their next adventure, the tears roll down my face and my thought is, *This is so hard. Why did I help her become so independent?*

The camper's mom on the phone knew on some level that having a successful independent experience away from home for a few weeks demonstrated positive growth in her daughter, but that same independence put a spotlight on the painful reality of feeling replaced by other people. When our child has been the center of our universe, our top priority, and our reason for being for many years, there is a strange dichotomy: We want our child to be happy and successful, and know that this requires them gaining autonomy, but that same happiness and success comes at a cost to us personally. Our life, which has revolved around them for so long—their events, their school-work, their extracurricular endeavors, their friends—can be turned upside down by them leaving. But that's how our kids' development is supposed to progress. If our child is going to become an adult who thrives and lives their own independent life, away from us, then they have to separate from us. This person we've poured our own life into for so long is not meant to reciprocate and stay by our side. In fact, if they do stay around, it stunts them (and us) from pursuing more of our life's purpose.

Why Do Our Kids Need to be Independent?

The central developmental task of adolescence is separating from parents and determining individual identity.[1] The psychological term for this, Separation-Individuation (S-I), describes the process of our kids moving from dependency on us to the more mature self-reliance of an adult. Successful separation from parents is critical for healthy adult relationships and emotional functioning, but this time of change in the parent–child relationship can be tumultuous. Ideally, we want our emerging adult children to gain functional and decision-making independence while still maintaining emotional closeness with us.

The process of separating from parents and determining their own identity can be viewed along a continuum. At the far end of the successful S-I continuum, the emerging adult stays connected to family while becoming psychologically and functionally independent. Homesickness and maladjustment to college are symptoms of disturbances in the normal S-I process. Especially for kids who struggle to separate from parents, it's important that we promote this normal developmental process.

In many families, the separation and move toward independence begins upon departure for college, but I believe that's far too late to help our kids develop their autonomy. Our kids need to be allowed to slowly unfurl their wings, not be abruptly shoved out of the nest. Continuing with the analogy, no bird is going to fly and thrive if one day they're having worms spoon-fed into their mouth and the next they're expected to fly on their own and feed themselves. Independence doesn't happen overnight.

Although it seems much easier to stay tightly connected and wound up in our children's lives and psyches until the moment we tuck in their college-dorm-room sheets (and far beyond, as many parents are now doing), we must let them go slowly, starting at a younger age, and allow them to figure out their own identity and destiny and feel pride in their growing independence, without us always hovering nearby.

Homesick

This was my nine-year-old's first time at sleepaway camp. He was quite homesick the first week, but he stayed and had a great time. When he got home, we saw how proud of himself he was for having worked through his homesickness, and he was more confident in his ability to do hard things. I love what he said in response to my question about what he did when he was homesick: "My friend comforted me."

—Kelly

One of the main reasons kids rapidly gain independence skills at camp is the simple fact that their parents are not there. Well-meaning parents (and I count myself among them) have been so involved with our kids that we sometimes have not allowed them to practice the autonomy that they need in order to successfully emerge into adult-hood.[2] We tend to pave the path for our child and help them avoid obstacles rather than help them face those obstacles themselves. I've heard terms like *lawn mowers* and *bulldozers* used to describe some parenting styles. Both descriptions illustrate this practice of preparing the path for the child, rather than the more effective technique of preparing the child for the path.

As a result of well-intentioned parents who can't help but try to mitigate their child's discomfort, many campers arrive at camp having never had to navigate a difficult situation without their parents' support. They have become accustomed to immediately seeking adult (usually a parent's) intervention when faced with any challenge or difficulty, whether it be academic, interpersonal, or physical. They text their parents, whine, complain, cajole, call, yell, cry, throw a fit, beg for intervention—and more often than not, their parents oblige by stepping in to help. The rocky, uneven dirt paths at camp offer the ideal metaphor for why campers experience so much growth in their independence in such a short period of time: They are allowed to stumble and trip, to experience some discomfort and difficulty without concerned parents swooping in to save them. While supportive counselors are nearby to assist, they don't clear the path but instead help the campers learn to navigate it for themselves.

A common challenge, especially among first-time overnight campers, is homesickness. Like many child care institutions (day care, preschools, kindergartens, day camps), we have become experts at coaching both parents and campers in different coping strategies to address the normal separation anxiety and homesickness that occur when a child is away from parents, especially for the first time. We expect homesickness in campers, prepare for it, and have confidence that every camper can overcome it. Some parents, knowing their child has the propensity toward separation issues, choose to send their kid to camp because they know the experience will help them grow by challenging them to overcome this crippling emotion that can limit future endeavors like going to a college away from home, joining the military, or participating in an abroad experience.

Many years ago, I talked with the mom of a twelve-year-old first-time camper, Greg, before he arrived at camp. Greg's mom anticipated that he was going to be extremely uncomfortable at camp, but she also was desperate to help him gain some separation and independence, and she thought a session at camp was a potential answer to helping her son in this area. We talked about how Greg might be really upset at camp, especially at first, and I reassured her that we could handle even the strongest homesick emotions. The mom's predictions came true. On the first evening, during the twilight hours as campfires were getting started, I sat in the center of camp listening to Greg sobbing and saying over and over, "I just can't do it. I can't stay here. I need to be home."

Over my years at camp, I've counseled countless homesick campers, and most of them say things along these same lines. They truly do experience extreme discomfort and do not believe they can survive being away from home and parents. They often complain of stomachaches and an inability to eat, as this severe emotional pain is manifested in somatic symptoms. In fact, often homesick kids will go see the camp nurses, convinced their physical symptoms are the reason they need to go home immediately. But Greg was one of the most extreme cases of homesickness I'd ever seen. His screaming and crying showed a high level of desperation and a complete lack of confidence in himself. Despite my belief that all kids can eventually master the emotional pain of homesickness and succeed at camp, I started to waver on whether this kid really *could* survive his monthlong camp session. I helped Greg get through that evening, and worked with his counselor to help him get through the next morning, the second night, and the first week—and then I watched as Greg not only survived, but ended up thriving at camp. It was truly like watching a caterpillar struggle out of its cocoon.

That summer, we installed a new radio station that broadcasted throughout camp. Greg was the DJ on the opening morning of his third week at camp, confidently exclaiming into the radio, "Gooooood morning, Gold Arrow Camp!" (The 1987 movie *Good Morning, Vietnam* featured Robin Williams as a DJ using the same voice modulation.) Greg returned as a camper for a few more years, then later joined our staff as a counselor (a twelve-week summer commitment away from home). I was proud to watch his progress—and proud of his mother, as well. They both experienced a lot of growth that first summer.

Why did Greg end up overcoming his extreme homesickness and become an independent, autonomous adult despite his early anxieties? His mother had the wherewithal and courage to let him feel the distress he needed to experience in order to complete his developmental task of separating from her, confident in his ability to be independent. It was as simple and profound as that. They both needed to experience discomfort in order to allow him to grow into an independent adult.

I've seen this same story repeated multiple times over the years. Unfortunately, on the rare occasions when a parent can't handle their child's emotional hardship at camp and instead comes to "rescue" their upset child early, I've seen and heard of the negative consequences of that course of action. I plead with parents not to send their child to camp if they are not going to follow through with letting their child experience homesickness, because the damage of remembering that they "couldn't make it at camp" serves as a painful reminder of their unsuccessful first attempt at independence. For some kids, the negative experience becomes an excuse not to attempt future independent experiences and to become comfortable with the label of "homebody."

At home, opportunities to teach our kids to be autonomous begin the moment they start to move on their own, and the opportunities continue well into adulthood. The same lesson of expressing confidence and not rescuing kids from summer camp can be applied to all aspects of our parenting. When a toddler is struggling to get the T-shirt over her head, instead of jumping in to do it for her, why not give some guidance and time, teaching the child not only patience for learning new tasks but also confidence in her ability to do things by herself? When crossing a street with your four-year-old, tell him he's in charge of looking both ways and telling you when it's safe to cross. When your kindergartener is anxious about being away from you, give her small "practice" opportunities away from you with a neighbor or friend.

Opportunities to teach children autonomy, by being patient and following through with confidence even when theirs is faltering, continue throughout childhood and adolescence. If we show and express confidence (even when we, too, are nervous on the inside), our children will be emboldened to keep trying. Instead of seeking us for rescuing, our children will gain reassurance and confidence when they see our confidence in them. The emotional pain of separation from each other is real, and so is the need for our children to feel confident and capable in facing the world without needing to get our approval or intervention at every step. Small opportunities to do things on one's own translate into confidence in being away from parents and autonomy over one's own actions and decisions—important traits for being a thriving adult.

These Precious Childhood Years

For many of us, letting our kids go is really hard. I see this play out all the time. At the beginning of eighth grade, my son's school takes the students on a five-day retreat to an outdoor education center near Yosemite. Following a parent orientation session for the trip, I found myself walking across the school campus with the mother of one of my son's classmates. She lamented that parents were not allowed to go on the retreat and told me that she had been on "every other school trip" with her son over his last eight years in school. I was slightly alarmed—and finding it hard to take off my camp director hat, told her I was excited for the trip and thought it would be a lot of fun for the kids to be without their parents for a few days. I explained that I run a camp where even small kids attend for two weeks without their parents and that I see a lot of growth in them during their time with us. She looked straight at me and said, "I would *never* send my son to summer camp. These years are too precious and go by too fast, and I want to spend as much time with him as possible." Despite my normal tendency toward being effusive about the benefits of camp and the independence kids learn being away from us, I was left speechless. This mom, like many others I have met over the years, proudly sees her ever-presence with her child as her calling, and I wasn't going to try to convince her otherwise.

I understand the feeling of loss many of us experience when our kids venture on without us. For some empty nesters, there's a deep sense of mourning over not having the children at the center of their home and schedule any more. Even with two teenagers still at home, I am keenly aware of the empty chairs around our dining table. Many years after my oldest child left home for college, I relish those few nights a year, usually around holidays, when we're all seven gathered around the table together. As a parent, it feels easier emotionally when our kids just stay put and choose not to go away, but that is not always what's best for our kids.

Regardless of how hard the process of separating and becoming independent will be for our kids and for us, unless they are severely disabled and unable to care for themselves, one of our most important parenting tasks is to help them learn to face the world without us. Parents of children with special needs—such as a severe food allergy, disease, physical disability, or mental illness—have a more challenging process to navigate in helping their kids become independent young adults, but it is still equally important. Regardless of how difficult it will be for our child to learn to navigate the world on their own, they need to learn to be their own person and take care of themselves.

I've witnessed the joy that kids with special needs experience at being away from home—diabetic campers proudly monitoring their own glucose levels, asthmatics using their own breathing machines, anxious kids practicing coping skills, allergic kids asking questions about what ingredients are in foods. When there are medical needs that parents have been closely monitoring for the first decade of their kid's life, passing the baton to the child by teaching them to care for themselves, and expressing confidence in their ability to do so, offers the child the gift of knowing that despite their illness or disability, they can handle independent life without their parents always being present.

Getting Help from Strangers

A thriving adult life includes mutual, interdependent relationships. Being able to trust and depend on others, and being available and reliable to offer the same support in return, are traits our kids need in order to have positive adult relationships. The independence we want for our kids is, therefore, not about being completely independent from all other people and relationships. It is instead the ability to develop a life separate from us where they have confidence in their own autonomy and the ability to rely on other trusted adults besides parents. In order for our kids to be able to thrive outside of our homes, we need them to gain a feeling of autonomy as well as the ability to seek help and guidance from trusted adults other than ourselves. That's why we need our kids to be comfortable talking to strangers— on the phone and in person.

In *How to Raise an Adult*, former Stanford dean Julie Lythcott-Haims writes that one of the most important life skills for eighteen-year-olds is that they "be able to talk to strangers—faculty, deans, advisers, landlords, store clerks...—in the real world." She recounts countless meetings in her office where the student would need to call or text parents before answering her questions or making any decisions. During my childhood, there was a "Don't talk to strangers" mantra meant to keep kids safe. We now know that learning to talk to strangers is an important skill required to function separately from parents. Therefore, encouraging our kids to talk to the checkout person at the store, the server at the restaurant, the delivery person, and other strangers encountered throughout a normal day is a way to help them develop the communication skills they'll need when they have to talk to other strangers without us throughout their childhood and adolescence.

Over my many years at camp, I have countless examples of campers who wrote letters home to describe a complaint or need. They would write in a letter to their parents that their lips were getting chapped. The parent would then call the camp office to ask us to help their child purchase a lip balm from the camp store. We would then help the camper. This process, of course, is absurd and took about four days as compared to the five minutes it takes for a camper to let their counselor know. But despite having a caring counselor right in front of them who could have met that need on the spot, the camper was not yet comfortable asking for help from anyone other than a parent. We now spend time, in our online precamp family orientation, reviewing with campers and their parents the different adults who are at camp to help ensure a positive experience. We talk about the counselors who will be living with them in the tent and going to activities with them, the experienced head counselors who will spend time with their group and can help with challenges, and the camp directors (me included) who never miss a meal or an assembly and are always available to talk.

We don't allow phones or phone calls home to parents, and one of the many reasons for this policy is that we want campers to learn to feel comfortable turning to adults other than their parents. And while this might sound harsh, the lack of ability to text or call Mom or Dad with every question, decision, or problem forces kids to reach out to other adults for assistance. And they learn how to talk to strangers. Summer camp is an extreme example of independence from parents, but there are opportunities at home where the same concept of allowing children to solve their own problem or make their own decision can be applied.

Phone Calls to Strangers

When my thirteen-year-old daughter accidentally locked herself out of her flip phone (in the blessed presmartphone days), she did not want to call AT&T customer service to get her phone unlocked. I refused to make the call for her. This was her phone and her call to make. Cleverly, she negotiated with her older sister and got her to make the call for her. She eventually overcame her fear of calling strangers, but it took some time.

My fifteen-year-old son and I recently walked into the DMV for him to take his driver's permit test. Before we went in, I told him, "I'll be here with you, but you're doing all the talking. If you're going to drive a car, you'll need to be able to talk to other adults, like people who you're involved in an accident with. So it starts now."

Those who know me well know that it is not in my normally take-charge, camp-director personality to step back, so those moments in the DMV while my son stumbled over responding to questions and needed to repeat himself a few times because of his inaudible mumble required a *huge* level of self-control. But I did let him talk to the various adults at counters 5, 21, and 17, who directed him on each step of the bureaucratic process. I stood a few steps behind him, not hovering over his forms. When the adult behind the counter would look at me for some type of verification or question, as if my son couldn't answer, I clenched my jaws and looked at my son. It worked! He did all the talking, and I'm sure he felt some pride at navigating the intricacies of a governmental agency. I know I felt pride in myself for keeping my big mouth shut (for once).

We need to empower our kids to get out of their comfort zone and talk to adults on their own. Question about a test in fourth grade? Go ask your teacher! Navigating a desired course change in high school? Set up a meeting with the school counselor! The convoluted communication where the kid texts the parent, who emails the teacher— when the kid and teacher are twenty feet away from each other—is ridiculous. We need to stop this madness and teach our kids how direct communication—with the person directly involved—is always the best course of action.

Starting at a very young age—as soon as they can say "mac and cheese"—teach your child how to order their own meal at a restaurant.

I've seen parents of teens ordering for them: "He'll have the plain cheeseburger." Again, I've been tempted myself, because my enunciation is much clearer than my teenage son's. But unless we let our kids stumble (and mumble) through things like ordering for themselves, they will never learn how to communicate better with strangers. They will eventually gain better skills, but not if we keep stepping in for them.

My then seventh-grade son was on a committee to plan an end-of-school celebration field day. He proudly recounted to me the phone calls he made to the bounce house purveyor and the taco truck man. He called them and arranged for them to come to the field day. He felt proud, and just a few weeks later he was presented the "Leadership Award" at the school year-end assembly. My son was recognized as a leader, which I honestly believe came from the fact that he was comfortable calling and talking to strangers when most kids his age were not.

"What Are You Going to Do?"

> Both our kids have a bit more independence and confidence they exude since returning from camp. There is an ease in the morning routines for our son, where we aren't having to ask him to do the things he needs to do in the morning; he now just does them.
>
> —Melanie

One of my favorite questions to ask my kids is, "What are you going to do?" This one question helps them learn to solve their own problems. It's a question we've taught counselors to use in response when a camper comes to them with a problem.

Erin, a friend of mine from college who's blessed with a calm, positive demeanor, shared a story that demonstrated brilliant parenting. Here's what happened: While packing to go to her great-uncle's out-of-town funeral, Erin instructed her daughter to pack a dress or skirt to wear, something nicer than her normal casual jeans or leggings. Her daughter, an avid reader, didn't want to take time away from her book, so she packed quickly. When they arrived at their hotel and were getting ready for the funeral, her daughter freaked out, "My dress isn't here!" She had forgotten to pack it. All she had in her luggage was a pair of jeggings, decidedly inappropriate attire for the event.

My friend remained composed and with a kind of wisdom 99 percent of us would not be able to muster in such a situation, said calmly to her daughter, "Well, you know you can't wear jeggings to your great-uncle's funeral, so what are you going to do about it? I'm going to get ready while you figure it out."

With that, my friend left to get herself dressed for the funeral. After she was ready and came back to her daughter's hotel room, her daughter told her of how she planned to solve the problem she had created. She had located a Target store that was on the way to the funeral where they could quickly stop to purchase a dress. She asked her mom, "Can I reimburse you by working it off?" She agreed to pay her mom back with a series of chores, including cleaning and vacuuming the interior of her mom's car.

The plan went off without a hitch, and they made it to the funeral, appropriately dressed and without any yelling or tears. The reason my friend had ended up sharing the story with me was that I had commented on how spotless her car was. It looked like a brand-new car. So not only had her daughter repaid the debt, she had done an excellent job cleaning the car.

My friend's daughter made a mistake, figured out how to solve the problem, and followed through with experiencing the consequences of her mistake. Not only did she practice valuable problem-solving, I'm guessing she'll be more careful with her packing next time they go on a trip.

I had a similar parenting opportunity when my eighth-grade son called from school just before his team was leaving for an away soccer game. He didn't have his soccer uniform shorts, because he had grabbed a white uniform top thinking it was shorts. I was at work, and our home is too far from school for me to help him. Besides, I've vowed not to do any more rescuing after reading so many articles and books about the damage we do by not letting our kids fail and deal with the consequences of those failures.[3] I had asked my son in the morning, "Do you have everything you need for soccer?" And, he had responded that yes, he did.

When he called with his shorts crisis, I channeled my inner Erin and calmly responded, "That's a bummer. What are you going to do?" He then told me he was going to the athletic office to see if they had an extra pair of shorts he could use. I told him that was a great idea, and we hung up. I never heard back, but when I showed up at the game later, he wasn't playing in his underwear, so he apparently had worked it out.

We parents are important to our kids, and we can have a positive influence on the choices they make and the path they take. We have a vital role in helping guide them through life. But how do we do that best, without hovering or smothering or nagging or yelling? Sharing our own stories and mistakes, and letting our kids know that we didn't just magically become the functioning adults we are today, is valuable. It's also valuable to stay calm when our kids make a mistake and help guide them to problem-solve on their own rather than freaking out or swooping in for the rescue.

Maintaining a close, supportive relationship with my kids is something I value. Fostering their responsibility and independence does not mean never communicating with them. But it is important that our relationship transitions, especially during their teen years, into one of a trusted advisor rather than rescuer and problem-solver. I want my adult children to think of me as a resource and someone to call when they need some support or advice. The tricky part is what to actually say when they do text or call with an SOS. It's important that we remain supportive while also giving our kids a vote of confidence in their own ability to solve problems and make decisions.

Memorize a line that's comfortable for you and that includes empathy for them and their problem, along with a question about how they plan to solve it. Something like, "That sounds really hard. I'm sorry you're going through that. What are you thinking about doing?"

In any given sticky situation (a failed midterm at college comes to mind), we know the steps our kids need to take because we learned them ourselves through our own mistakes and failures back when we were their age. When our kids ask us what they should do, instead of telling them our opinion and advice, we often serve their growth better by instead asking questions to help them come up with their own solution. Help them brainstorm ideas to address the issue by saying, "Tell me what ideas you've already thought about trying," or asking, "What are some different options you're considering?" Be a sounding board. Encourage them to try their different ideas, and suggest others if they're really stuck. Praise them for what they come up with: "That sounds like a great first step" or "I like that tactic! Great problem-solving!"

Our kids will not become confident, high-functioning adults if we constantly rescue them from their mistakes and don't allow them to practice solving their own problems.

Observable Changes and Core Transformation

My son has been at camp for three years now, and each year has been an important part of his development. He is proud of going off on his own and being part of a community where he has greater latitude to make his own decisions than when he is at home. He is more confident with his peers and is able to handle most all challenges that surface day-to-day independently.

—*Mina*

The surface, observable independence skills kids learn when they are forced to navigate a situation on their own include the ability to ask adults other than parents for assistance, the ability to make decisions without conferring with parents, and the ability to do more things for themselves. Without a parent stepping in to solve every problem, kids figure out how to do the things the parent has been doing for them.

The deeper and lasting transformations kids experience when they start having independent experiences away from parents are even more important. The sense of autonomy and newfound confidence kids gain from doing things on their own, without parents, creates new patterns of behavior. No longer does the child feel they need to call parents for every decision. Instead, they gain a confidence in their own ability to handle the situations that arise in their lives.

Bringing Camp Home: Activities to Promote Autonomy

> The greatest gifts you can give your children are the roots of responsibility and the wings of independence.
>
> —attributed to Denis Waitley

Here are some ideas for promoting the kind of autonomy required for kids to grow into independent adults.

One Simple Thing

Get off the treadmill of saying yes to every opportunity to be with your child during their school day and out-of-school experiences. I'm all for helping out and volunteering in class and contributing to parties and school events, but our kids desperately need some fun experiences *without* us there snapping pictures, commenting about everything, and wiping peanut butter off their chins. If you're a parent who's participated in every field trip your child has ever been on, one simple thing you can do is say no to the next one. Hold yourself back despite your desire to be there, and then listen to your child with rapt attention as they recount their independent adventure.

The Sticky Note Solution

"What are you going to do?" Write yourself a note as a reminder how to respond when your child reports their next problem, challenge, or decision to be made. The question you want to remember is "What are you going to do?" Put the sticky note in a few different places, and the next time a problem comes up, express empathy and then ask your child what his or her plan is for solving the problem.

Make It Fun

"Talk to strangers!" needs to be our new mantra for independent kids. We need to teach our kids to be discerning and aware about who to talk to in different circumstances. There are people we don't know who we need to talk to every day in order to be functioning adults in life every time we do an errand or call a company with a question.

One way to make learning the skill of talking to strangers fun is to set up a family "Be the Adult" game. Using index cards, brainstorm some things adults usually do that your kids haven't started doing yet. Ideas of things you might include: ordering food at a restaurant, making a haircut appointment, checking in at a doctor visit, calling a repairperson about something that's not working, scheduling the dog for grooming, preparing dinner, writing a check, putting something on the calendar, writing a grocery list, doing the household laundry (cleaning rags, kitchen towels, etc.), inviting grandparents to dinner, running the morning routine (telling people when it's time to go, etc.), and getting everyone together for a family game. Once you have a good pile of cards, set up a fun point or reward system. If each card is worth 10 points, maybe after each child earns 50 or 100 points, they get a special adult "date" with one of the parents to practice being an adult. Maybe a trip out for coffee or a bike ride.

Around the Campfire

Sharing stories is one of the best "around the campfire" family activities. Everyone, including parents, has stories of our most difficult independent experiences. I remember my six months studying abroad in France during the sunless European winter. While I had many fun and memorable experiences, I also felt some profound loneliness being so far from home. Because of the expense of international calls (this was way before the internet and FaceTime!), I had limited opportunities to call my parents. I mostly wrote long letters. And while there were times I really wanted to just go home, I stuck it out and now remember that time as one of the most impactful experiences of my college years.

Our kids need to hear our stories of overcoming the challenges that go along with becoming independent adults so that their feelings of separation anxiety are normalized. There may also be some benefit in sharing stories from their preschool or day care years when they struggled to say good-bye and then had positive experiences. If the kids are open to it, they can share their stories of overcoming separation fears and being independent from parents. Depending on their age, the independence can be as simple as going to kindergarten without clinging or crying anymore or successfully spending the night at Grandma's without calling parents.

Family Meeting Topic: Independence and Responsibility

Our kids won't intuitively understand the relationship between increased freedom and independence and increased responsibility. Oftentimes, teenagers complain that they want more freedom, but they don't always grasp that increased freedom needs to be paired with more responsibility. For example, the teenager who wants to drive the family car needs to also start helping with some of the family errands. The child who wants to go on a sleepover needs to make sure their at-home chores are done before they leave or are covered by a sibling. The kid who wants their own phone (paid for by parents) needs to contribute more to the household chores.

A conversation about how independence is not a function of chronological age is important. Our kids need to understand the relationship between their increased responsibilities and their increased privileges and freedoms at home. Eventually, and hopefully sometime in their early twenties, we want our kids to be fully grown, thriving independent adult humans. That end goal of our parenting means our kids need to start gradually learning how to take on more and more responsibilities and freedoms until they reach the point of living with complete freedom as well as full responsibility for themselves.

Diving Deeper

Our kids' independence, as I've discovered in hundreds of conversations with parents struggling with having their kids away from them, is as much about us as it is about our kids. I know this from experiencing my own ambivalence as well. It's hard to let our kids go. As I've already launched three of my five kids into the world of college and career, I've often found myself feeling down. I stare around my dining table at the empty seats and feel a sense of grief for what I now refer to as the "family years"—and I still have two kids at home! But what has ended up helping me cope is returning to my own purpose, separate from my role as my kids' mom. Reframing the empty nest (or, in the case of larger families, the "emptying nest") as an opportunity to return to hobbies and passions that have been put on the back burner due to lack of time has been a big help in coping with my kids not needing me as much.

Since my kids started leaving home for their own independent lives, I returned to school for a master's degree I had started pursuing before my first child was born; I began writing regularly on my blog; I returned to reading prolifically like I had before I got busy with kids; I started scheduling regular walks, coffee dates, and lunches with friends; and I started taking guitar lessons. This book itself actually represents part of my finding my individual, non-mom-focused purpose during this new season of my kids' growing independence. As a side benefit, while I've been pursuing these various goals and interests, I've modeled for my kids the process they'll need to go through in order to successfully separate from me and discover their own, individual identities. The process I've shown them over the past decade of getting outside my comfort zone, setting goals for myself, and working hard toward those goals all demonstrate another important character trait our kids need in order to flourish—grit.

Camp Secret #5
Grit Is Grown Outside the Comfort Zone

My fondest camp memory would have to be from this past summer, my last camper summer, when I got up on a wakeboard for the first time. This memory was significant to me because I had set this as a goal for myself many years before and kept trying to reach it. I kept building up the confidence to continue trying and build up my skill. This was also very memorable for me because my friends continuously supported and encouraged me through it. This could also be an example of growing grit, because I gave myself a goal and didn't give up until I reached it.

—Remi

In the early days of our camp's sailing program in the 1940s and 1950s, kids were crashing boats into the rocks near shore and capsizing frequently, because the camp staff did not know how to teach sailing. But in the 1960s the sailing program was dramatically improved when an amazing couple, experienced college sailing coach Boris Gregory and his wife, Irene, together with their four teenage, superstar sailing offspring, joined the camp staff and transformed the program. Better instruction and more sailboats led to many kids developing a lifelong love of sailing that they fondly attribute to their lessons with the Gregorys. Some campers went on to participate in and win sailing regattas and join college sailing teams. A basic expectation of the Gregory sailing program was that each camper must sail—by themselves in their own small boat—the first time they visited the camp sailing dock.

Boris, originally from Germany and still carrying a distinct accent, would blast instructions from the dock to campers whose sails were luffing (heading straight into the wind and flapping wildly). "Your sail is *luffing* at you!" he'd yell through his megaphone. His most common refrain was, "Push the tiller towards the sail!" To a crying camper, Boris gave brisk instructions to "buck up and sail." No camper was permitted to leave their boat, regardless of the number of tears or the intensity of their terror, until they managed to tack across the lake a few times on their own.

This old-style philosophy of forcing kids to just buck up and do things regardless of how they were feeling prevailed among teachers and coaches of Boris's generation. And while this strict style worked well for many kids, there were some kids for whom the "no choice but sail" technique was not a positive experience. These kids did not become avid, lifelong sailors. Instead, some became so terrified after losing control of their boat or capsizing in heavy winds that they vowed to never get in a sailboat again. The prevailing coaching philosophy of the era succeeded in getting many kids to master and enjoy sailing, but it also led to unintended negative consequences for those kids for whom the stress and pressure of the style were too much—those kids were just too far outside of their comfort zone to learn. Coaches of the era did not yet understand why their "one size fits all" approach wasn't ideal for all kids' growth and development.

In the mid-1990s, I discovered that one of my own kids wouldn't have thrived with Boris's "sink or swim" approach to teaching. My two oldest daughters were taking swimming lessons at our neighborhood pool from "Coach Bob," a renowned Southern California swim instructor. His method, like Boris's, was sink or swim (literally). At their very first lesson, Coach Bob put kids under water about ten feet from the pool's edge and forced them to swim to the steps. They flailed around a bit and he gave them a gentle push—as needed—to get them to the edge. For my oldest daughter, Gretchen, Coach Bob's technique worked perfectly. She was relaxed and felt proud of being able to swim on her own right away.

But for my younger daughter, Meredith, Coach Bob's swim lessons were traumatic. She sat terrified on the swim step, tears quietly streaming down her face, waiting for Coach Bob to put her under again and again. She followed the rules and did her lesson, because she was obedient to teachers and didn't want to disappoint him, but she was miserable for every swim lesson, and it was torture for me to watch. After several lessons, I knew that, despite his great reputation, Coach Bob's style just wasn't working for my younger daughter. We switched to a gentler instructional approach, and she learned to swim at her own pace with no further tears. I had learned, with my own kids, that the old-school philosophy of just forcing kids do things in order to learn doesn't work with every child.

While Boris, Coach Bob, and other teachers and coaches of their era have hundreds of success stories of children who revere their instruction and attribute their love of sailing, swimming, or other activities, to their coaching, there were some kids for whom feeling such a high level of fear and a lack of control was traumatic. These are kids who, as adults, might break into a sweat remembering their frightening times on the lake or in the pool. In the 1990s, I did not yet understand the neuropsychology and personality differences that explain why some children experience terror while others learn and grow with the same instructional method. I did know, however, that I did not want our camp instruction—in any activity area—to produce the kind of distress I had seen in my own daughter at her swim lessons. I was keeping up-to-date with the research of the burgeoning self-esteem movement. And, so, in the mid-1990s our instructional philosophy in all activities (not just sailing) swung from the "you have to try this" side of the coaching spectrum to the other extreme, the "let's just have fun" and be comfortable approach. Like many youth development professionals of the era, I became convinced that keeping campers comfortable and happy was our top priority. My reasoning went something like this: Camp experiences are supposed to be fun, and being scared isn't fun, so we should make sure kids are never scared and are always having fun.

I trained counselors to help campers feel comfortable and to never force them to do an activity that frightened them. Crying campers were quickly rescued from luffing sailboats and rock climbing ledges. The goal was to minimize fear and restore happiness as quickly as possible. Counselors were clear about their role: "swoop in and save" campers from discomfort.

While our new, more easygoing philosophy about activity participation led to fewer tears, it also led to some unintended and undesirable results—foremost of which was that hesitant campers were not trying as many new activities. Unintentionally, by keeping these kids super comfortable all the time, and preventing them from facing fears, we were also preventing them from capitalizing on growth opportunities. By not encouraging kids to get outside their comfort zones, we were preventing some of the great things that happen only when you get uncomfortable. Backpacking trips became optional and nearly disappeared from the camp schedule. Very few campers would voluntarily sign up to hike for a few miles with a heavy pack on their back when they could be doing a far more comfortable activity like driving a motorboat or making a friendship bracelet instead. We watched as the most popular activities shifted from the more adventurous ones like backpacking, sailing, and rock climbing to the more comfortable activities like archery, crafts, and kayaking. Once campers were no longer required to participate, some opted to just watch their peers from the sidelines rather than face their fears and their discomfort.

This new counseling philosophy was mirrored by parenting trends of the same time. Swept away in the self-esteem movement, parents and teachers became primarily concerned with children feeling good about themselves. At the same time, sensational stories about child kidnappings, sexual abuse, and razors hidden in Halloween candy produced a perception of increased child endangerment (that was actually not statistically true).[1] Keeping children safe from both emotional and physical harm became parents' top priority. And while keeping kids safe is, on the surface, an excellent goal, this new parenting style had unintended negative consequences that are still being felt in the adult workforce today.[2] By not preparing kids to face the discomforts that inevitably come up in life, parents unintentionally crippled many kids with a profound lack of resilience, stifling the development of what is now commonly referred to as "grit." Being sheltered from challenging situations did not leave our kids safer. Instead it led to a generation of adults who hesitate to take risks, fear failure, turn to substances to stifle difficult emotions, and want rewards and promotions for average performance.

But we didn't know about these unintended outcomes back in the 1990s. The term "helicopter parent," coined by Foster Cline and Jim Fay in 1990, didn't become mainstream until the 2000s, but the helicopter parenting movement was gaining steam a full decade earlier. Similar to our camp counselors who were on the lookout to stop any distress in their campers, the helicopter parent hovers nearby to make sure everything is going smoothly for their child, and swoops in immediately to rescue their child at the earliest sign of fear, pain, or any other uncomfortable emotion.

Many parents, myself included, got caught up in a trend that equated great parenting with keeping our kids happy and comfortable at all times, which meant being super-involved, constantly helping, and in constant communication with our children. There were (and are) some benefits to this modern parenting style. We know our kids well and have developed close family relationships, in many cases much closer relationships than we had with our own parents. We also know each of our children's homework assignments (and assist with a few of them), the drills they did at soccer practice (because we either coached their team or stayed and watched), and what snacks they ate at school.

The downside to this overparenting, though, is it makes it difficult for our children to develop their independence as well as their problem-solving and decision-making skills. When parents and other adults jump in too quickly to assist, kids don't have the opportunity to develop the important skills necessary for a thriving adulthood, including the ability to deal with mistakes, the capacity to problem-solve, and the skill of making independent decisions without needing to confer with parents. This points to one of the main reasons why kids experience surges of growth at summer camp. They are unable to access immediate parental guidance. Without all-the-time access to parents, campers learn to rely on their own resolve and thinking skills to navigate situations and make decisions. The experience often gives them a boost in confidence as they discover for the first time that they are capable of doing many things without a parent present.

In the 2000s, my newfound knowledge about what kids need to develop into thriving humans led to a shift in both my parenting and camp counseling philosophies. While I was working to buck the helicopter trend with my parenting style at home and allow my kids more freedom to experience discomfort and growth, I also intentionally adjusted our camp counseling style away from constant hovering and protecting from discomfort toward a style that encouraged growth in confidence and resilience.

This was, in effect, a third philosophy, balanced between the "sink or swim" of the 1960s and the "never feel uncomfortable" philosophy of the 1990s. While I was being more intentional in my parenting and attempting not to constantly rescue my own kids from their mistakes, I also didn't want our camp counselors to mirror the over-parenting trend in their leadership style. I knew that campers needed to be allowed to experience times of discomfort in order to experience growth and that, depending on where their parents fell on the over-parenting spectrum, camp might be one of the only places where they could experience this kind of growth.

Today, campers are guided by caring counselors to face their fears and learn to get outside their comfort zone. We talk to kids about how the feeling of being uncomfortable and taking risks is the only way we grow. At camp and at home, I have watched kids thrive under this style of adult guidance, which differs from both past coaching philosophies and the current overinvolved style.

Learning Our Kid's "Zones"

It's not easy for children to overcome their fears and try something new. There are some kids who take a few summers at camp before they attempt certain things. Waterskiing, wakeboarding, sailing, and the zip line come to mind as some of our top fear-inducing activities. Riding the "RAD" (a tube-type thing towed behind a boat that requires no skill) gives many kids a stepping-stone to work up to the things they fear. During a recent summer session, there was a boy who must have told me ten times that he was *not* going to try waterskiing or wakeboarding; his goal for the summer was to "feel satisfied," and he felt that the RAD would give him that.

I understood his trepidation to try something that scares him. Nobody likes trying something new that seems either too hard ("It might be super-embarrassing if I'm terrible at it"), too scary ("This is too high [or *hard* or *deep*] for me"), or too dangerous ("I might get hurt"). Keeping ourselves feeling comfortable and safe is, for the most part, a good inclination; it often prevents us from doing things that are dangerous. When it comes to jumping off a dangerous cliff or riding on the top of a teenage friend's car, we want our kids to autonomously choose *not* to try new, risky activities that could lead to injury or death. However, for the most fearful and anxious kids, that inclination goes too far and keeps them from discovering new and fun people and things.

For most of life's challenges—reaching out to someone for a job we're interested in, approaching someone who we think could be a good friend, trying a new outdoor sport that could be fun—facing a bit of trepidation is actually required. And, in fact, the bit of anxiety we have often helps fuel our success. Most growth and learning happens in that magical space just outside our comfort zone, where we are just a bit scared or challenged. Our slightly elevated heart rate and nerves actually propel us to work harder and do better.[3] To understand how important it is to help your fearful child get out of their comfort zone, ask yourself this question about your own life: If I had never done anything that made me nervous, where would I be today?

For fearful kids to grow (and get less fearful), we need to help them learn to give themselves small challenges. A place to start is figuring out what your child's comfort zone is. Like all people, comfort zones vary greatly depending on the temperament of the child. Even within my extended family, we have kids and adults who are the first to jump off the zip line platform, those who spend thirty minutes on the platform before building up the courage to jump, and those who end up climbing back down the ladder.

How do adults who work with and parent kids figure out what each child's comfort zone is? During a recent summer season, a Dutch counselor sketched a graphic of how to think and talk about our comfort, growth, and blackout zones (see graphic below). I found her illustration helpful and have been using it to train counselors. All children have a zone of circumstances, behaviors, and actions where they feel very comfortable. Those activities and events are within their comfort zone. Depending on their personality, kids can naturally have a very

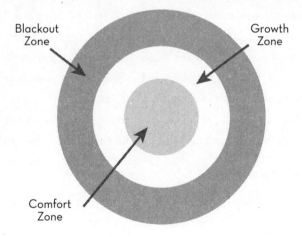

small or very large comfort zone. Things that are new and challenging take kids out of their comfort zone and into their growth zone. Kids feel more anxiety and often express fear when they are in their growth zone, but they may be there because they've set a goal for themselves and want to reach it. They are usually happy with themselves after trying. The blackout zone is the emotional place where kids are unable to learn. They are so far outside their own comfort zone that they are overwhelmed with fear and anxiety. Activities that take kids high off the ground (like a ropes course) can often send some kids into the blackout zone, so we caution our staff to encourage kids to climb only as high as what's still comfortably within their growth zone. Public speaking is an example of something that strikes fear in many hearts and stays in the growth or blackout zones throughout our lives.

As a ninth grader in speech class, I remember the anxious feelings leading up to the day I had to give a short talk about how to bake blueberry bars. I was petrified, and I can still remember how my stomach felt upside down as I waited to speak. But the experience of speaking in public, which was definitely on the border of the blackout zone for me at that point, led to it moving more into my growth zone. Much of what I now do in my profession involves public speaking, and while doing so in front of a large number of campers is well within my comfort zone, there are other groups (e.g., one hundred–plus adults) that definitely put me right back into my growth zone, which motivates me to prepare better and work harder for those gigs.

For some of us, and for kids as well, the comfort zone is quite large, and trying new things is not such a leap. But for others, the comfort zone may be very small; that is, there are very few things they may be willing to try, since so many things make them uncomfortable.

"I don't like waterskiing."

It's not that hard to tell when a child is out of their comfort zone. A fearful kid will often say they don't like a certain activity. Sometimes they will even try to convince others that it's not fun. "I don't like going in the lake," they'll say, or "Water sports aren't that fun." It's simply not comfortable (nor cool) to say, "*I am so scared of going in the lake that I'm freaking out right now!*"

Questions to ask when a child voices this kind of concern include:

"What don't you like about the lake?"
"Is there something I can do to help make you feel more
     comfortable?"
"What if I go in with you?"
"Would you like to watch some other kids try it?"

It's also helpful to explain the concept of "challenge by choice." Let your child know that you want them to grow, and that growth occurs when they try new things and overcome some fears. Encourage them to try, but let them know that it's ultimately up to them to decide how much they want to challenge themselves.

Why Kids Need to Grow Their Grit

It turns out that grit predicts performance better than IQ or innate talent. Grit makes our kids productive and successful because it allows them to reach their long-term goals despite life's inevitable setbacks. This ability to overcome challenges makes them stronger and more masterful at their tasks. Moreover, the ability to cope with difficulty—to be resilient—paves the way for long-term happiness.

—Christine Carter

When Manny Vezie, our camp's founder, started his all-boys camp in the 1930s, he was concerned that boys were getting "too soft." His brochure tagline, "The Last of the Rugged Camps," emphasized that kids would get toughened up by attending camp. Long pack trips, cold showers, and time away from hovering mothers, Manny believed, was what boys needed to toughen up. *Grit* was what Manny and other camp directors of the early twentieth century wanted to develop in their campers.

Although Manny passed away in 1985, I often reflect on what he would think about the twenty-first-century kids attending camp today. My guess is that he would still be concerned about them being too soft and would want camp to continue to provide the opportunity for campers to build the grit, or persistence or resilience, that Paul Tough identifies as one of the character traits distinguishing children who successfully navigate life's difficulties from those who do not.[4]

I have seen this firsthand in the campers I've worked with. The kids who struggle the most with adjusting to camp and pushing themselves to try new things are often the same ones whose parents experience extreme distress when hearing about their child's discomfort. In recent years, I've had more than a few parents say to me, "I just don't want him to be uncomfortable." Unfortunately, being uncomfortable is a prerequisite to growth, and parents who have trouble dealing with their child's discomfort often are setting the child up for much bigger setbacks in the future. The minor discomforts of childhood often don't compare to the stressors of difficult coworkers, challenging relationships, and tasks that require trial and error. Grit is an important character trait all kids need to develop.

The research of psychologist and author Angela Duckworth further cemented the importance of focusing on this important trait of "mental toughness" and found that grit trumps talent in all fields of work.[5] Our challenge as parents, teachers, and others who work with and care about youth is providing our children with opportunities to develop the character traits that will help them find success in life, and grit is one of the most important.

Knowing how important it is for kids to grow their grit, I chose that as one of our summer themes. The summer of "Growing Grit," we talked openly about challenging ourselves to get uncomfortable and try new things. Campers and counselors shared stories of persistence. One Dutch counselor shared the story of the trials and challenges she faced leading up to her national water polo team winning a gold medal at the Beijing Olympics. When we share stories with our kids that tell about not just the successes but also the setbacks and hard work, they learn that doing great things often entails overcoming many obstacles along the way.

How can we grow our children's grit, especially if they, like many in their generation, seem to lack the persistence and drive that are its hallmarks? Here are some ideas we've used at summer camp that you can incorporate at home.

Five Ways to Grow Grit

> I would not be the person I am today without camp. I am much more confident, my communication skills are a million times better, I've learned to embrace failure and grow from it, I've developed grit, I'm a better problem-solver, I'm more likely to take initiative, I understand people better, I'm better able to understand and control my emotions. This list goes on and on!
>
> —Chloe

With all the research backing the importance of this character trait, there has also been a growing body of evidence that grit is not an innate trait but can be developed through practice. Summer camp offers the perfect environment for growing grit, and there I've witnessed five key ways kids do so. Some of these observations are helpful and informative for parents who want to help their kids grow grit at home.

#1. Learning self-reliance and responsibility grows grit.

Encouraging kids to be more independent (covered in Secret #4) and more responsible and capable (which you'll read about next in Secret #6) are both great ways parents help kids to grow grit. When kids start to clean up, make decisions, solve problems, face social challenges, and remember their own sweatshirt on a cold day, they can use these opportunities to gain self-reliance and the accompanying grit. Learning to do more things for themselves—and seeing that they *can* do things without parents' help—grows children's grit.

#2. Experiencing mistakes and failures grows grit.

So often, parents step in and stop a failure before it occurs; how often have we rescued a homework assignment left behind on the desk or put the finishing touches on a procrastinated science board project? It's just really hard to stand there and watch our children crash and burn when we know the easy fix, usually involving our intervention. Unfortunately, by not allowing our kids to feel the pain of the forgotten assignment or the sting of the lackluster science board, we deprive them of the chance to learn from their mistakes and, more important, *not make them again* (or at least not too many more times!). Instead, our kids learn about "parental rescue," which is not something we want our children to take with them into adulthood. Allowing our kids to make non-life-threatening mistakes, and educating them that failure is part of growth, is another way to grow their grit.

#3. Talking about, setting, and reaching goals grows grit.

Encouraging our kids to talk about and reach goals can serve as a guidepost and motivation for our children and is another way to grow their grit. Campers experience amazing gratification when they reach a goal such as overcoming a fear of heights or breaking through their shyness to make a new friend. Each of the goals our kids set and reach, whether big or small, grows their grit.

#4. Facing new challenges grows grit.

When we conquer fears or are faced with new, unfamiliar activities or places (such as a new school, a new team, or a new teacher), these are opportunities for our kids to grow their grit. Some of our most negative life experiences, like a difficult summer job, grow a lot of grit. My first summer job during high school was scooping ice cream at a Häagen-Dazs shop. I liked my coworkers, but I was scared of the manager, who yelled at us a lot, had the video security camera focused on us, not our customers, and definitely did not ever offer us a scoop of free ice cream. I spent my shifts feeling nervous, with my heart racing. I was constantly worried about making a mistake. But looking back, that experience was a good one. I stuck with the job throughout the summer and learned a lot about managing other people—mostly in the "what not to do" category! Every new experience, whether easy or difficult, grows our kids' confidence in themselves about approaching *other* new and challenging experiences.

#5. Feeling emotional and physical discomfort grows grit.

Unfortunately, growing grit is not comfortable or easy. One way our kids grow their grit is through experiencing emotional pain and physical discomfort. Hiking up a long trail with a heavy backpack may feel unpleasant, but once the pack is off, we've caught our breath, and as we sit by a fire overlooking a majestic view, we see that our hard work and physical discomfort led to a memorable and life-changing experience we would not have had otherwise.

Three Things Parents Can Do to Help Kids Get Out of Their Comfort Zones

#1. Let them do it alone.

Many parents marvel at the new things their kids try at camp—activities they've refused to do with their family. They ask, "How did you get him to go waterskiing? We've tried for years and he wouldn't go." The answer is really quite simple. As parents, we seem to bring out the most fear in our kids. Maybe it's because we've been taking care of them since they were babies, so they naturally feel less courageous when they're with us. I've been convinced through my observations of kids at camp (and through personal experience with my own five children) that kids are, for the most part, *much* better at trying new things and getting outside their comfort zone when parents are not hovering nearby, and this is especially true when those parents have worried expressions on their faces.

One simple idea is to figure out other trusted adults with whom your child might try something new. This is a hard truth for parents to swallow: that much of the growth our kids will experience will be when we're not around. It's natural, though. After all, we are wired to help and support and keep our children safe and comfortable, and when we're around, we can unwittingly impede growth and limit opportunities.

We can be there for our kids, prepping them, cheering and encouraging, and debriefing with them after challenges. And yet, for some reason, our presence often serves as a crutch our kids fall back on at the slightest feeling of discomfort.

#2. Practice "baby steps."

The boy who wanted to be "satisfied" and not try the watersports? He did the RAD several times and ended up trying kneeboarding, as well. The pride in his voice when he reported to me about it was yet another example that it was, in fact, a good thing for him to try something a bit more challenging. Feeling comfortable and satisfied is good, but the greatest things in life happen in the growth zone, whether at summer camp or anywhere else.

Many of my favorite moments at camp are when I get to witness a previously fearful and hesitant camper in the moments just after they've tried something new. Their confidence and joy are at a high as they tell the story of how scared they were, how they tried anyway, and how much fun it was! The refrain is often the same: "I was so scared of heights and didn't think I could do it, but everyone encouraged me, then I tried, and now *I love it!*"

#3. Remember the "blessing" of the least favorite activity.

Finishing up an online camp orientation meeting for our first-year campers and their parents, I got asked a question that I've been asked hundreds of times by prospective and new campers: "Do I have to do every activity?" My answer, as always, was not a simple one.

"No," I tell the activity-avoidant camper. "You won't be forced to try every activity, but we will still have you go with your group to the activity, and once there, counselors will encourage you to give it at least a small try. For example, if you are scared to go waterskiing, we may encourage you to put on the skis, on land, to see how they feel. Then we'll encourage you to see how you feel holding the ski rope handle and having an instructor pull you up to the standing position while on the beach. We'll have you go in the boat and watch others try waterskiing, and when you're feeling ready—whether that's this summer, next, or three years from now—we'll encourage you to give it a try."

The underlying message we continue to give campers is that it's okay to be nervous and we don't want them to ever feel forced, but we will continue to encourage them to try new things, especially those things that scare them a little. And we don't ever excuse them from the activity altogether, because we know that if we did that, they will never gain the courage to overcome their fear. I often remind parents about the "blessing of the least favorite activity." I coined this phrase around the time of publication of Wendy Mogul's best-selling book, *The Blessing of a Skinned Knee.*[6] Among the variety of activities at camp, some induce fear or discomfort in children. For some children, the lake—with its deep waters—is scary. For others, the climbing activities that require going up high are frightening. Still others had a previous negative experience that has made them not want to repeat a certain activity.

And while personal preferences need to be acknowledged and honored, as it is natural to enjoy some activities over others, there are reasons to encourage kids to try activities that they *think* they won't like. Often, when a child (or adult) says they don't like a particular activity, it is because they have never tried it and assume they won't like it. It seems scary to them, or they do not think they will do well at it, or they may be fearful of being embarrassed by their lack of skill, and they are therefore hesitant to try.

Figuring out the reason why the child doesn't want to do an activity is important, as there are often good reasons to try a "least favorite" activity. Overcoming a fear, discovering a new hobby, and gaining confidence are among the blessings that can come from trying something new. There may be a hidden blessing in what a child thinks they won't like, so it's important for parents to remember that there are many reasons for a child to dislike an activity, and at times it may not have to do with the activity itself, but instead is about a fear or another issue.

Making Another Lanyard

There are some kids who, without encouragement, would choose to spend their entire time at camp making lanyards. These are often the same kids who are hesitant to try a new activity, club, or sport. Because of this, our camp's program is set up to require kids to go to every activity, with their group, even the activities they would not choose to sign up for. While they're not forced to participate, they do still need to go with their group, see what the activity is about, and watch their cabin mates participate. In most cases, because they feel comfortable and encouraged by their counselor and friends, they end up giving the new activity a try.

This story from long-time camper and counselor Stevie Goodrich, about helping one of his campers overcome his fear of waterskiing, shows the magic of overcoming fears and trying something new:

Slightly homesick, scared to enter the cold blue water, petrified of being unable to ski after all his peers had tried and succeeded, my camper Sam cried and hung on to me for dear life, resisting all my attempts to calm and coax him into the lake. We sat on the edge of the boat dangling our feet in the water for over an hour, talking about what it would feel like to try it, why he might be so afraid, what his favorite movie was, and even the way his dog looks when she jumps into his swimming pool. Eventually his tears subsided when I told him about my own first bumbling experience on water skis. Finally, Sam summoned up enough courage to slip on the skis and jump in, but not without my promise that I would jump in at exactly the same moment he did and be right there with him in the water. The momentary look on his face when he hit the water and popped up looking astonished he had actually survived the jump was one of the most poignant yet funniest moments of my summer.

After talking Sam through his fears on the back of the boat and watching him slowly gain confidence with my encouragement, I probably felt secretly more joyful than he did when he signaled the boat driver to start moving. I remember, waving to him as he rode away on his skis, how amazing it felt to have helped him overcome his fears. Watching him continue to grow from that moment on, easily trying archery or the ropes course for the first time, feeling the comfort of being "equal" to his peers now, grinning at me when he ran by laughing with new friends, was incredible. I know I will never forget that huge smile on his face and the high five that I gave him when we both climbed back into the boat.

In order to foster the grit kids need to thrive as adults, parents can foster a family environment where the *courage of trying* is celebrated, and mistakes and failures are viewed in the positive. Most of us are not good at things we try the first time, and our kids need to know that venturing outside their comfort zone to try something new can be difficult. In those times when a kid is saying, "I can't," a great word to remember is *yet*. If your child is struggling to ride a bike and saying, "I can't," you can respond with, "You're right—you can't ride a bike *yet*. It takes time to learn something new."

Embracing Hard Emotions and Teaching Growth MindSet

One of the most difficult things as a parent is not being able to protect our children from the bad things that inevitably happen to them. A kid at school says something mean; they don't get on the team they wanted to be on; they lose a school election.

Instead of jumping to anger and trying to force the world to be nicer to our kid (which is extremely tempting but also impossible to do), we can view our role as parents not as fixing all the negative circumstances our kids face but comforting and guiding our kids. Getting with our kids in their discomfort and helping them learn to face and embrace all of their emotions—both the positive and the negative ones—offers our kids the chance to learn an important life skill. When they are uncomfortable or sad, we can let them know we're here for them: "I'm right here with you. I see this is really hard for you." We can also reinforce that their feelings are valid while not offering a quick fix.

While it's tempting to tell our kids how amazing they are (they are, after all, so amazing!), we need to avoid constantly giving our kids positive labels in our praise. Kids may get the wrong message and start believing in a fixed mindset when we tell them they're smart or the best. Instead, when we focus on the effort and character traits behind accomplishments and use growth mindset praise, our kids learn that they can do hard things and overcome obstacles. Rather than tell them they're smart, we can talk about the effort, time, and planning we saw them put into a successful school project. Rather than saying they're the best on their soccer team, we can point out specific skills they have developed over the season through persistent practice.

Observable Changes and Core Transformation

At camp, we see kids trying many new things. The kid who thought of himself as more of a lanyard maker than a rock climber discovers that he likes climbing. The one who is obsessed with horses discovers a love of sailing. Some kids experience new adeventures that help them discover places they've never been and want to explore more. At Catalina Sea Camps, teens dive deep underwater in scuba gear. At AstroCamp, they study space, experience zero gravity, and learn what it takes to become an astronaut. At Wilderness Adventures and other outdoor adventure programs, campers tackle whitewater rivers and mountain peaks. Discovering that there are new things to experience and try beyond the comfortable zone of the known is something kids learn at camp. And much of the growth we witness in them happens at what are often considered scarier, riskier activities.

More important, trying new things and learning to tolerate being uncomfortable teaches kids a more lasting and important skill. Trying new things and overcoming fears translates into confidence to try *other* new things, often in unrelated areas. Our kids will experience hardships throughout childhood and adolescence. Helping guide them through these experiences without jumping in to rescue them provides them with the opportunity to grow their resilience and overcome the inevitable obstacles of adulthood.

Young Adults Need Grit, Too

Children aren't the only ones who need to grow their grit. Several years ago, I had just finished running a marathon and had flopped onto the grass to rest. I was so tired that I hadn't registered that the tired runner sitting next to me was a former camp counselor. He had worked at my camp eight years earlier and quit after just three weeks. He was a well-liked counselor who had been doing a great job, so I remembered feeling disappointed that he had not completed the season. I had not, however, given him or his departure any thought since the time he left. He had apparently been thinking about it a lot. He reintroduced himself and proceeded to tell me how much he regretted leaving camp early. He said that he had not, in fact, had to go home to deal with a sick family member as he had reported at the time. Instead, he had been feeling homesick. He said he had really enjoyed the work and the people he had met, and he knows now that staying for the summer and working through his homesickness would have been a better choice.

I was struck that we need to help even our young adult counselors recognize that it's okay to feel uncomfortable sometimes and encourage them to work through the difficult feelings which may mean they are growing, just like their campers. Several years after not mustering the grit to stay at camp, this young man had found the resilience to finish a marathon! I was reminded that we never stop growing our grit.

Bringing Camp Home: Growing Grit

A ship is safe in harbor, but that's not what ships were built for.
                                        —attributed to John A. Shedd

A memorable episode of one of my favorite TV shows, *Modern Family*, features the dilemma of daughter Haley not having any hardships to write about on her college application. Her mom created one by dropping her in an unfamiliar location and making her walk home. It was a humorous example of a real problem: Colleges want to see that our kids have some grit, because they will need it to complete college. But for many kids, their lives have not been conducive to developing that particular trait. Life is often too easy, especially for kids on the higher end of the socioeconomic spectrum whose parents have hovered, saved, and protected so much that there haven't been enough opportunities for their kids to develop grit. Here are some strategies you can use to develop this important character trait in your kids:

One Simple Thing

If we want to raise kids who are resilient and persevere through difficulties, we need to model how that's done. One thing (perhaps not so simple) that you can do to raise a gritty kid is to show them—through your own example—what it looks like to set a goal and work through the inevitable stumbling blocks to reach it. Regardless of what you choose for your goal—running a 5K race or reading a certain number of books in a year—let your child know what you're doing by posting a chart or discussing your progress. If your goal requires some coaching or help, let your child know what you are doing to get that help.

Because I'm a runner, and training for a race offers an ideal example of growing grit, I'll use the example of the "Couch to 5K" training plan. If you have never run a race, announcing to your family the goal you have to complete a 5K, putting it on the calendar, and printing out the training plan for all to see shows a tangible example of how one perseveres to reach a goal. I caution you not to recruit the rest of your family (including your spouse or kids) until you have conquered the goal yourself. Our kids learn much more from what we model for them than how we lecture or prod them.

If you'd prefer a nonphysical goal, there are many ideas that come to mind: taking a class to learn a new language, learning to play a musical instrument, getting some training to advance in your career, or starting a regular volunteering practice. Letting your child see you study, practice, and invest time in reaching a personal or professional goal is an impactful way to teach them what it looks like to persevere and reach goals.

The Sticky Note Solution

Our kids know when we're offering untrue parental platitudes. When we tell our kids that they're good at something when they really aren't, they know. When your child is facing a disappointment or struggling with mastering a skill, an encouraging sticky note, strategically placed on their pillow or their bedroom door, can provide the boost they may need:

> I know you're disappointed that you didn't do well on your chemistry exam. You don't have all the understanding you need **yet** to do well in the class, but I've seen how hard you are working, and I am confident that you will continue improving your chemistry skills if you keep at it.

Make It Fun

Family movie nights are a fun tradition, and there are many movies where the protagonist overcomes a challenge to reach a goal.

These movies, which show examples of grit, are a fun way to reinforce the value of perseverance and hard work. A few years ago, when our camp's summer theme was "Growing Grit" and I was talking a lot about grit at home, we watched the movie *The Martian*. My then ten-year-old son said, "The Martian had grit." In the movie, Matt Damon's character has countless failures and disappointments as he tries to survive alone on Mars. I remember thinking that watching that movie and talking about it was much more powerful than my dinner table lecture about Paul Tough's book, *How Children Succeed*, in which he gives compelling evidence for the importance of grit.

Countless books and movies feature gritty characters. Some that come to mind for tweens and teens include *Raiders of the Lost Ark*, *Rudy*, *Everest*, *Gandhi*, *The Grapes of Wrath*, *Rocky*, *The Karate Kid*, *Groundhog Day*, *The Princess Bride*, and *October Sky*.

For younger kids, gritty movies include *Finding Nemo*, *Homeward Bound*, *March of the Penguins*, *The Land Before Time*, *Babe*, *The Little Mermaid*, *Hoosiers*, *Spellbound*, *Dark Horse*, *Oliver*, *The Pride of the Yankees*, *Fly Away Home*, and *Chicken Run*. The list of inspirational movies featuring one or more gritty heroes goes on and on. In fact, if you think of your favorite movies, I'm guessing that what you love about the main character is their grit in overcoming failure and obstacles and pushing through to eventual success. So for a fun way to get inspired together, gather around the TV, get your popcorn and hot chocolate ready, and enjoy a gritty movie!

If you're looking for a nonscreen way to learn about grit, there are, of course, many books that feature stories of both fictional and real people overcoming failure to eventually succeed. Many now-famous people experienced multiple and enormous failures before ultimately succeeding and becoming household names. Sharing the stories of these individuals can be helpful for our kids, who often falsely assume that success comes overnight. Even more inspiring for your kids will be your own failure stories. Ever lost a job? Failed a test? Tell the story and emphasize what you learned from it and how you found a different way to succeed. By reframing your own failure as a learning experience, you'll teach your kids to do the same.

Around the Campfire

For a family dinner table conversation, I like the idea of creating a "Courage Box." This can be an actual box or a jar, or it could just be an area on the family bulletin board. Each family member has one index card on which they write "Conquer My Fear!" On the card, they write a fear they want to overcome. It can be a social situation, a daunting physical challenge, or a new thing they have wanted to try but have been afraid to. To set the example, have a parent go first and share a fear you want to conquer—such as public speaking at a large meeting at work. This example will be powerful in helping your kids understand that *everyone*, even seemingly confident adults, has fears.

Next, go around and have each family member share what they fear. As a family, brainstorm ideas about overcoming or confronting the fear. It's important that no teasing or shaming is involved, so be sure to set those ground rules by explaining that everyone has fears and that fears are a normal part of life. After discussion of the fear, let each person come up with their own plan for addressing the fear and write it on their card.

Set a date (one month away is a good benchmark) to check in on how each person is doing with conquering their fear. If someone overcomes their fear, have a celebration and some kind of ceremony, like ripping up the card or throwing it in the fire. Perhaps the Courage Box can become an ongoing family tradition that encourages the sharing of stories of courage.

Family Meeting Topic: Setting Goals

In order to grow grit, we need to stretch ourselves with a goal. We set goals at work and on our sports teams, but we rarely set personal goals that we talk about at home with our families. An excellent dinner conversation (or, even better, an ongoing conversation) can revolve around our individual goals. There are many different ways to approach goals, but some important reminders as we teach our kids about goal setting, and model for them our own goals, are as follows:

- Use the SMART acronym to make sure goals are:
  Specific (simple, sensible, significant)
  Measurable (meaningful, motivating)
  Achievable (agreed, attainable)
  Relevant (reasonable, realistic and resourced, results based)
  Time bound (time based, time limited, time/cost limited,
  timely, time sensitive).
      "Getting better at soccer" is not a SMART goal, but "Dribbling with both feet down the length of the field by the end of the soccer season" is.
- Focus on the GAIN not the GAP:
      We tend to lament when we don't reach a goal, when we are far better off celebrating how far we've come. One way to think about this is thinking of our goals in the *Good, Better, Best* model. For example, when training for a 5K, a good goal is completing the race regardless of speed, a better goal is running the entire race without stopping, and a best goal would be running the race in a specific time. Even if we reach our good goal, we've done something much better than if we hadn't set the goal in the first place!
- Share the goal and write it down:
      People with written goals are 50 percent more likely to achieve them than those who don't write goals down.[7] The act of writing down a goal is a powerful motivator. And sharing your goal with a close friend or family member increases the likelihood of reaching the goal even more. Once someone else knows about your goal, they can provide the encouragement you'll need to persevere through the hard parts of reaching your goal.
      Talking about and writing down individual goals at a family dinner or meeting, either on individual papers or a family goal sheet, is an important part of the goal-setting process. I love the idea of making recording our goals a fun family project. Each

family member can create their own collage or list, or each family member's goal can be put on a "vision poster" that hangs in a prominent location. If younger kids want to participate, they can draw pictures of themselves achieving their goal (I envision a six-year-old drawing a picture of themselves reading a book).

Diving Deeper

Each of us is uniquely made with a starting comfort zone point. Observing our kids and how they respond in different situations is an excellent way to get to know how big or small their comfort zone currently is. Once we have that knowledge about our child, it's important that we communicate with the other adults who work with them; coaches, teachers, school administrators, and camp counselors need to know whether to "push" or "cushion" kids.[8] Kids with a very large comfort zone who are rarely scared or uncomfortable need to be pushed to get into their learning zone by trying new, more challenging things, while kids with a very small comfort zone who are anxious need to be gently encouraged to take baby steps toward new tasks. Knowing our own children, and communicating with them about their own comfort zone, helps them understand that being uncomfortable is part of growing up, and that it's okay to be uncomfortable but that they also need to let people know when they need a break or a moment to regroup so they don't get into their blackout zone.

As I learned about the green, red, and blue zones Dr. Daniel Siegel and Tina Payne Bryson, PhD, describe in *The Yes Brain*,[9] I was reminded that our children's behavior provides us with important clues as to where they are in terms of their comfort, learning, or blackout zones. A child who is completely relaxed is definitely in their green zone. A child who is slightly nervous but still responsive and engaged is still in their green zone and can be encouraged to keep trying. Referring to the circular graphic (see page 109), the child is likely outside their comfort zone and in the sweet spot of their growth zone, where they are being appropriately challenged to expand their comfort zone. Alternatively, a child who is screaming or crying (in their red zone), or unable to talk or move (in their blue zone) needs to be comforted and not pushed further. Each of us, and our children, have different zones of comfort and different widths of our green zone. Both of these zones—the comfort zone of activities and the green zone and ability to stay calm—are things our children need us to assist them with in growing larger throughout their childhood and adolescence. Rather than condemning our kids for how small either zone is for them, it is important that we help our children grow those zones, and grow their grit, at their own pace.

Camp Secret #6

Kids Are More Capable Than Parents Think They Are

Confidence 101! Sending your child to camp rewards you with a child capable of taking care of him-/herself and wanting to do it. Without any parental guidance (or interference, sometimes), for two weeks, your child realizes he/she has all of these abilities which they normally don't need to tap into—because they rely on you to do things for them. Once you both see this, it's another step in your remarkable journey together!

—Basia

One summer in the early 2000s, a group of ten-year-olds was getting ready to go sailing on the first day of camp. One of the campers, Theo, couldn't find his bathing suit, and was becoming increasingly distressed. He anxiously told his counselor, Buddy, "I don't think I have a bathing suit." Buddy helped Theo pick through his footlocker—and found Theo's clothing perfectly packed and beautifully organized. Theo had no clue what was in his luggage and didn't even recognize some of the clothing items, which had been purchased for camp.

Theo was not alone in being unable to find things in his own luggage. Many of our campers' parents, doing what they thought was best, spent hours organizing and packing their children's belongings for camp, carefully following the packing list we provided. These parents did a much better job than their child could have done, and many took great pride in the organized luggage they loaded onto the bus at drop-off. Some parents, overtly or secretly, viewed their child's well-packed camp trunk as a reflection of their excellent parenting skills.

There was one major problem with this parental packing trend: Without their parent nearby to assist them, these campers didn't know how to manage their own clothes and supplies. Like Theo, these campers required a lot of assistance and reassurance from counselors, just like they required a lot of assistance and reassurance from parents at home. Seemingly simple instructions like "Put on your bathing suit" sent them into a tailspin. These problems were manageable—Buddy and Theo eventually came across two carefully folded pairs of swim trunks so that Theo was able to go sailing—but Theo, like other campers, missed out on a critical lesson: how to take responsibility for his own things.

The lesson we learned from Theo and many of his contemporaries is that unless a child has actually placed the item in the luggage himself, he likely will not know or remember its location. Another thing we learned is that unless a child is specifically asked to do something for him- or herself, the default behavior most likely will be to wait and watch as someone else (usually a parent) does it. On the first day of camp, counselors can spot the difference between kids who are being taught to do for themselves and kids who have parents who constantly do things for them. They can tell the first time they ask kids to put on their bathing suit and get out their towel and sunscreen. As a result of these lessons, we now ask parents to support us in encouraging campers to do more things for themselves—including packing—before they come to camp.

Managing your own belongings is one of many skills a responsible human adult needs. Even small humans, and most definitely ten-year-olds, can learn to be responsible for their own belongings. In order to allow kids to learn new skills, adults need to remember to give them small responsibilities and lots of guidance starting at an early age. We also need to understand that they will not initially do the tasks as well as we (fully grown adults) do. Being patient in giving instructions and allowing kids time to practice skills until they become competent at doing them on their own is what kids need from parents and other adults in order to grow into capable, responsible, thriving adults.

For the past decade, in our precamp, online orientations for our first-year families, and in our parent handbook, we have been very specific in our packing instructions. In addition to making sure campers follow our suggested packing list, bring old clothing they don't mind getting ripped or stained, and label all their clothing and equipment items, we emphasize the importance of the kids doing their own packing for camp. For older campers, that means having them do their own packing from start to finish (with parents okaying the clothing they've selected and making sure there's no contraband packed) or, in the case of younger campers, having them participate in every step of the packing process, *especially* placing the items in the luggage. We explain to parents that packing for camp is an important first step toward the many new responsibilities and skills their child will develop through their summer camp experience.

Milk Crates Full of Water Bottles

Parents weren't the only adults doing too much for our campers back in the early twenty-first century. Our counselors, meaning well, had also fallen into some of the very same traps of "overhelping." One of our most responsible, dedicated counselors developed a new, innovative practice to prevent lost water bottles: he got a plastic milk crate from the kitchen, loaded it up with the kids' water bottles, and lugged that crate around with his campers from activity to activity. Now, on the surface, this seemed like a fabulous innovation—not only did he get some serious weight training in, but his campers had their full water bottles at every single activity. Other counselors of our youngest campers caught on to this trick and started lugging their own milk crates around camp. The result? A huge reduction in the number of water bottles lost and left lying around camp.

The other, unintended result of the new practice, however, was that the campers were not learning to be responsible for their own water bottles. Carrying their own water bottle is a very simple, age-appropriate responsibility for even our youngest campers. The milk crate solution was robbing them of that opportunity. And so, to the well-meaning counselor who thought of the idea, I explained that I understood where his idea came from, that he showed great initiative and very good intentions, and that the outcome he was getting was much better than when he let the kids carry (and forget) their own water bottles.

But I also explained that these kids were getting too much help already—at home and from us—and that we needed to be more concerned about the lifelong responsibility skills we are teaching campers than the short-term outcomes. I explained that at camp we need to think as much about the *process* of how we do things, and what kids can learn, as we do about expediency. The quote "Life is a journey, not a destination" came to mind as I talked with the counselor. Competency takes practice. But how will our kids ever learn to do anything as well as we do if *we never let them try*?

Our kids are on a journey toward becoming more capable and responsible, and we adults need to assist them in that process by sometimes *not* assisting them. They will not do it as well as we do for quite a long time, but we need to consciously choose to do things in a way that is less efficient, and possibly has fewer positive short-term outcomes, so that we can teach the greater long-term goal of personal responsibility. Keeping our eyes on our campers' *eventual* competency has changed the way we do certain things at camp and can provide inspiration for parents who want to raise competent, responsible future adults.

Missing Water Bottles

Children feel capable when they have a sense of power,
competency and control over their lives, believe that they can

handle challenges and that they are able to make a contribution to
their environment, and when they feel pride in accomplishment.
                                    —The Center for Parenting Education[1]

Due to our "no milk crate" policy, we have a lot more missing and misplaced water bottles around camp, especially in the first few days of each session. In fact, a commonly heard refrain while groups are walking between activities is, "I forgot my water bottle!" The same holds true for beach towels, sweatshirts, and lip balm. Kids forget stuff wherever they are, and camp is no exception. I don't have scientific data to prove it, but my guess is that the kids who forget stuff the most haven't been required to keep track of their own belongings as much in the past. But even these frequent visitors to the lost-and-found table learn to keep better track of their belongings during their few weeks at camp when they are *required* to be responsible for those items themselves. By giving campers control over their own water bottles, they grow their competency at keeping track of them.

We now teach our counselors about the value of mistakes and natural consequences, and how they can use something like a missing water bottle as a growth opportunity. Parents can learn from the missing-water-bottle example how they, too, can promote learning from mistakes. When a camper forgets his or her water bottle, some or all of following may happen:

• The child notices the water bottle is missing, which means he is thinking about his own belongings and not counting on an adult to think about and take care of his belongings for him.

• The child has to think through where she last remembered using the water bottle. She is figuring this situation out on her own.

• The child has to do some extra work—for example, walking back to the archery shed to retrieve the water bottle or checking the lost-and-found table. He is working toward solving his own problem rather than asking for an adult to solve the problem for him.

• If the water bottle is not found, then the child has to find an extra one (we keep a collection) or purchase a new one at the camp store. Again, she is problem-solving.

All of this is rather inconvenient and takes more time (and sometimes a portion of the camper's store account balance) than if the counselor carries all the water bottles or jumps in and solves the problem for the camper. But with each lost sweatshirt or water bottle, the camper becomes more aware, more responsible, and less likely to forget at the next activity (or at some point in the future). Once the camper knows that he is responsible for his own water bottle, and that no one else is going to take care of finding it for him if he loses it, he learns to be more careful and responsible about keeping track of it. Not always after the first time, or in some cases the tenth, but eventually the camper gets better at keeping track of his own belongings. Everything takes longer, but we understand that trying to do things faster and more efficiently doesn't give campers the opportunity to grow.

At home, work on prioritizing learning from mistakes over the convenience of doing things for your children. Simple messages that express confidence in your child's ability to do something for themselves, even when the child doesn't yet feel capable, help develop responsibility and the related feeling of capability. We don't want to ever call our children irresponsible. Instead, we want to promote a growth mindset in our kids about their growing level of responsibility. The Center for Parenting Education calls the best messages we can give our kids "'doing' messages."[2] Messages of praise need to help children understand both their special areas of talent and the areas where they have potential to grow.

And so, to the camper who retrieved the missing water bottle, the counselor might say, "You are practicing being responsible for your water bottle. I bet you will not forget it next week." The camper's belief in their own capability increases and the label of "irresponsible" starts dropping away. As parents, you can think about areas where you currently view your child as irresponsible and think about messages you can give to encourage growth.

Training for Responsibility

> At camp, my son feels the joy, freedom, and independence of doing things on his own. Trying so many new things—away from us—builds up the confidence we know will help him in adulthood.
>
> —*Stacie*

Responsibility at camp is not just learned through keeping track of belongings. Campers are also given daily jobs both within their cabin group and around camp. One of those responsibilities is "KP" (Kitchen Patrol). For each day of camp, two campers are assigned to set the dining table, scrape and clear dirty dishes, wipe down the table, and clean up trash from beneath and around the table. This is, remarkably, the first time some of our campers have experienced these simple cleanup tasks. As we do with the water bottles, we train our counselors to use some restraint and not step in too much, even though the table would be cleaned better and with more efficiency if the counselors just did it themselves. Counselors follow a simple, step-by-step process to train and mentor kids on their KP duties. It goes like this:

• At the first camp meal, counselors tour their group around the dining porch, showing them where to find the cutlery, drinking glasses, and water pitchers that get set on the table by the KPs before each meal. Counselors also instruct campers on where to place the napkins and cutlery and how many places to set.

• At the end of the first meal, counselors demonstrate where to get the KP buckets (large commercial tin cans) in which to put all food scraps and trash.

• Finally, the counselors show campers where to empty the buckets, drop off dirty dishes, pick up the cleaning cloths, and wipe down the table.

Just like kids often do at home, some campers will drag their feet in fulfilling their KP duties, perhaps subconsciously hoping that an adult will step in and do the job instead of letting the camper do it himself. Many kids have mastered the art of hesitating, because they've had good results in the past. Frustrated adults often just jump in and do the task themselves rather than finding the extra patience required to encourage the kid to step up and act, but we teach our counselors to stand back and let the often painfully slow and inefficient process unfold. Parents, too, can benefit from stepping back and allowing the process to unfold. If your child is accustomed to you stepping in and doing, this may take some extra resolve to show that you are no longer going to step in and do for your child what they can and should be doing for themselves.

As an added motivational tool, for meals that have a dessert involved, all KP duties need to be completed in order for the counselor to go pick up the platter of gooey brownies. Counselors sometimes make the task fun by challenging campers to try to beat the best time of KP cleanup. Some use a fun chant or song to keep the campers entertained while working.

Keeping up with growth mindset praise that promotes greater capability and responsibility in this area, counselors say things like, "I really appreciate how you wiped down the table without my needing to remind you. That's what I call being responsible." By noting the desired trait—doing an assigned job without being reminded—counselors reinforce in campers the sense of pride and accomplishment one feels from a job well done. Again, parents can mirror this at home by acknowledging when the child successfully completes a task.

Lessons in Delayed Gratification

Getting the table cleared and cleaned before dessert is served offers another important lesson in responsibility—delayed gratification. The ability to make sacrifices now in order for some future better outcome is one that is not easily learned in our era of maxed credit cards, same-day Amazon delivery, and ubiquitous screen distraction. In the now-famous 1960s Marshmallow Experiment, Walter Mischel gave four- and five-year-olds two options: Wait fifteen minutes and *not* eat the marshmallow in front of them in order to get a second treat later, or, eat the one marshmallow and not get a second one. Mischel's simple test was followed up by more than forty years of longitudinal research following the original participants, which showed that the ability of a young child to delay gratification predicted a lengthy list of positive outcomes, including lower levels of substance abuse and better social skills. As James Clear sums up in a review about Mischel's experiment, "Success usually comes down to choosing the pain of discipline over the ease of distraction. And that's exactly what delayed gratification is all about."[3]

Most kids I know, including my own, will not choose discipline over distraction unless required to do so by consistent routines. Whether they are getting the table cleaned for dessert, tidying up their rooms before heading out for fun, or helping a friend or sibling succeed at an activity while waiting for their own turn, kids need consistent practice in delaying gratification. At camp, counselors allow this practice to occur naturally by providing a structure and routine that repeatedly cycle through getting jobs done well *before* moving on to the next fun activity or event. Cabin cleanup precedes morning activity. KP table cleanup precedes dessert. Sunscreen application and filling up water bottles precede heading out on the lake. Campers get swept up in the cycle and routine of attending to required tasks before the fun event. And in this daily, repetitive process, they gain both skills to do the tasks and a belief in their own competency and responsibility.

"What Else Can I Do?"

During the summer of 2010, I was visiting our camp's water sports outpost, which is located on an island at a lake about fifteen miles from where our main camp is located. Because of its remoteness, I don't get out to the outpost very often, usually just once every few weeks. On my first visit of the summer, I found myself chatting with a first-year British staff member named Tristan. He had come to work at camp through a camp exchange program and was working as a water sports instructor and boat driver at the outpost. While chatting with him and asking about how his summer was going so far, he asked me, "What can I do to improve at this job?"

I'll never forget that moment—and not just because Tristan ended up being a valued, longtime counselor and even spent a year working for us during the nonsummer months. Tristan's question struck me, because I could not remember a single counselor asking me anything like that in any setting other than during a formal evaluation meeting. Tristan, a high-performing counselor with outstanding people skills, got that way because he actively sought to learn how he could do better. He wasn't afraid to ask how he could improve.

Recently, when I told Tristan about my memory of him asking me how he could improve, he told me, "I have gained valuable insight over the years and it [asking the question] has helped me identify areas of personal improvement." Tristan has excelled and advanced quickly in his career as a sales manager. While working for Cintas as a senior sales representative, Tristan was recruited by a head hunter to work for a large, privately held manufacturing company that supplies equipment to the food and pharmaceutical industry. He now oversees more than $15 million in annual revenue in six states. Tristan loves his company, the people, and the culture. I'm not at all surprised that he is advancing rapidly in his career.

Some of Tristan's counterparts, other young adults who've worked for us as camp counselors, have not stepped up to their job duties nearly as well. Many need step-by-step guidance in order to complete even fairly basic job responsibilities. Our biggest struggle with some of our counselors is that many start projects but leave them unfinished. They lead a super-fun bingo game and then leave all the supplies out. They brainstorm a fun new game or activity they want campers to play but then fail to collect all the necessary supplies. They plan a fun hike but neglect to request lunches from the kitchen. My husband and I refer to this as the "waiting for Mom to clean up after them" effect. Fifteen-year-olds who have not been required to finish jobs at home become twenty-year-old employees who need a lot of guidance (or their moms to come to work with them). For many years, we found ourselves spending inordinate amounts of our time reminding our employees what they have been trained to do and what they are supposed to be doing on the job.

I stumbled upon a solution of how to better train our staff and my own kids in following through on tasks while at a camp conference listening to a keynote talk from pediatrician Dr. Deborah Gilboa ("Dr. G"), a well-known parenting expert and speaker.[4] She told us about teaching her four sons to always ask the simple question "What else can I do?" before being released from whatever household task they were helping with. Dr. G gave the example of getting home from the store with a trunk full of groceries. Her boys know to help unload the bags, but they also know to ask their mom the important question ("What else can I do?") before leaving. If they forget to ask the question, they must put all the groceries away by themselves.

I introduced this brilliant question at camp right away, and I also introduced it to my kids at home. I explained to them that I want them to be the kind of employees people really want to hire and promote—those unique individuals who stand out because they ask what they can do not just to complete a job, but to exceed expectations. Every night at the close of kitchen cleanup, my kids ask the question, "What else can I do?" and my husband or I have the opportunity to let them know what tasks still need to be done. They resisted the new habit at first—and only reluctantly asked the question with a sarcastic tone and some eye rolling—but by getting into the practice of asking this question, they've learned to see for themselves what needs to be done so our answer now is most often a quick "Nothing else. You're done."

"What else can I do?" is a magic question that teaches the important life skills of taking the initiative and finishing a job well. We can become more effective and less frustrated as parents when we take the time to teach our kids to do for themselves rather than waiting for someone else to do for them. We also set our kids up for future success by teaching them to be self-starters who require neither moment-to-moment supervision nor constant reminding.

Observable Changes and Core Transformation

Camp has had the single greatest impact on my daughter's growth. She not only loved camp but she came back with a keen sense of competence, confidence, and independence.

—Robin

The surface, observable skills kids learn at camp include being responsible for their own belongings, problem-solving when something goes missing, and participating in assigned cabin group chores. Daily cabin cleanup time requires campers to keep their own belongings neat and help with group chores like sweeping the deck, stacking campfire wood, and hanging towels. Being KP requires practicing some basic kitchen cleanup skills.

The deeper and lasting transformations campers experience are even more important. Campers learn how their actions impact others in their group, how to be a contributing member of a team, and the importance of following through on tasks. Looking around, seeing what needs to be done—without being reminded or supervised through every step—sets apart the best team members in any setting. People described as self-starters or as having a good work ethic are the ones employers most want to hire and the ones fellow team members most want to be partnered with for projects.

Bringing Camp Home: Activities That Grow Kids' Capability and Responsibility

It is not what you do for your children, but what you have taught them to do for themselves, that will make them successful human beings.

—*Ann Landers*

People sometimes ask how I have been able to parent five kids—which seems overwhelming to them. The simple answer is that I've needed to teach them to do for themselves, because I can't do as much for each of them as I could if I had fewer children. I also have a parenting partner who does the same amount of parenting and housework that I do, which is a luxury I know not all parents enjoy. The more complex answer is that I've had my ups and downs with teaching these lessons to my own children and haven't been consistent through my parenting years. As I've gotten older (and more tired) I'm not as on it when it comes to all things parenting.

A few years ago, for example, as I sliced strawberries early in the morning and placed carefully measured servings into individual ramekins for my two school-aged children (the ones still living at home), my husband teasingly said something about how the kids would starve if I didn't cut up their fruit. What had happened to my resolve to teach responsibility? Eighteen years prior, I had instructed my then four-year-old firstborn how to get her own breakfast in the morning. I placed a liquid measuring cup full of milk on the lower shelf of the refrigerator and watched as she proudly got herself a bowl of cereal.

Part of the shift in my parenting mindset came with the arrival of our adopted son. He was ten years old when he joined our family, and for his entire life had been living in foster care or an orphanage in China. I knew that we needed to make up for the lost years of nurturing he hadn't experienced. So I regressed in my parenting back to when my kids were toddlers and served him a lot more than I had the previous ten-year-olds in my family. My younger son, who was seven at the time, got carried along with my new mode of helping.

In addition to the fruit-cutting gig, I was getting ever more resentful about how much time I was spending serving and doing for the boys while they were (sometimes) doing homework but mostly playing on a computer or an Xbox. I would be in the kitchen peeling and chopping vegetables, and hear a yell from one of the boys in another room, "When's dinner?" Worse, they would sometimes complain about what was on the menu.

While grocery shopping with my boys, I asked one to get some romaine lettuce, the kind we usually put in our dinner salad. He came back with a prewashed bag. Annoyed, I said, "That's not the kind we get. We get the heads of romaine and wash it ourselves." As I watched him standing there, baffled, I asked, "Haven't I taught you how to do that?" That was a wake-up call. It was *my* fault that he didn't know what kind of lettuce we use. I had not taught him. While I had been washing lettuce for the past six years, he had been playing in another room. And so that day, I taught him how to cut, wash, and prepare the romaine for our nightly salad.

Now he does this task regularly—and well. The romaine salad incident was a reminder that I need to be much more cognizant of what I have taught each of my kids and what they still need to learn. That is one of the biggest challenges of having a lot of kids—it's hard to remember who's been taught what. The last thing I want is for my kids to be like the students that advisors bemoan at college, who don't know how to work a can opener or operate a washing machine. We have to check ourselves and make sure to get back on track when we find ourselves still doing things for our kids that they are capable of doing for themselves.

A side benefit of requiring kids to take on more responsibilities is that it can make life less stressful and more relaxed for parents. By getting more help with household chores, you free up more of your own time to pursue activities and interests that shore you up to be a more present and pleasant parent. Here are a few ideas to increase your kid's levels of competence and responsibility.

One Simple Thing

Who's doing what around here? Depending on where you are on the spectrum of doing for your kids versus letting them do for themselves, you may have fewer or more steps to take in this area to help grow your kids' responsibility level. A great place to start is with a simple assessment of what your kids are currently doing versus what you and/or your parenting partner are doing. My "Household Task Audit" (see the "Resources" section) will help you see what your kids are currently doing and where you can give your kids more responsibilities.

If your kids are still young when you're reading this, you can save yourself some heartache later by adding responsibilities at each birthday, starting as early as eighteen months. Young kids are excited to take on increasingly grown-up jobs. Toddlers can start helping with many tasks, including keeping their toys put away, sorting laundry, and simple meal preparations (with your support). By the time your kid starts driving, they should also be ready to shop at the grocery store and prepare a meal for the family. The "Household Task Audit" is a great way to see where your family can make some changes and shift more responsibilities from parents to kids. If your kids are older, you may need to delve into some more intense interventions (see "Around the Campfire" and "Diving Deeper" that follows).

The Sticky Note Solution

Because I get really tired of nagging and reminding (and it doesn't work, anyway), I like to use a "Saturday Sticky" (or whatever day it is) to let kids know what needs to happen and what their deadline time is. Rather than barking at them to clean up their room or unload the dishwasher, I write a quick note with some open boxes to the left of each item (so they know these are items to actually check off). Here's a sample of one of my Saturday sticky notes:

> Good Morning! Here's what needs to get done today by 5:00 p.m. (when we're leaving to go out to dinner):
>
> ☐ Dishwasher Unloaded
> ☐ Laundry Done
> ☐ Bathroom Cleaned
> ☐ Patio Swept

By giving a deadline time (rather than yelling, "Right now!"), it gives kids the opportunity to practice some autonomy. They get to decide how and when to get the tasks done. If at 5:00 p.m. something isn't done, instead of a big lecture, it's a simple "Oh, that's too bad. Now you won't get to go out to dinner." I learned this technique from the *Love and Logic* parenting curriculum, which cautions parents not to get in the habit of multiple reminders and also to always follow through on appropriate, predesignated consequences delivered with empathy, not anger.[5]

So when a child does not follow through on a task, you let them know that you are bummed that they won't be able to get the fun privilege (because you really do feel bad). Kids learn quickly when they are held accountable for their actions (or inactions). I've seen many posts on social media with notes to kids with a list of chores that need to be done before they get the day's Wi-Fi password. That's also a good idea, as Wi-Fi is a privilege (not a right) kids can have when they're doing their fair share of work. Of course, all those Wi-Fi password changes sound like a lot of work, so I prefer to use a simple sticky note and tie actions to daily privileges.

Make It Fun

What about making some chores into a game? Or having humorous monthly "awards" for different chores? Or, maybe you can make the chore assignments themselves into some kind of game? You could have a "draft" for chores, with the winner of a family ping-pong tournament getting first pick at chores. Be creative and make either the selection process or the chores themselves more fun. The ability to make mundane tasks more fun is a useful, positive life skill many outstanding leaders possess, so teaching kids from a young age that chores don't need to be dreaded is helpful.

Around the Campfire

Talking about delayed gratification, especially as it pertains to dreams and goals we each want to pursue, is an excellent family discussion topic. Each family member (parents included) can share about a goal they have as well as steps they can take now to reach that goal. For many kids, the goal could be saving money for something they want to buy in the future, such as a phone, a computer, or a car. Saving money for something is a great opportunity for kids to practice delayed gratification. They might need to spend more weekend days babysitting or doing other work they can do at their age. Or they may need to forego trips to Starbucks or the movies. In any case, talking about and planning for a future goal is an important skill that leads to a growth in responsibility.

As with all discussions of this type, I think it's best if parents are prepared to talk about one of their own goals and what they're going to do to reach it. Alternatively, parents can share a story about a time they had to sacrifice to achieve a future goal. It doesn't need to be a monetary or savings goal. In fact, talking about something like learning a new instrument, training for a vocation or sporting event, or gaining new knowledge that will help you advance your career are each examples of how parents can model specific actions they are taking in order to achieve a future goal. My husband and I have both completed numerous running events, including the Boston Marathon, and our kids have grown up watching us train for and complete many races. They've witnessed the steps we've taken and the discipline required to reach the goal of running a very long race. During the writing of this book, our youngest daughter signed up to run her first marathon. When we model for our kids the work we're willing to do now to reach an eventual goal, that provides them with an excellent example of delayed gratification.

Once you've talked about each person's goals, you can write the goal and the action plan (including sacrifices to be made) on index cards. These can be posted somewhere and reviewed regularly so that family members can hold each other accountable and encourage one another.

Family Meeting Topic: Sharing Household Duties

If you have been packing for your kids for family trips (or summer camp), doing their laundry, or preparing dinner without their assistance, it's time for a family meeting on the topic of sharing household duties. Start by apologizing to your kids and letting them know that you have made a mistake that you are ready to correct. Then you can explain that for your home to run more smoothly, everyone needs to be pitching in to help. Here's a sample of what you might say:

> "We need to talk about how our family is working together to keep our home running. I've made a mistake by not requiring you to learn the skills you need in order to help out more. Now I've gotten resentful that you are not doing work you are fully capable of doing. I'm also concerned that you have not learned some important skills you will need as an adult. I'm ready to correct that now. Here's what we're going to do."

Next you can explain the different tasks and responsibilities required to keep your home running smoothly. You can let your kids know that you are committed to making sure that in the time they have left at home (whether that's two months, one year, five years, or more), you are going to make sure they gain the competencies and independence they need to prepare for adulthood. You can use the chores list from the "Household Task Audit" (in the "Resources" section) or print them their own copy of my "Ready for Adulthood Checklist" (also available in the "Resources" section and at http://

happycampersbook.com). Go through the chores list and figure out how to divvy up household responsibilities like cleaning, laundry, and cooking. Include grocery shopping and other errands on the household chores list. If your kids aren't old enough to drive, they'll see that those are your chores now but could be theirs in the future.

It may be that kids have a preference for certain chores or would prefer a rotation (if you have more than one child). Oftentimes, it's better for a chore to just belong to one kid semipermanently, so that they get in the habit of doing that same task daily. In her book *How to Be a Happier Parent*, K. J. Dell'Antonia shares extensive research she did about how to make chores stick. She discovered that yearly chores (or chores covering some other very long period) for kids work far better than any kind of daily or weekly rotation. The longer length of time gives kids the opportunity to master the skill, make it a habit, and make it slightly less likely that you'll need to constantly remind them to do it.[6]

In the end, it probably doesn't matter how you divvy up chores—whether everyone helps out with dishes every night or individuals are assigned their own night or specific task—as long as they start helping out more and taking on responsibilities around the house. For the past several years, my teenage sons have kept their same kitchen cleanup roles—one putting the dishes into the dishwasher and cleaning the counters, and the other doing all the hand washing of pots and pans. They also both do their own laundry and clean their bathrooms. Let the kids help determine who is going to do which chores, and then post the list so that everyone is reminded what they are responsible for. It's best if one of the kids writes up the list while you're having the meeting so that they are actively involved and more likely to take some personal ownership in the process. But to save your energy and keep the chores consistent, make the household assignments last for a long time!

Diving Deeper

There are many areas to think about when it comes to raising our kids to be competent and responsible adults. Many recent parenting books have addressed some important considerations.

- In his book *The Opposite of Spoiled*, Ron Lieber makes a good point that teaching our kids about money and financial responsibility—including how to work and make money—are excellent ways to teach them to be responsible humans. He teaches parents to raise "grounded young adults with financial habits that reflect maturity beyond their years." As he describes how to talk about money with our kids, his underlying premise is that "every conversation about money is also about values."[7]

- Julie Lythcott-Haims's *How to Raise an Adult* offers a list of life skills she found lacking in college students when she was a dean at Stanford. The list includes adult responsibilities like making their own appointments and managing their own bank accounts. Lythcott-Haims outlines a simple way to think about teaching our kids these and other life skills:
    - First we do it *for* you.
    - Then we do it *with* you.
    - Then we *watch* you do it.
    - Then you do it completely *independently*.[8]

As we consider areas where we want our children to eventually do things independently, Haims's list offers an excellent model for learning. Learning to drive, which is what is happening now with my sixteen-year-old, offers an example of one area where there is a formal process in place that helps parents follow this model. First, we drive our kids around. Next, we show them how it's done (and have them take the necessary driving course and lessons). Then, we let them drive for a period of time under our close supervision. Finally, they take a test to check their competence and are allowed to drive completely on their own. Applying this same process to other areas of responsibility helps us raise responsible and capable kids.

Regardless of what areas of responsibility you want to focus on with your kid, there will be unique considerations based on your family and your child's personality. I have a few kids who have never lost anything in their lives, and I have one forgetful soul who has trouble keeping track of things, so I know firsthand that kids are born with differing propensities toward personal responsibility. I also know my job as a parent is to help as best I can with their development of skills they'll need to thrive in life.

My forgetful one needs the most guidance—and natural consequences—in the area of personal belongings. Recently, after returning home from a trip to his sister's college graduation, he realized he had left his computer charging cord in the hotel room. I talked him through the process of calling the hotel, telling them the room he had been in, and making arrangements to get his cord back. While I easily could have made the call myself, I knew that it was important for him to make the call and take care of it himself. I am hopeful that he will be more careful with his packing the next time he's in a hotel, but if he remains forgetful, at least he knows how to remedy the situation.

Here are a few additional notes and considerations as you think about growing competency and responsibility:

What if your kids are "too busy" with school and sports to help out at home?

Many parents balk at the idea of having their teenagers help with things like cooking dinner because, they say, their kids are too busy with sports and academics. My kids are busy, too. So am I. Isn't that how a full life is? As adults, we have a lot of different responsibilities, and we still need to go to work, feed ourselves, and do some basic daily chores. Learning how to balance and schedule work, leisure, and household responsibilities is an important life skill competent adults need. Many meals are quick and easy to prepare, so even a teenager with limited time can make a dinner for the family once a week. I would also argue that if the family schedule does not allow time for kids to do any chores, then the schedule is too busy and something needs to change.

What about car washes, housekeepers, and other outsourced services?

When I was a kid, my friend Kristy and I ran a neighborhood car wash in my driveway during the summer. I think we charged five dollars per car, and we would wash the exteriors and vacuum and clean the interiors. We hauled in some good cash on those summer days, and we also perfected our car-washing skills. We learned about shammies and Armor All, and we mastered streak-less window washing.

I knew all about how to wash cars because I had washed cars at home and this was a skill I made sure my own kids also learned. Vacuuming the car interior and washing windows are helpful chores young kids can easily accomplish. But the reality is that my kids have washed far fewer cars than I did in my childhood. Instead, they have been passengers driving through a car wash far more times than they've hosed down cars in our driveway. Due to the convenience factor in our busy lives and a long drought in our state (and our understanding that going through a car wash that recycles water is better for the environment than letting all that hose water run down our driveway), we now pay for our cars to be washed more than we wash them ourselves.

Another conundrum I faced as a parent was about cleaning our house. I cleaned countless bathrooms and vacuumed many floors during our early married years. But in recent decades, with both my husband and me working full time and a full family schedule, we've turned to a weekly housekeeping service to keep up with deep cleaning. In order to figure out how to manage this situation—that we wanted and needed the housekeeping help but also wanted our kids to learn how to clean and be responsible for cleaning—we came up with a unique solution.

We determined that we (the parents) need a housekeeper but our kids do not. What we do is have a housekeeper who comes weekly to clean and vacuum the common areas of our home as well as our master bedroom and bathroom. Our children are responsible for cleaning their own rooms and bathrooms and keeping the kitchen, office, and other areas they use clean. This is a set-up Ron Lieber describes in *The Opposite of Spoiled*. He advises us to explain to our kids that although we can afford to pay a housekeeper to clean their rooms, we are deliberately choosing not to so that they can learn these skills.[9] Here's a script of what you might say in explaining this to your kids:

"We [the parents] have decided it's important that you learn how to do some basic household chores. Starting now, you will be responsible for keeping your own room and bathroom clean. Although we can afford to pay a housekeeper to do this work, we realize that that is not in your best interest. Moving forward, you will be responsible for [list specific tasks, for example, vacuuming their floor, washing and changing their sheets and towels, cleaning their toilet] each week."

If you start having your kids do these things at a young age, they won't ever know any difference. In my family, weekends are when their cleaning duties need to be completed. I just let the kids know that they need to be done by Sunday at 5:00 p.m. They get to choose when, over the weekend, to get their laundry washed, folded, and put away and their bathrooms cleaned. Because I started this practice when my kids were young, I found them to be receptive to the idea. They were actually excited to have their own toilet brush, bottle of toilet cleaner, and window cleaner. I got them each their own set of cleaning supplies so that they'd feel a sense of ownership.

The enthusiasm for cleaning has definitely waned as they've gotten older, but my adult kids are competent at cleaning kitchens and bathrooms and have been at times frustrated at the lack in these skills they've witnessed in some of their dorm and apartment mates. This year, two different parents who've hosted my thirteen-year-old son at their homes have commented on his excellent dishwashing skills. These compliments mean more to me than a goal on the soccer field or an A on a test, because they represent an important lifelong skill—not just washing dishes but also seeing what needs to be done and taking care of it.

If you're needing to catch up in this area because your kids are older and haven't been helping out around the house much, I'm certain that this idea might be wildly unpopular when you first introduce it to your kids. That's okay—they will get used to it. You can use the script in the "Family Meeting Topic" section to explain how you're getting your family back on track in this area. Just remember that our ultimate goal as parents is for our kids to develop their competence at doing specific tasks as well as their ability to see what needs to be done and taking the initiative to do it without being asked. We can help them grow into competent adults and valued employees by taking simple steps at home, when they're young, to instill these basic household skills and the accompanying character trait of responsibility. One way we help instill these and other important skills and character traits is by providing the structure they need to thrive as children and adolescents and to become capable, responsible adults.

Camp Secret #7
Kids Thrive with Structure

Most of all, I love camp's consistency. While summers come and go, styles change, and children grow up into adults, summer camp always stays the same. Every year I know I will hear "Circle Game" and make memories with my best friends. This same stability has guided me down my own consistent, reliable path. In fact, every revered tradition at camp has helped me be a "constant" for somebody else.

—*Katherine*

Have you noticed that some people don't like it when you change the schedule or plans at the last moment? While reading Gretchen Rubin's *The Four Tendencies*, I had a light bulb moment about why my husband, one of my kids, and my closest coworker get irritated with me when I switch the schedule or plan at the last minute. They are each what Rubin describes as "Upholders." They meet both external and internal expectations with ease, and they are awesome to work with or do a project with for that very reason. They get things done and are consistent and loyal. They also love order and consistency. When they have a schedule or task list, they want to stick to it.

I, on the other hand, am an unintentional plan changer. I really love my rainbow-striped planner and my bullet journal, and I truly desire to follow the many to-do lists, action plans, projects and priority lists that I create. I just have trouble sticking to any of my original schedules, plans or lists. Writing this book offers a perfect illustration. Stephen King's *On Writing*, the #amwriting podcast, and many other writers' resources promote the importance of writing every single day, at the same time.[1] According to the experts, this practice is the best way to improve writing skills and complete an entire book, yet I have never been able to stick to a strict writing schedule. My best writing has emerged unexpectedly, when unforced, and usually in very long, binge-like spurts. At times I've found myself up early in the morning with an idea, sitting at my computer with my coffee, and I've busted out a few thousand words before my family wakes up. Other times, I've sat down in the evening, intending to revise a few paragraphs and ended up writing ten new pages. Almost always, I can't seem to get the fire to write unless I have a strict deadline.

My latest writing hack has been writing on the treadmill desk I received for Mother's Day. If I can get myself to open the Word doc before I open any other files or apps, I can get sucked in to writing most of a chapter without even noticing that two or three hours (and six to eight miles!) have gone by. Walking and writing on my tread-mill desk have been the closest thing I've come to a routine; however, I haven't even been able to consistently stick to my treadmill writing habit. I've often gotten on the treadmill intending to write and started answering my emails instead. Then I've gotten myself sucked into the vortex of emails and social media. The same two or three hours go by in a blink, but I never made it to my actual writing project. So, even my beloved treadmill desk writing habit hasn't been entirely consis-tent. I've learned I'm more of a binge writer. I can write for four or five hours when the ideas and urge strikes, and I haven't yet been able to consistently stick to a "I write between 7:00 and 9:00 a.m. every day" plan. That's how I roll, and for a long time I felt bad that I'm not like Stephen King. But I've learned to accept that my chaotic, burst-like writing style works for me.

I have attempted to squash my scheduling inconsistency when it comes to family life. As much as possible, especially when my kids were young, I created and stuck to a consistent family schedule and predictable routines. I modeled our family structure and routines after the place where I found so much stress relief and happiness myself during my tumultuous college years—summer camp. Camp life, like most other institutional cultures (think schools, hospitals, prisons) is *extremely* predictable and structured. Meals are at the exact same time every day, with the same side options available. Kids who like their daily plain bagel with cream cheese or vanilla yogurt with fruit know that it will always be there, in the exact same spot on the dining porch. After the predictable breakfast, campers and counselors see what activity they have for the morning and head back to their tent cabins to get the appropriate clothes on for the activity, clean up their cabin, brush their teeth, and put on their sunscreen.

Morning assembly is next. The whole camp gathers together as a community to talk about the day, sing a few songs, and have some laughs together before we head off to our different morning activities. Lunch is followed by a daily rest time, where some campers (and most counselors) rest, read, play cards, and relax. Evening activities, without fail, end with groups gathered around their campfires for some chatting and together time before following the same bedtime routine that they've followed since the first night of camp, which varies by age group. Our evenings always end with each camper being given a hug or high five as one of their counselors "tucks them in" to their sleeping bag. Then counselors read aloud from a book they've been reading (*Wonder* by R. J. Palacio has been a favorite for all ages). Even our oldest campers—fifteen-year-olds!—love being read to at night by their counselors. They consistently say it's one of their favorite parts of camp. Every night at camp, kids of all ages sleep between nine and ten hours per night, with our youngest campers in their sleeping bags from 9:00 p.m. to 7:00 a.m. and our oldest from 10:00 p.m. to 7:30 a.m. Counselors get a minimum of seven to eight hours of sleep, with a consistent lights-out time of 11:00 p.m., which we start before the campers arrive so that they can get into their new, earlier sleeping habit (most are college students who are rarely in bed before midnight when not at camp).

What's also predictable about the camp structure is not always to be found in other institutions—the daily, predictable *fun* that is built in to our daily routine. We have times every day when we sing together, dance together, and play games. For campers, the trade-off of giving up their screens for a few weeks becomes a nonissue when they experience the fun of camp life. I've had many kids comment to me how much they enjoy not having their phone with them all the time. Said one fifteen-year-old camper, "Camp is a place where, without the distraction of my phone, I can have a clear mind about who I am and what I want."

Why Do Kids Thrive with Structure, Routines, and Clear Expectations?

Although it may seem counterintuitive to people who believe spontaneity is the spice of life and rules are meant to be broken, the consistent and predictable structure and expectations at camp allow campers to relax and enjoy themselves. Expectations and schedules, outlined and reviewed clearly, actually make campers feel safe. When we explain to campers that we value "living healthy," and that means we do not allow any alcohol, illegal drugs, or tobacco at camp for our campers or staff, they get it. We give them one night of amnesty to turn in any contraband without punishment, because we want to give them a chance to follow through on meeting our expectations. Many high schoolers feel a great sense of relief that for the few weeks they are at camp they won't have to face the social pressure to drink or engage in other unhealthy activities with their peers.

The reality is that our older campers (and even some of our younger kids) are being exposed to or are participating in dangerous activities at home, without their parents being aware. These kids choose to return to camp each summer because of the feeling of safety they experience. Experienced campers often articulate this, and I have learned from these kids that teenagers—who will naturally push against rules and expectations—feel safer and more secure when they are being held to a high standard, even when they may vociferously complain about rules. My teenage sons often complain that we are "the only parents" who don't allow phones or other electronic devices in bedrooms, but they also share that they'll subject their own future kids to the same rules. One time my sixteen-year-old angrily told me, "You care too much."

"Yep, I do" was my response. While he was fuming at me on the outside, I gave myself an internal high five. I know that I'm not in this parenting gig to make my kids happy with everything I say and do now but to help grow kind, self-disciplined humans.

Campers themselves are part of the process of determining their group's rules of living together. Because they have ownership in the process as well as an understanding of exactly what is expected, they tend to behave appropriately. Schedules and routines, many of which are outlined in the counselor handbook, are implemented consistently. A secret that parents can learn from camp is that a set schedule, clear expectations, and simple routines around daily events make family life less stressful and more fun and relaxed. This is especially true for parents like me whose personalities and approaches to life lean away from following a set schedule. Research has clearly shown that a high-nurture-with-high-standards parenting approach, often referred to as "authoritative," is ideal for helping kids thrive.[2]

One of our greatest successes at camp is convincing screen-addicted tweens and teens to willingly and completely unplug for two full weeks. We explain and promote our core value of "unplugging and connecting face-to-face" long before campers arrive for their first summer stay with us. Our campers and families know that we are focusing on developing close friendships and improving social skills, and that we believe devices can get in the way of these important and valuable things that happen at camp. Similar to how we explain our alcohol and drug policy from the perspective of our "healthy living" value, we explain our screen and other rules by making sure our campers know the underlying value behind the rule. When they know *why* a rule is in place and have internalized the value behind it, kids are much more likely to follow the rule and even promote it.

In the case of the camp-imposed break from all of their screens, I've heard hundreds of campers and counselors share that the time at camp became a pivotal point for them to alter their screen habits outside of camp. One of our eighteen-year-old former campers, Henry, proudly told me he was the only kid at his high school with a flip phone. He said his smartphone broke and he decided not to replace it after realizing how much he enjoyed not having to deal with social media all the time. He found that he preferred focusing on his face-to-face connections at school.

One brave camp parent, Jill, decided to extend her ten-year-old son's unplugged time beyond his two weeks at camp. She especially dreaded the long, screen-free seven-hour drive in the car after picking him up from camp. But she said it didn't end up being hard, and three months following camp, her son is still screen-free except for schoolwork. Jill reports that her son is "a different person." He is more engaged socially, he's more pleasant to be around, his behavior and attitude have improved dramatically, and he is more curious and inquisitive about his surroundings. He's become an avid reader who always has a book on hand. While Jill has taken an extreme approach to limiting screen use, she has found that for her son—whose screen use and addiction she was convinced were playing a role in some behavioral issues—it was the right decision. The improvement in her son's behavior, she says, was well worth the new family screen restrictions, and family life for her is far more pleasant now.[3]

Kids thrive with structure for the same reason most adults do—when we know what to expect, we feel less stressed and more relaxed. The unknown causes stress, and there are many unknown things in life for which we cannot prepare. While the process of setting up structure, rules, and routines in your family might stress *you* out if you are a parent with a more free-flowing personality, know that you are taking an important step for your children's well-being by bringing calm and predictability to your family's daily life. If our kids can depend on some predictability and structure in that very important place called home, we provide them a safe, calm buffer against a chaotic world.

The Power of Simple, Predictable Routines

Routines, when followed regularly, provide a sense of security that make everyone more relaxed. Routines also help our kids develop the self-discipline they'll need to thrive as adults. Waking up, making good food and exercise choices, and getting homework done are all examples of routines we can help our kids learn in order to thrive as adults later in their lives. "Hot spots" in family life—where the stress level is especially high—tend to be consistent across families, even with different ages of kids. These high-stress times include weekday mornings, homework time, and bedtime.

People fear many things, but a fear of the unknown is one of the greatest, behind only death and public speaking, for most of us. Children show us their fear of the unknown through their behavior when faced with trying new foods or experiencing new things, like going to a new school or participating in a new activity. Many of the rapid changes our kids experience are completely out of their control—moving to a new school or city, being required to learn new skills at school and in other activities, new siblings arriving, or strange bodily changes that make them feel different. So, it's understandable why they try to take charge in areas like what they eat or wear or how they spend their playtime. Just like most adults, our kids handle change better when they know what is expected and it occurs in the context of a routine. If we can keep some family routines predictable during the other inevitable changes, we can provide our kids with a much-needed sense of safety and mastery that will help them handle future challenges.

Unpredictable changes happen in life, and these can't be planned. Grandparents die; parents get divorced; military parents are deployed; older siblings leave home. Kids themselves suffer from unexpected illnesses, injuries, or setbacks that change their schedule and activities. With these unpredictable changes, kids can become anxious and their sense of safety can be eroded. Their stress level rises when they sense things being out of control. Says Dr. Laura Markham, author of *Peaceful Parent, Happy Kids*, "That's why we offer children a predictable routine as a foundation in their lives—so they can rise to the occasion to handle big changes when they need to."[4]

Instead of thinking of routines and schedules as a negative thing, parents need to view them as an important tool to help kids learn to cope with life's changes and stressors. When kids can depend on their nightly bedtime reading with Dad, they feel less stressed about the other, out-of-control things happening in their lives, including difficult class assignments, mean kids, and social pressures. Establishing predictable routines in one or more of these areas can improve your family's happiness level by reducing stress and creating more calm during potentially chaotic times:

• *The Morning.* A morning routine that's consistent and predictable is a family stress buster. Plan out routines around what time everyone needs to wake up (which varies from kid to kid based on their snail-like or speedy morning pace) and the specific tasks each person does until the moment people get in the car or walk out the door.

• *After School.* What works for your family? Snack time and playtime before homework or getting homework over with first? There's no right answer, but what is important is having the process be the same most days so that stressful nagging and discussion aren't a daily occurrence.

• *Dinner.* If you can muster the energy for only one family routine, then make it dinner. The routine can be simply that you all sit down together at approximately the same time to eat dinner together each evening. You can add in some cooking and cleaning up together for bonus family time. Whatever you do, having dinner as a family is one of the most important routines. Kids who eat dinner with their families on a regular basis:

   • Are more emotionally stable,
   • Are less likely to abuse drugs and alcohol,
   • Get better grades,

- Have fewer depressive symptoms, and
- Are less likely to become obese or have an eating disorder.[5]

If that isn't a compelling list, I don't know what is.

• *Bedtime.* Good sleep habits start early, and kids benefit from a consistent evening bedtime routine. Reading aloud to your child, even older ones, or just talking together at bedtime for few minutes, are a wonderful way to provide a daily, predictable one-on-one check-in and connection with your child. Some of the most meaningful conversations I've had with my kids have been in the dark of their bedrooms right before they drift off to sleep.

People often think of family traditions as related to holidays, but the most important family "traditions" are the things you do together regularly, not just on holidays. Some families have a weekly movie or game night. Others have a weekly unplugged Saturday activity or attend weekly religious services. Like your other routines, having some regular practices or traditions are an important way to create structure and reduce stress for your family. Especially for kids who really like to know what's happening, knowing that they can depend on their Friday movie night, snuggled on the coach next to Mom, is important.

Looking at Your Family's Pace of Life

My friend Sara, who is also a camp director, does a parenting workshop called "Family Pace and Space." She told me that she's had to scale back her approach because of the horror she saw on parents' faces upon learning the harm their overscheduled family lives was doing to their kids. With multiple club sports, tutoring, hours of homework, short nights of sleep, and a full extracurricular schedule, these parents were desperately trying to do everything right for their kids by doing what it appeared everyone else was doing. Instead of benefiting their kids, it became clear that their family's schedule was not good for their kids or themselves.

Sara learned to take a gentler approach with these parents to help guide some reflection about their family's schedule and pace of life. The questions she now asks them to consider after taking a few minutes to look at a typical week's family schedule are as follows:

- Does the balance of activities reflect your family's values?
- Do activities reflect each family member's temperament, interests, and energy level?
- Does each family member's pace and schedule bring out the best in him/her?
- Are there any activities that your family engages in only because "that's what everyone else does"?
- Are there rituals or traditions that can be established to ensure playtime, downtime, and family time?
- Are there activities that can be eliminated regularly or seasonally?

You can download and print Sara's questions at http://happycampersbook.com.

These questions serve as a catalyst for parents to reconsider some of the activities they have been thinking they or their children have to do. Sara has heard many success stories from parents who've attended her workshop, asked these hard questions, and adjusted their commitments accordingly. These parents have expressed a great sense of relief about cutting out an activity that doesn't fit with their values. The reality is that our culture has created a crazy pace that many families are struggling to keep up with to the detriment of both adults' and kids' mental and physical health.

Author and psychologist Daniel Siegel, together with David Rock, a leader in organizational consulting, created a "Healthy Mind Platter" that is shared in *The Yes Brain*. Their platter consists of "seven daily essential mental activities to optimize brain matter and create well-being." Their Healthy Mind Platter list of daily activities includes focus time (think "work"), playtime, connecting time, physical time, time-in (quiet reflection), downtime (relaxing), and sleep time.[6] If you're like me, as you read through Daniel and David's list, you can see some daily essential mental activities that are getting short-changed either in your kids' lives or your own. What's missing from your family's schedule?

In my family, we seem to all sometimes lack time-in, or quiet reflection. But some of what's missing on our daily platters differs for my husband and me compared to our kids. We (the adults) are often lacking in playtime and downtime, while our kids are, on some days (especially weekend days with no sports), lacking in physical time and connecting time.

I'm guessing that other families may share some of these same issues. Looking at how we do spend our time, perhaps going back to Sara's "Family Pace and Space" questions may help get our lives a bit more balanced. For our own and our children's mental well-being, we don't want to sacrifice important mental health activities on the altar of mindless activities.

Communicating Your Values and Expectations

In her keynote address at a camp conference I attended in 2017, Tina Payne Bryson shared a story about parents who came to her when they were shocked to learn that their fourteen-year-old daughter, an exceptional, well-behaved student and young lady, had gotten drunk at a party. When Bryson asked the daughter what her parents' expectations were around drinking alcohol, the girl responded that she didn't know and that they had never told her. How many important things have we just *assumed* our kids know we believe or expect? I know I'm guilty of not discussing some important issues with my kids, and I'm going to keep working to change that. Many of these discussions are awkward, but sometimes a book or documentary can help promote the discussion.

Perhaps you value service to others and have expectations around family volunteer time. Or it could be that you love art or theater and want your children to be exposed to a certain number of cultural experiences. I'm certain that you can come up with other values and things that are important to you above and beyond this list. Think about your values and how they relate to expectations you have for your kids. Then, in a discussion with your kids, clearly articulate those values and expectations that are most important to you. In this chapter's "Family Meeting Topic," I offer some topics and questions to help you figure out which values and expectations you wish to model for and teach your children.

Observable Changes and Core Transformation

The surface, observable changes we see in kids once they experience more structure are clear: They follow rules better (because they know and understand them), don't need to be nagged as much to do things (because we've helped them develop a consistent routine), and they start doing more things for themselves because they know what's expected. Kids who know and follow a balanced schedule, including enough sleep, are much more pleasant to parent.

On a deeper and lasting level, more structure and clearer expectations at home help kids feel more relaxed and less stressed and pave the way for a better ability to self-discipline when it becomes important for them to take care of themselves and manage their own schedule and time as young adults at college. The implementation and consistent following through of predictable schedules, expectations, and routines improves the mental health and behavior of children. Our kids, when they have a safe, predictable life at home, are better able to handle the chaos they will inevitably have to deal with.

Bringing Camp Home: Using Structure and Routines to Reduce Stress

Our children are counting on us to provide two things: consistency and structure.

—Barbara Coloroso

Changing something as fundamental as your family's daily schedule and routines won't happen overnight. I recommend starting small, perhaps with implementing just one new routine. Besides your family's daily schedule and routines, it is equally important to look at the pace and balance of your family's life. Are you all getting enough sleep? Downtime? Playtime? By making small tweaks to your family's daily life or weekly schedule, you can reduce stress and help make your home calmer and your kids' behavior more pleasant. Here are some ideas to get started at bringing more structure and reducing stress for your family.

One Simple Thing

As with many of the "simple things" I've shared, this one is only simple because it does not require you to get buy-in from other family members. It does require you, however, to spend some time reflecting on the current state of your family's stress level. I recognize that this kind of introspection can be hard, especially when you're buried by—well—all the things that are going on! Sometimes it seems easier to shove problem areas under the proverbial rug and keep plugging along as usual. But if there is a consistent hot spot in your family's day, taking time to figure out what time of day that is and how you can structure it to make it more calm and pleasant will go a long way toward promoting your kids' (and your own) well-being.

One clue to your hot spot is people's moods. When do you find that you or your kids are consistently unhappy or angry? Is it the morning? When it's time to turn off screens? When you're trying to motivate people to help clean the house? Think about the time of day or week that is your personal least favorite, and plan on starting there to create a new routine. If applicable, discuss the routine with your co-parent. Write out your ideal routine. For example, your ideal evening routine to make mornings less stressful, could look something like this:

- Lunches are made and put in the fridge.
- Backpacks are packed and put by the door.
- Outfit for school is laid out.

Note that all school-age kids can do all of the above activities themselves. Just give them guidelines for each. I included a "what goes in your lunch" list for my kids when they were little that offered different choices but prevented Doritos and an applesauce being called lunch. You can download a pdf of my "Lunch Packing Instructions" at http://happycampersbook.com.

Here is a sample morning procedure:

- Kids get themselves up by 6:30 a.m. This may require you get them their own alarm clock (an old-fashioned one, not a smartphone).
- Everyone gets their own breakfast from assorted daily choices that are always in the same locations: bagels, toast, cereal, yogurt, fruit, eggs.
- Teeth are brushed and faces are washed.
- Beds are made and rooms are tidied up.
- Everyone is in the car, ready for departure, before 7:30 a.m.

A great way to introduce a new routine, once you've figured out what it is, is to present it when everyone is calm and getting along. Outline the new routine, provide a written sign with bullet points, see if kids have any questions, and end with something like, "I will allow kids who are in my car and ready to go before 7:30 a.m. to use their screens during playtime after school." Do not nag or cajole them through the routine, and you may even secretly hope that one of them is late on one of the first days of the new routine. That way, calmly and without any yelling or nagging, you empathetically let your late child know, "Oh, what a bummer." After school, when you remove the screen, ignore any subsequent whining and complaining. Follow through on the consequence for them not sticking to the schedule, and they will learn quickly to follow your new morning routine (or whatever new routine you decide to implement).

This process, although now listed in my "One Simple Thing" category of activities, is not a simple process. So, perhaps, for the time being, just do the prework of deciding what one of your family's main hot spots is, and think about what new routine could improve family life for those daily moments. Perhaps even jot down some notes or confer with a friend who has implemented a successful family routine during the time of day you're looking to improve.

The Sticky Note Solution

Because none of us like surprises, getting in the habit of writing a sticky note to remind your child of any events that are out of the ordinary is helpful. Reminders about school picture day (if you know when it is scheduled), or a reminder about an appointment they have after school are both examples of things that might be good to communicate via sticky note in advance, especially if they need to bring a special item.

For example, your note could say, "You have an ortho appointment at 3:30 today. Bring your retainer so it can be cleaned!" A simple sticky note reminder can be especially helpful for kids who tend to be more rigid or anxious. Letting them know ahead of time what unusual or unexpected events are coming up can reduce their stress level.

Make It Fun

While many kids today do not perceive getting off their screens and going outside as fun, I know from personal experience that most do end up enjoying the time and benefiting from it. If your family is like mine and lacking most in the more reflective, quiet times, try incorporating a weekly mindful activity that involves getting outside: Go for a short walk or hike, gaze at the stars together, or go bird-watching with some binoculars. If the weather isn't conducive, or you prefer some inside family time, do a yoga pose or two together, practice taking some deep breaths, or just do some family reading time with real books (park the devices in another room). This can be either quiet reading to yourselves or a family group read with parents reading or everyone taking turns.

I recently heard a good definition of mindfulness—"paying attention on purpose"—that doesn't conjure up the usual images I've had of the word—of people with crossed legs chanting, "om." Instead, this definition reminded me that mindfulness is the opposite of the state of distraction many of us find ourselves in almost constantly. If we take some time, with our family, to pay attention to the moment we're in and to each other, that is practicing family mindfulness. This important practice is getting exceedingly rare in our distracted, fast-paced world, but we can create some fun, calm moments for our families by being intentional about taking some family time together, ideally outside. These times can serve as an antidote to the distraction and pace of our normal routines and model for our kids a practice that will help them thrive as adults navigating a profoundly unmindful world.

Around the Campfire

How do you relax? What gets you in that great state of flow where you lose track of time? Is there a craft or creative activity that is your go-to relaxation and rejuvenation activity?

A great family dinner discussion can be on the topic of how people relax and refresh themselves in different ways. For some people, a long run is actually relaxing. For others, time alone is key to getting refreshed. Our kids may not know how they best relax, but opening up the discussion helps them to recognize that it is important to include some of this type of time in their daily Healthy Mind Platter of activities.

Family Meeting Topic: Values and Expectations

Depending on the age of your kids, an important topic to cover at family meetings is your values and expectations. When our kids understand the why behind our rule, they are more likely to follow it and complain less. Following are some questions to consider as you determine what your family's values and expectations are, so that you can figure out how to clearly articulate those expectations—and the reasons behind them—to your kids:

Sleep: How many hours of sleep do you want yourself and your children to have? How important is sleep to you? How much do you see lack of sleep negatively impacting yourself or your kids?

Eating and Nutrition: What do you want to teach your kids about healthy eating? Do you want your family to be less wasteful? Eat whole foods? Learn to cook? Focus on whole grains? Eat lots of fresh fruits and vegetables? What about dessert—is it a nightly thing or only on weekends and special occasions?

Manners: From table manners to social skills like introducing themselves, what manners are important to you? If you really value people looking others in the eye and shaking hands upon meeting someone for the first time, teach your kids how to do this.

Chores and Helping Out: What are your expectations around how much your kids help out around the house? Do you want regular, daily chores, weekly ones, or both?

Screens: How much are screens a part of your family's life? What parts of the day do you want to be unplugged times for your family? Where do screens get charged and stored at night? What are your expectations around what is shared and what comments are made on social media?

Driving: When your teen starts driving, what are the rules? Where can their phone be while they drive? How often do they need to check in with you? Who can be in their car? What are the consequences if they don't follow your driving rules?

Academics and Going to College: How important are academics to you? Do you want all your children to go to college? What minimum educational requirements do you want your children to fulfill? How much of your family's time do you want spent on academics (tutoring, homework, etc.)?

Athletics: Do you value being healthy and fit? Are competitive sports an important part of your family? How much exercise do you expect your children to get? Will your family participate in club sports that require a big commitment of time and resources?

Alcohol and Drug Use: What are your values around alcohol and drugs? Are you okay with your teenager experimenting, or do you expect them to follow the law? Do you have any family history of addiction your kids need to know about?

Sexual Activity: When your teen or young adult becomes sexually active, how do you want them to behave? Are you supportive of multiple sexual partners or do you value monogamy? What are sexual health practices you want your child to know? What are your religious beliefs and values around sexuality?

Diving Deeper

Thinking of your family like a business, with you as the CEO (or co-CEO with your co-parent), is a helpful analogy. Knowing your important role as your family's leader (or coleaders), you can approach problem areas—like stressful daily hot spots, an overscheduled life, or too much screen time—the same way business leaders and consultants turn around struggling companies. Much of the education I've received as a business leader in training, motivating, and managing employees has been informative to me as a parent, too. As with any company, a family's culture can be improved through good leadership.

What is your family's current culture? Is the attitude and atmosphere in your home what you want? Can you articulate your vision and goals for your family? What about some strategic priorities for the next year, five years, or ten years? It may feel silly, but treating your family more like a business, and taking these things seriously, can lead to positive changes. Stepping back and reflecting on what's going well in your family and strategizing areas to improve upon are great first steps to turn around a family culture that you're finding to be too stressful and chaotic.

There are many different ways you can approach this family strategic planning process, but here are a few ideas:

• Attend a parenting talk sponsored by your school or religious institution. Often listening to a speaker serves as a catalyst to review or discuss important points.

• With your co-parent or a friend, read through and discuss a parenting book that elaborates more on positive, authoritative parenting (the one in your hand is a great start!).

• Consider taking a parenting class (either in person or online) together.

• There are trained parenting coaches available who can help you strategize how to address common parenting issues or family stress points. Seek a recommendation from a friend or look at reviews online. Many reputable parent coaches have written books about their parenting philosophy. If you have a parenting author whose advice has resonated with you, check if they offer any coaching or consultations.

• Ideally you have at least one trusted friend with whom you can share those "me, too" moments about your kids. I've found it especially helpful to seek advice from friends who have children a few years older than mine. Hearing how their kids have successfully come out the other side of some challenging years, and what the parents did to assist with that process, is helpful.

• Especially during the turbulent teen years, many families benefit from counseling, either individually or as a family. When I found myself feeling squeezed on all sides by aging parents and hormonal teens, I sought counseling from a therapist who helped me think through my priorities and reframe some of what I was considering bad behavior. Getting some outside, objective support can be extremely helpful.

Taking the time to intentionally work to create the calm, structured family life you desire will have a lifelong, positive impact on both your relationship with your kids and their individual growth and development. It's well worth the investment of time and energy to create some structure and routines, especially if you veer toward the less-structured type of personality. One trait you may want to focus on, as you think about the future adult you are raising, is where kindness falls among your family's priorities and values. That's what we'll cover next.

Camp Secret #8
Make It Cool to Be Kind

Because of camp, I've become a more aware and caring human.

—Paige

Several years ago, I received a call from the father of one of our long-time campers. The child was joining us for her final summer at camp and, due to a sports commitment, she was arriving two days late to her two-week camp session—a practice we discourage due to the disruption in the bonding and forming of friendships in the cabin groups. The session had started the day before, and the father and daughter had browsed through the pictures from the first evening's campfire to see who would be in her cabin group. They had noticed that a camper with Down syndrome was in the group, and the dad was calling to request that his daughter be moved to a different group "without any special needs campers."

My camp is not specifically set up for any one specific group of special needs campers; however, our philosophy has always been to accommodate campers whose special needs do not negatively impact other campers' experiences any more than different personality types and severe allergies can impact a group. One of our past longtime campers, Jake, could not walk around camp or hike as fast as other kids due to a physical disability. His cabin groups over the years slowed down for him, just as they would for a camper whose fitness level or asthma required a slower walking pace. In addition to learning to look out for and think more about their fellow campers, Jake's cabin mates also witnessed an incredibly inspirational example of perseverance. They felt inspired by Jake and learned to be better people themselves due to his upbeat attitude and his grit.

Many of the special needs campers we've hosted over the years have had a profoundly *positive* impact on their fellow campers, who often, for the first time in their lives, make a new friend who is different from them. Living with someone who is differently abled helps kids learn that people who look, act, or move differently from them can still be their friends. The positive impact of making small accommodations to host a few kids with special needs each summer have, I believe, far outweighed any inconveniences. Prior to that phone call, I had heard nothing but positive feedback from the campers and parents of kids who experienced living with and befriending a differently abled child.

I've also learned—after working with thousands of kids and parents—that *all* kids have special needs, but most of these needs are not visible on the outside. Some kids have a special need because they've just gone through a rough year socially at school and are feeling sad and lonely. Others have a medical need, like diabetes or a severe peanut allergy, that they need to learn to live with. They (and their parents) are often anxious about being away from home for the first time, but their parents know that their kid needs to learn to handle their illness or allergy in situations without their parents present in order to thrive as young adults. Many other children have behavioral or mental health issues—both diagnosed ones and ones that have not been identified—like ADHD, depression, or anxiety. Some kids are sad and withdrawn due to a negative event such as their parents' recent divorce, a grandparent's death, a move to a new school, or a severed friendship, and they may need some special care and attention from camp counselors. But whether or not the parent lists a special need or diagnosis on their child's camp forms, I know it's most realistic to view all kids—and people—as having some "special needs."

Nicole, the camper with Down syndrome whom the returning camper wanted to avoid, had joined us at camp for several years. She was high functioning due to the intense therapy and interventions her parents had provided, and she was able to thrive in most mainstream life settings, including school and camp. While she did at times need a little extra help, and was not as good at some of the camp activities that required balance and athleticism, Nicole's attitude and influence on other campers was overwhelmingly positive. She was kind, funny, and great to be around. Her maturity level was not the same as the girls in her group, as she was more innocent and—well, let me be frank here—kinder than a typical fifteen-year-old. We had learned in past summers that her presence within her cabin group led to the group being more cohesive and kind to each other, and less self-focused. They were better people after having been with Nicole.

I felt strongly that Nicole's special needs did not negatively impact any other campers' experiences. I also felt strongly—and still do—that what *does* negatively impact other people's life experiences are unkind kids and adults who are not welcoming to others and prefer to be siloed with only their own type. I refused to move that dad's daughter to another group. I also offered them a full refund of their camp tuition if they decided to no longer attend camp. The camper decided to still come to camp despite my denial of the request to change to a different cabin group, and her final camp experience with us was a positive one.

But their request and her late arrival left a bad taste in my mouth. Two weeks of camp didn't quite fit into this family's already crammed schedule, but they didn't want their child to miss out on summer camp, so they forged ahead with their plans. This parent seemed unaware of how his daughter's late arrival could negatively impact a group that is well under way on their bonding and adventures. What does overscheduling and being late to camp have to do with the topic of kindness? Arriving on time to an event that involves a large group of people is a common courtesy—a kindness because we're thinking about our impact on others' experience.

Why would any parent intentionally block their child from an opportunity to learn about and practice more kindness and compassion for others? Would parents rather raise self-focused kids who don't want to be inconvenienced to think about or make sacrifices for others? Unfortunately, for many parents, even those of us who think we are prioritizing raising kind human beings, the answers to those questions aren't as clear as we would like. In the cutthroat, competitive world in which our kids are growing up, kindness and caring appear to be mostly afterthoughts.

Richard Weissbourd, of the Harvard Graduate School of Education, set out to understand children's perceptions of what they and their parents value. He surveyed ten thousand children and asked them to rate how they felt about the importance of "caring for others," "achieving at a high level," or "being a happy person (feeling good most of the time)." They were also asked to rate how they believed their friends and parents perceived these same values. Eighty percent of the youth surveyed agreed with the statement, "My parents are prouder if I get good grades in my classes than if I'm a caring community member in class and school."[1]

Perhaps as adults we understand and see the benefits of kindness and caring for others, and have learned to value it in our friends, partners, and children, but as Weissbourd's research shows, we are not doing a good job of teaching kids how much we value kindness. Unless we want to continue on the current trajectory of increasingly more self-focused, uncaring, polarized, depressed, anxious people, we need to focus on raising kinder humans.

What would your kids say *you* value more—grades and achievements or kindness? A clue can be found in how your family spends your time and what your conversations revolve around. When was the last time you complimented or celebrated your kid for doing something kind? What about the last time you complimented them on earning a good grade or scoring a winning goal in soccer? When was the last time you or your family did something kind for a neighbor or volunteered to help with something that didn't directly benefit you? If, upon reflection, you don't like the answer, do not fear!

Regardless of the age of your kids, or where you and your family currently are on the "kindness meter," kindness is something that you can promote and grow at home. And the resulting positive changes in your kids will be well worth the effort. Kindness makes us happier, healthier, better people.

Why Is Kindness Important?

The concerns I had when I witnessed parents not setting an example of kindness for their kids, coupled with the rising tide of articles and stories about bullying and meanness, led me on a lengthy quest to learn about the science of kindness. And what I've learned backs what I intuitively knew: Kindness matters. A lot.

There are many measurable health benefits to kindness, including a longer life span and a younger-looking appearance (take that, Botox!). People fifty-five and older who volunteer for two or more organizations have a 44 percent lower likelihood of dying early.[2] This "kindness effect" has a stronger correlation with longevity than exercising four times a week! In fact, giving help to others serves as a better protection to overall health than taking aspirin protects against heart disease. Some of that longevity can be directly attributed to the beneficial chemicals and hormones produced by acts of kindness. Witnessing acts of kindness produces oxytocin, a hormone that both lowers blood pressure and increases heart health. Just like the antidepressants one of every nine people in the United States take,[3] kindness stimulates the production of serotonin, which heals wounds faster, calms us down, and makes us feel happier. Engaging in acts of kindness also produces endorphins, which serve as the brain's natural painkiller. Additionally, people who are "perpetually kind" have 23 percent less cortisol (the stress hormone) and age slower than average.[4]

If all that's not enough to convince you that kindness is good for our health, brain scans have shown exactly what is happening when we do something nice for someone else: Our brain's pleasure and reward system lights up as if we are the *recipient* of a good deed when we are the *doer* of the kind deed.[5]

When our kids witness or are the victims of ugly name-calling or aggressive, mean-spirited behavior (or posts on social media), how do we teach them to respond? In an interview with my favorite happiness guru, Dr. Christine Carter, I asked her how parents can teach kids to respond to unkind kids. I was thinking she might say, "Ignore them," and "encourage them to hang out with other people," which was what I advised my daughter to do when some of her friends started acting like mean girls in fourth grade.

Instead, Carter explained that the best way we can raise kind kids is to teach them to respond to people who are being unkind with compassion:

"Give them their own sense of personal power that's positive in the face of a situation that might otherwise make them feel powerless...Give them a way to look at the unkind behavior that is actually probably more true and quite different from the way that they see it. The goal is so that it doesn't trigger fear in them. Somebody's being unkind to them or somebody else, and it triggers a pretty big fear response, which is stressful for kids and doesn't necessarily lead to them doing the right thing in the face of that. But if we can teach them to see that all unkind behavior comes from a place of real pain, all of a sudden, they can see the unkind person's pain, and instead of just feeling afraid of them, they might also feel compassion. And compassion is a very powerful positive emotion, and it has the opposite effect on our nervous system as fear. So helping them break down unkind behavior, spending time talking with our kids about that person, what they might be going through, imagining what kind of pain they might be going through builds their compassion skills."

We can talk with our kids about how the kid who's being mean to other kids at school might have something difficult going on at home.

It's possible he is in pain from problems with siblings or parents. Instead of feeling like a victim, our child can realize that the mean kid might be behaving the best he can given his difficult circumstances. How do we teach our daughters to respond to the girl going out of her way to exclude people and make them feel left out? We can have a conversation about how people who feel loved, valued, and appreciated don't feel the need to put others down and be exclusive. Perhaps the mean girl is doing and saying mean things in an attempt to be accepted or popular.

In her song "Mean," Taylor Swift asks, "Why you gotta be so mean?" and talks about ending the cycle of being pushed around. I loved belting out that song with my kids. It served as a kind of catharsis, but also a good reminder not to sink to the same level as mean kids.

While our hackles will naturally rise, and our protective instincts will kick into gear upon hearing about someone saying or doing something mean to our precious child, it serves us well to remember that, unfortunately, mean people will be a part of our child's world *forever*. Instead of jumping in to intervene and rescue our child from the pain, we usually serve them better by teaching them how to respond with compassion and curiosity. Launching a school-wide, adult-driven attack usually doesn't work, because adults are notoriously bad at figuring out the root causes of meanness. Often, the kids perpetuating the cruelest acts are the ones viewed in a positive light by adults. Our kids' social lives are extremely complicated, and often the kid committing the unkind act is doing it at the urging of another kid. We need to encourage our kids to talk with us about negative social experiences, explore the possible whys together, and ensure that they don't get led down the road to meanness.

Teaching our kids to be discerning about friends, and finding kind ones, while also viewing kids who do mean things through a lens of compassion and empathy, teaches our kids an important life skill. Instead of teaching our kids to see themselves as victims of meanness, we can transform negative situations into opportunities for our kids to learn and practice more kindness themselves. Of course, we don't want our kids pursuing friendships with kids who they know are mean. And that means, in some cases, avoiding being part of social groups where negative behaviors to others are the norm.

The world in which we are living—and raising our children—clearly needs more kindness. It can start with us and our families and produce a ripple effect outward to our schools and communities. Given the rising depression and anxiety rates, and the ever-increasing use of psychotropic drugs, isn't it worth trying out a little more of the proven cure? Kindness.

It's Not ALL Bullying

Before I talk about modeling and practicing kindness with our kids, I need to address the B word. Like all adults, I have been horrified by the well-publicized stories of kids who were so aggressively taunted and bullied for such a long period of time that they committed suicide. The antibullying education, however, has created a social landscape where kids and parents call almost any unkind act as "bullying." Several summers ago, a ten-year-old camper wrote a letter home telling his parents he was being bullied at camp. His irate mother called to let us know. I was very concerned, so I went to talk with the camper right away. I expected to find a sullen boy sitting in the corner of his tent, but instead I found him in the middle of a friendly card game with three other boys. I waited for him to finish then asked if we could chat for a few minutes.

We found a bench where we could talk privately. I told him his mom had called because she was concerned he was being bullied, and I asked him what was happening. For a few moments he sat and pondered my question, and then he told me about two different incidents that he was referring to when he wrote the letter to his parents. The first incident was when two boys in his cabin group didn't want to play the card game he wanted to play. The second incident was when a boy touched his shoulder from the seat behind him in the van on the ride to our outpost camp. I asked him if anything else had happened.

Had anyone called him mean names? Had he been left out from games or events? Had any of these three boys done anything else on another occasion? He said he couldn't think of anything else. I asked him if he was making friends and having fun at camp, and he said he was. And I started wondering, *When did not getting your way or a one-time annoying behavior become "bullying"?*

According to speaker and children's book writer Tracy Ludwig, "Bullying is comprised of the following key elements: the intent to harm; an imbalance of power; repeated aggression and/or the threat of further aggression." I experienced bullying, or maybe more specifically sexual harassment, when I was in seventh grade. A man-sized eighth grader who sat behind me in math class bothered me daily by saying rude sexual comments and snapping my bra strap. I dreaded the class, and it really made me miserable having to be around that kid. I didn't report it, because this was the late 1970s and I didn't know that was a thing to do. I complained to my friends and counted the days until I was done with seventh grade, math class, and that kid. I'm glad that teachers and other youth professionals work harder now not to let bad behavior like that continue unchecked, but I'm getting tired of kids and parents referring to every behavior they don't like as "bullying."

Back to my conversation with the "bullied" camper: I asked him if he had ever said or done anything annoying to the other kids in his group. He admitted that yes, in fact, he had.

"Were you bullying them?" I asked.

"No!" he emphatically responded.

"So why are you being bullied but they're not?" I asked.

He thought about that for a while and then decided that, in fact, he wasn't being bullied after all.

But how did we get to the point that I was even having this conversation? When did a kid who doesn't get his way become a victim of bullying? And why are parents so certain that if their child uses the B word he must be being mercilessly harassed? Psychologist Signe Whitson distinguishes between rude, mean, and bullying behaviors:

Rude = Inadvertently saying or doing something that hurts someone else.
Mean = Purposefully saying or doing something to hurt someone once (or
    maybe twice).
Bullying = Intentionally aggressive behavior, repeated over time, that
    involves an imbalance of power.[6]

Parents and youth development professionals need to know this distinction and teach children that not all negative behaviors toward them qualify as bullying. Kids who don't have the same interests, don't want to play the same game at recess, or don't want to be close friends with another child are not all bullies. We need to teach children the important friendship skill of finding friends with like interests who reciprocate their feelings. We also need to help them learn to cope with the heartbreak of unreciprocated friendships. These are some of the friendship lessons covered in the next chapter. All children are the recipient of one or more mean comments or actions at some point during their school years, but unless it's ongoing, repeated intimidation, it's not bullying. It's a kid who's being rude or mean.

When my son came home with a story about something mean another child did to him at school, I listened and asked if the meanness was only directed toward him or also toward other kids—an important way to discern whether the incident can be defined as bullying. He said the kid treated everyone badly. I encouraged him to steer clear of the kid as much as possible. I want my son to have the ability to handle occasional mean comments and be discerning about who he spends time with. This is an important life skill he needs because, unfortunately, mean-acting people are part of life.

When we focus on the character traits we want children to be developing, like kindness and compassion, and model for them what those character traits look like, we raise kids who positively contribute to their relationships and their communities. We are wise as parents to clearly understand and distinguish between whether our child is dealing with the unpleasant but common experience of rude or mean behavior or is being systematically bullied by a person or group who is more powerful physically or socially. I'd love for parents to encourage schools to be pro-kindness rather than antibullying. We need to focus more on what we *do* want kids to be doing instead of what we don't want them to do. We need to model and teach kindness, acceptance, empathy, and compassion, which are all the antitheses of bullying. After all, we don't just want kids to stop bullying each other. We want them to be kind and caring, to include kids who are new or isolated, and to reach out to children who need social support. Instead of assemblies and motivational posters with the "Stop Bullying" theme, I'd like to see assemblies with titles like "10 Ways to Be a Great Friend" that cover ideas on specific things you can do to be a good friend. And what about having a bulletin board where kids can post "Acts of Kindness Seen This Week"?

Making It Cool to Be Kind

Meanness is contagious, and kids, especially in group settings or behind the perceived anonymity of social media, will say and post incredibly mean and hurtful things. But kindness is contagious, too. One good deed in a crowded area (or a Starbucks drive-through line) can create a domino effect and improve the moods of everyone who witnessed or participated in the act. Think of all those brains lighting up from the kindness!

Each year we have a theme we focus on at camp, and the summer following that infamous phone call mentioned at the start of this chapter, we chose "Cool to Be Kind" as our summer theme. I wanted to communicate clearly to our entire camp community that kindness is an important and valuable character trait, and I wanted kids to experience the good feelings you get from caring for others so that they would be inspired to continue their kindness practices after they returned home. I also firmly believed that kids needed to hear the message that being kind is actually much more cool than being mean.

The examples and messages kids get from the media (and their school hallways) often do not promote kindness. Many kids learn that the quickest route to popularity is putting others down or leaving other kids out. In the perceived zero-sum social worlds of middle and high school, one person being put down means you get on a higher rung of the social ladder. Social media posts, political discourse, and cultural norms often promote name-calling and being mean, gossiping, and telling jokes at the expense of others. That's what our kids are seeing and hearing every single day, and that's also why many kids start to consider it cool to perpetrate mean behaviors. It's no wonder that while adults are sending hateful messages through tweets, our kids are practicing a similar level of meanness on their own media. Why are adults so shocked to hear about horrendous stories of cyber and in-person bullying when we as adults are modeling that very same behavior? But there is hope for our world, because kids intuitively understand the benefits of kindness and can be taught to be kinder when we take the time to model, talk about, and practice kindness with them.

Can Kindness Be Taught?

It's kind of like weight training, we found that people can actually build up their compassion "muscle" and respond to others' suffering with care and a desire to help.

—Helen Wang, University of Wisconsin

Kindness can be taught at home, at school, and at summer camp. In order to roll out our "Cool to Be Kind" theme, we came up with specific ideas to promote and practice kindness. There are a plethora of resources available. One of my favorites is the website, The Random Acts of Kindness Foundation (https://randomactsofkindness .org), which features stories and ideas to promote kindness. At camp, we knew that the best way for our campers to learn kindness was to see our counselors modeling it. There were specific issues we needed to address. A common practice—especially for adolescent males—is to "dis" (disrespect) each other with negative jabs. Girls, too, often say something mean followed by "JK" (just kidding) or some other caveat that still leaves the recipient of the negative comment feeling awful. Commonly, adolescent and young adult relationships are full of these kinds of negative interactions. Instead of allowing an environment where put-downs were overlooked or encouraged, we trained our counselors to flip the script on friendly interactions and talk to each other in a way that was not common in their college halls—with compliments, kindness, and what we call "put-ups."

Gossip is another negative, unkind, and hurtful practice. Unfortunately, it is prevalent in all age groups—including adulthood. We knew in order to reduce gossip, we needed to be proactive in teaching our staff and campers how to be more direct in our communication and talk with the right person when we have a problem or concern. When a counselor or camper was upset with another counselor or camper, we taught them appropriate ways to handle the situation, talking directly to the person involved or an adult who could help—not gossiping to someone else. Spreading negative things about others becomes gossip and does not resolve conflicts and, in fact, usually exacerbates the conflict.

Most kids need help learning to resolve their own conflicts. In my research on social skills, I learned that kids who have difficulty responding appropriately in challenging social situations generally have trouble making and keeping friends. They are often rejected by other kids due to their inappropriate overreactions to minor conflicts. A post I wrote on my website many years ago called "5 Steps to Help Kids Resolve Conflicts" continues to be my most searched-for and viewed post of all time, so I know that parents and educators are struggling with helping kids learn how to respond appropriately in heated situations. At camp we tackle this as part of our "kindness curriculum," where we include lots of coaching on conflict resolution skills, including teaching kids about different ways they can choose to respond in conflict situations. The options counselors present to kids included:

Use an "I" message. For example, "I feel _____ when you _____."

Walk away or go to the cabin "chill spot" (a designated place where campers and staff can go when they needed a moment alone) and cool off (calm down). (It's a good idea to designate a chill spot for you and your kids at home.)

Go play with someone else.

Take turns or share.

Talk together. Work it out.

Think or write about what the camper can do to make the situation better.

Use kind words and friendly voices.

Count to ten.

Talk to a grown-up.

Whether we are helping facilitate a discussion between campers who have a conflict or coaching them individually on how to resolve the conflict themselves, the steps the counselors assist campers with always included:

1. Help the child calm down.
2. Have one or both children state the problem.
3. Encourage the children to apologize as needed.
4. Promote solution finding.
5. Follow up to be sure the children are getting along.

Parents can follow these same guidelines in addressing conflicts between siblings or between your child and a friend. You don't have to be a professional conflict resolution expert to help kids learn to talk about and work through conflicts!

Making Kindness Part of Family Life

Parents can implement the same kindness focus at home and make it cool to be kind. Being intentional about modeling and implementing kindness practices with your kids will lead to all of you *feeling* and *being* kinder. In our families, the simplest place to start is with teaching our kids common courtesies. For example, show your child how to hold a door open and explain that it's kind to hold the door for the people behind you. Practice at home and then give the door holding a whirl at a local mall or doctor's office. Your child will learn—from the appreciative thanks of others—that it feels good to hold the door open for others.

There are other common courtesies that we often wrongly assume our child will just learn on their own. Helping someone pick things up when they drop them is an example. If a kid drops their binder and their papers go flying in the middle school hallway, we want our kid to be the one who stops to help pick those papers up. But our kids might not naturally do this if they don't understand that it's the kind thing to do.

At a high school football game, I witnessed the actions of Logan, a perpetually kind boy I know. He was walking toward the student section of the bleachers and stopped in front of two new foreign-exchange students who were sitting in the row in front of us and several other parents. Logan said hello and encouraged them to move to the student section and sit with him and the rest of the kids. I remember thinking, *That is how I want my kids to be. Looking out for opportunities for kindness!* But how did Logan get that way? I need look no further than his parents, who are kind people who often volunteer to help others. To raise kind kids, we need to look for opportunities to offer courtesies and kindnesses to both friends and strangers. Before the start of a new school year, talk with your child about reaching out to new kids. Remind them what it felt like to be new, and encourage them to spend time with and welcome the new students. If your school has a formal "buddy" program that pairs older students with younger ones, or returning students with new ones, encourage your child to participate.

Bringing Camp Home: Activities to Promote Kindness

We need to care less about whether our children are academically gifted and more about whether they sit with the lonely kid in the cafeteria.

—*Valerie Williams*

Viewing both our own and our children's kindness through a growth mindset lens is extremely important. Rather than labeling ourselves or others as "kind" or "unkind" people, we can recognize kind behavior and promote the concept that each of us can get better at being kind through intentional practice. The surface level changes that occur when kindness is practiced regularly is a quieter, less volatile family environment. On a deeper level, everyone feels less stressed and happier when we are both the givers and receivers of more kindness. At home, parents can do both small and big things to encourage more kindness. Besides making your home life more pleasant, you'll be raising kind humans who likely will bring positive changes to the world.

One Simple Thing

When you get cut off by another driver, treated rudely by a store clerk, or snarled at by a cranky neighbor, how do you respond? Do you stay calm and friendly and keep your voice low?

If we want to raise kind kids, they need to see us model kindness, even with people who don't reciprocate. Because we want our kids to learn to view mean acts by other kids as an opportunity for compassion not retaliation, we need to show them how to practice kindness even with unpleasant people. If you struggle with flipping your lid and getting angry when people do unkind things to you, the most important thing you can do is work on your own reactivity. What can you do to show your kids that you are working on staying calm and kind, regardless of the circumstances? Take a few minutes to think about common scenarios that make you lose it, and brainstorm alternative, kinder responses.

Perhaps to the driver cutting you off (and after you grip your steering wheel and take a deep breath): "Wow, that guy is really in a hurry. Maybe something stressful is going on at his job."

To the rude clerk: "Thank you for your time. I appreciate your assistance. I hope the rest of your day goes more smoothly."

To the cranky neighbor: "I'm sorry we were too loud for you when we were playing in the yard. We just made a batch of cookies. Would you like one?"

These responses, of course, do not come naturally to most of us. More common is the "eye for an eye," angry, hateful discourse, where people respond to violent acts, anger, or meanness with retaliation. But responding with kindness not only teaches our kids how to deal with mean people, but will also make them healthier and happier people. They'll learn kindness more from how we actually respond to rude, unkind behavior from others than how we *tell* them to respond.

The Sticky Note Solution

> Unexpected kindness is the most powerful, least costly, and most underrated agent of human change.
>
> *—Bob Kerrey*

Online, you can find hundreds of ideas for doing Random Acts of Kindness (RAK) either alone or with your kids. When we had our "Cool to Be Kind" theme, I created an entire Pinterest board on the topic and printed out many camp-friendly ideas for RAKs.

Many of the RAKs are simple and involve leaving an uplifting note. How about keeping a pad of sticky notes and a good pen in your car, along with a list of ideas for RAKs? You and your kids can leave uplifting messages around—on lockers at school, the ATM machine, the mirror or stall door of a public bathroom. The fun part is making sure you do it secretly, and usually to someone you don't know. Messages you might want to consider leaving:

- "There are many beautiful people in this world. Never forget you are one of them."
- "Do what makes you happy!"
- "Only in the darkness can you see the stars."
- "You rock!"

Alternatively, you can use your sticky note to pass along a surprise gift. Pay for the Starbucks for the person behind you in the drive-through *and* have the cashier give them a sticky note that says, "I hope this coffee brightens your day and brings you happiness." If you're out to dinner with your family and see a younger family or person eating alone, consider buying their dinner and wishing them well with an encouraging sticky note. Think of all the kindness your family can spread with a stack of sticky notes in your car, at the ready!

Make It Fun

Acts of kindness like the sticky note idea can be super-fun family activities, but there are always opportunities to do some nonrandom acts of kindness to the people closest to us. Keep a box or drawer full of supplies to create postcards or greeting cards, and make it a family habit to gather and each send one card of appreciation to someone who you want to lift up. It can be a friend, teacher, or relative. Each of you create and write a note, and together send out some happiness into your community. If you enjoy cooking together, you can make this activity even more fun by linking it to cooking a batch of cookies or your favorite banana bread, or jarring supplies to make cookies, to share along with your note.

I copied a great idea shared by my friend, Ashley Peters. During the holidays, shop with your kids for some items (or make some cookies or banana bread loaves) and leave the wrapped goodies or store-bought snacks with some water or other drinks on your front porch with a large sign thanking your delivery people. Our poster board sign in front of our tub full of goodies reads, "Attention: UPS, FedEx, and USPS Mail Carriers, All day (year!) long you've been on your feet, so please pick out a much deserved treat. A sincere thank you for all that you do and Merry Christmas from us to you!" During their busiest time of year, brighten their day by leaving some cheer for them! This could be a fun thing to do randomly in the middle of the year, too.

What other fun ways can you think of to surprise a grandparent, neighbor, or friend? Have your kids help you leave something special on the front porch "just because." They'll have fun going on these kindness adventures with you, and they'll be developing their own kindness habit, too.

Around the Campfire

Once you decide that kindness is a value that is important to you, an excellent family dinner conversation and activity can be on the topic of kindness. For this activity, I think having a place to record your ideas is a great idea. If your kids like to write, have them record the kindness ideas you come up with. Use a legal pad or blank piece of paper. Younger kids can even draw the kindness activities you think of.

The book *Have You Filled a Bucket Today* by Carol McCloud[7] is a great read-aloud for younger children. After reading the book together, a new question to ask kids is, "How did you fill someone else's bucket today?"

For older kids, the discussion can be a brainstorm, where together you come up with ideas of ways to be kind to others. Questions to get the brainstorming started include:

- What is something kind someone has done for you?
- What are kind things you can do for others?

After each family member shares, create a "Family Kindness" poster or list with all of your kindness ideas. Post it to serve as a reminder that kindness is important in your family.

Keep the conversation about kindness going by adding a question to your regular dinner or bedtime conversations. Ask: "How were you kind today?" or "How did you fill someone else's bucket?" By talking regularly about kindness, your kids will truly understand how much you value it, and not be in that majority of kids who think kindness is not important to their parents!

Family Meeting Topic

In Ron Lieber's book *The Opposite of Spoiled*, he urges parents to be more upfront with our kids about money. Many of us learned from our own parents that it's not polite to talk about how much money we have. Growing up, I did not know how much money my dad made. I did notice, however, that we started doing some cool things as I got older. Ski trips. Hawaiian vacations. I knew that we did not have financial worries. I also knew that my dad valued work and was not going to give us large amounts of money. I realize, looking back, that I took for granted having my college education paid for. But I also worked throughout college to earn money for all the extras that I wanted (but did not need). Movies, clothes, and outings with friends were on my own dollar.

I have become convinced, like Lieber advises, that how we talk about and spend our money is a great opportunity to teach kids about our values. If we want our kids to learn about giving, we need to talk with them about how we give. According to Lieber's compelling argument, our kids don't become spoiled by wealth but instead by not knowing how to steward it well. We also don't serve them well to lie and say we can't afford something they want. For example, when they ask for an obnoxiously expensive pair of shoes that we can, in fact, afford, we need to take the opportunity to share our values. We can explain, for example, that we think it's wasteful or showy to spend that much on shoes, and we'd rather buy good shoes that allow us to donate for kids who don't have any shoes.

A great way to start the money discussion doesn't have to be about your net worth or mortgage statement. Instead, you can have a family discussion about your values and philosophy around giving financial donations. Do you have a budget for annual giving? Is it a percentage of your income or do you use another formula? Do you regularly give to a specific organization? If so, share with your kids what that organization is doing, why you believe in their work, and how long you've been giving to them. If they have a video online talking about the work they are doing, show it to your kids. If it is a local place, like a homeless shelter, take them to see it.

Ask your kids what causes they're interested in. Are they concerned about a specific group of people? There are a multitude of great organizations to which you can individually or as a family donate your time or money. Start with the people closest to you. If you have an elderly family member who could use some help with house or yard work, or would enjoy a visit from your kids, that's a wonderful, tangible way for your kids to experience giving. During natural disasters, go online and make a donation together specifically toward relief in that area. There are many people and families who are in need of support. Find a population or group that resonates with your family's values, or what you and your kids are most concerned about, and research ways you can help.

If you value kindness and giving, and want to pass along a legacy of giving to your kids, make giving a family conversation as well as a family action. Dedicate time as a family to serving others, and you will instill the value of kindness and giving in your kids.

Diving Deeper

With kindness, a positive upward spiral can occur in your family that creates a momentum that can last for decades and improve people's health and happiness. If you start some family kindness practices, my suspicion is that the kindness will continue to spread like wildfire. To dive deeper into kindness as a family, consider doing one of the RAK challenges—like thirty days of kindness, where you commit to doing one act of kindness a day for thirty days.[8] Or, challenge your family to write fifty-two thank-you notes or letters—one a week for an entire year. These kinds of bigger kindness challenges will keep kindness in the forefront of your family's minds and remind you all to seek out opportunities both small and big to help others.

Another great way to promote kindness is to ask scenario questions. For example, ask your kids what they would do if there was someone sitting alone at school lunch. Or ask what they would do if their friend told them something mean about a mutual friend? When other kids are being disrespectful to a substitute teacher, what can they do that's kind? Share stories of times when you've witnessed unkindness or had to make a decision to be kind. Alternatively, share about a time you regret being unkind and what you wish you had done differently. Open up the discussion with your kids about how it often goes against the grain to be kind and is sometimes perceived as uncool.

Kindness and bravery are often closely linked, because sometimes being kind means going against what others are doing, and that can be hard. Talk about scenarios where they might have to do something different from their friends in order to choose kindness. The book *Wonder*, by R. J. Palacio, is an inspirational story of kindness.[9] As I mentioned earlier, it's one of our most popular read-aloud books at camp, and I highly recommend reading it as a family. There is also an excellent movie, but I recommend reading the book first, as it has even more details about what it feels like to be the victim of meanness, and what it looks and feels like when people choose kindness instead. By the time your family has a sustained focus on being kind, your kids will have already learned that kindness makes them a better family member and friend. And while kindness attracts friends and makes kids a desirable friend, there are other skills kids need to make and keep friends, too. Those friendship skills are what we'll address next.

Camp Secret #9

Coach Kids to Better Friendships

I've learned the qualities of true friends and how to maintain strong connections with them not through technology but through real human interaction. This skill I will continue to use for the rest of my life.

—Izzy

I couldn't believe my fourteen-year-old son's rudeness one day when his twenty-year-old sister had just walked in the door, having come home on college break after being away for two months, and he didn't stop playing his video game to greet her. In the past, my response to this type of socially inept behavior came from the emotional, fight-or-flight part of my brain—*I cannot believe such a selfish heathen has been raised in my home.* I'm a camp director, so having kids who lack social graces feels profoundly embarrassing and shameful. But this time, I didn't let the words actually come out of my mouth. Instead, I took a few deep breaths and using my thinking brain's knowledge of how kids learn social skills, reflected on the situation and realized that the blame for his lack of appropriate greeting skills lay not with him but with me.

I had never taught my son the appropriate greeting for when one of his siblings comes home after being away for a long time, and this was the first opportunity the social situation had occurred. Therefore, instead of expressing my frustration at his lack of appropriate greeting skills, I let him know, privately, that the next time one of his sisters was arriving, the appropriate thing for him to do was to stop whatever he's doing, stand up, and greet her with a hello and a hug. Years later, without fail, upon the arrival of one of his siblings who had been away from home, he cheerfully greeted them with a hug and a hello. He learned this skill not because I berated him for his lack of social graces, but because I coached him on what was appropriate in that specific social situation.

I now understand that I need to step back and view each social snafu as a teaching moment—a mistake to learn from—rather than a referendum on my parenting. It's not about us as parents. What it *is* about is helping our kids learn the social skills they need to make and keep friends. As parents, we need to stay focused on the goal—which is raising kids who thrive in relationships and in life. The great news is that we know our kids better than anyone else does, and most of us have a lot of life experience in social situations. We have experienced social successes and failures throughout our lives and have learned and honed our own social skills. Therefore, we are the ideal guides for our children in the area of social skills and relationships. We are their ideal "Friendship Coaches."

Why Kids Make Their Closest Friends at Camp

> The great outdoors can be a great experience for children only if they know how to live and play together in a cooperative and collegial manner.
>
> *—Anne (teacher*
> *and camp parent)*

Why do campers and alumni frequently say that they consider their camp friends, many of whom live far away and they see for only a few weeks each summer, their closest friends? Most camp experiences are intentionally set up to foster friendships as one of the top priorities, if not *the* top. At schools, on sports teams, and in other settings, there are usually other goals for kids that supersede social growth and fostering friendships. But at summer camp, making friends is the overarching and most important goal, so we take it seriously.

Kids who are socially adept and good at making friends thrive at camp, just like they do in other social settings. But it is the kids for whom social interactions are more challenging, whose social life presents a daily challenge, who have benefited the most from their camp experiences. Because counselors view themselves as their campers' "Friendship Coaches," understand their important role in helping campers learn to form close relationships, and provide ample opportunities for practicing, campers often improve their social skills while at camp. Counselors assess kids' skills, identify social strengths and deficits, and use proven coaching techniques to encourage campers to learn and practice important friendship skills. Conversations about friendship are prevalent at camp, friendships are celebrated, and continuing connection outside of camp is encouraged. Many kids report that their camp counselors are the first adults who ever talked with them about making friends and being a good friend.

Why Are Children's Friendships So Important?

Making friends is the primary task of childhood. The importance of quality childhood friendships as a predictor for psychological well-being both during childhood and later in life has been clearly documented in numerous research studies.[1] Friendships during childhood and early adolescence are where kids learn important skills like cooperation, altruism, and empathy.[2] Children with friends are more confident, more involved at school, and more work-oriented.[3] Friends open up kids' affective world, fostering self-awareness, self-respect, and self-esteem.[4] Friends provide support during the often-challenging transitions of adolescence and also serve as a buffer against family risk factors like divorce and peer victimization.[5] The importance of quality childhood and adolescent friendships cannot be understated. These early positive relationships predict psychological well-being both during childhood and later in life. The research is clear: Friendships, not pop-ularity, *are* the key to happiness.

Children who don't have friends are referred to by psychologists as "low on the sociometric spectrum." They are socially rejected or neglected. Rejected children are kids who other kids specifically name when asked whom they dislike. Neglected children are almost invisible to other kids.[6] Regardless of how they are described, children who lack childhood friendships suffer from long-term, negative con-sequences. When childhood social connection issues are not resolved, these kids are more likely to have psychiatric diagnoses both during childhood and later in life. They are at a higher risk for addictions and suicide.[7] Taking it to a frightening extreme, being socially rejected or isolated is the description that fits most of the adolescent perpetrators of school shootings.[8] Rejected children tend to be more verbally and physically aggressive. They show disruptive, withdrawn, or submis-sive behaviors.[9] As parents, we need to view these behaviors in our own children as red flags indicating that they need help. Understand-ing the importance of helping kids with their social skills as much as you help them with their academic or athletic skills is an important paradigm shift parents and other caring adults need to make in order to help kids who are struggling to make or keep friends. Thinking of yourself as your child's friendship coach is a good first step toward addressing your child's social skills deficits.

Being Your Kid's Friendship Coach

It's painful to watch our children suffer social rejection, and our inclina-tion as parents may be to jump in and blame other kids (who can behave horribly), teachers, or coaches for our children's social troubles. But no matter how hard we try, we can't make all the other kids respond differ-ently to our kid. We can't make our kids' friends for them.

If you have a socially adept child who makes friends easily, be grateful and praise their pro-social behaviors. But there are many kids who need extra support in the area of social skills and friendships. If our child plays baseball and needs to work on their catching skills, we willingly head to the park to play catch with them for an hour. When our child struggles with a math concept, we sit with them and try to figure out how the heck they're teaching long division these days, guiding them until they (and we!) are able to master the math skill. Viewing social skills in the same way can be helpful. Once you identify a social skill your child needs to work on and determine what coaching techniques you're going to utilize, you can help your child improve that specific skill. Just like our kids need to be coached on and practice their skills to improve in sports and academic subjects, social skills need to be coached on and practiced regularly.

During my college years, I learned a lot about friendship. At the start of my freshman year, I traveled to Stanford University convoy style for the seven-hour drive from Southern California with two friends; one was a family friend I'd known since childhood, and the other was a good friend from high school. We were three peas in a pod for the start of school, going to football games and parties together, making new friends, and navigating college life as a team. I loved our time together, but I was naïve in my understanding of adult friendships. They were males, and as soon as they each found a girlfriend, the girlfriends didn't want either of them hanging out with me anymore. Our close friendship gave way to superficial greetings in social situations for the remainder of our college years. I had lost my two best college friends.

The same year, I developed a new friendship with a fun, vivacious athlete from Texas. I served as her life coach and counselor, which was a friend role I'd honed in high school. When she and her boyfriend were having some issues, I talked with them together. I did what I knew best to do as a friend—I provided empathy, comfort, and guidance. But the following fall, at the start of my sophomore year, I was having my own troubles. Looking back, I was depressed and would have benefited from counseling. But I turned to my friend instead. Turned out she wasn't interested in the kind of friendship where she would need to serve as my counselor. She preferred being the helpee, not the helper. That friendship waned, because she couldn't deal with my pain, and I learned a lesson about the importance of the mutuality of friendships.

I'm sure you have friendship stories of your own—stories of great friendships, stories of being betrayed. Happy friend stories and sad ones. As adults, we have a lot more experience than our kids do learning about and navigating relationships. We've had social successes and endured social mistakes of our own or others. Our children do not have the same awareness of how their social actions impact others, nor do they have the ability to see their own role in social challenges. We can't assume that our kids will learn social skills by osmosis, nor should we fall into the trap of having a fixed mindset about our kids' social skills, labeling them as introverted or as homebodies. Berating them, or comparing them to other kids who are more socially adept, also will not help them grow their skills.

As parents, we play an important role as our kids' first and most important social skills coaches. The way we model, talk about, and teach relational skills to our kids can have a powerful and lasting impact on their lives. Our kids' relationships with each other and with us provide the training ground for all of their future relationships, including romantic relationships and marriage. How we model for them and help train them in social skills will have a positive, long-term impact on their overall well-being. Viewing ourselves as our kids' friendship coaches, and approaching social skills the same way we would academic or athletic ones, is an important shift in thinking. When we see areas of social skills deficits, or our kids talk about their social challenges, we help our kids most by approaching the situations with the mindset that these challenges are opportunities for social growth. Just as Carol Dweck's research about the importance of instilling a growth mindset in our kids holds true for academics, it also holds true for social skills.[10] If we let our kids say, "I'm just not good at meeting new people," or, "I can't talk on the phone," we're allowing them to have a fixed mindset about their social skills and we're doing them a disservice.

As our kids' friendship coaches, we can approach social skills the same way we would approach coaching or tutoring them in an athletic or academic area:

- Understand which social skills they need to make and maintain friendships.
- Assess their current skills.
- Coach them using proven techniques, including modeling, discussion, instruction, and role playing.
  We'll explore these coaching techniques next.

Understand the Skills Kids Need to Make and Maintain Friendships

The first thing you need to do to become your kid's friendship coach is to educate yourself on the social skills that predict success in friendships and other relationships. As you read through these skills, think about your child and which of the skills are their strengths and areas for improvement. This will help you when you get to the point of assessing your child's current social skills, which will be explained in the next section.

Think about your own skills, as well. What are your areas of social strengths? What about areas where you can improve? One of the most powerful ways you can mentor your kids with their social skills is showing them that good relationship skills can be difficult to practice and are learned and honed throughout our lives. Showing your kids that you are working on your skills makes them more likely to be enthusiastic about working on their own.

Fundamental to our children's ability to make friends is their knowledge about what skills are necessary to make friends. We can refer to these as "friend-making" skills. These skills include the basic social skills of greeting people, introducing yourself and others, conversation skills, and extending invitations. Many kids falsely believe that the fault for lack of friendships lies with other kids. They think that because people aren't coming over to talk to them, inviting them to play, or including them in games, the other kids don't like them. What they don't see is that *they* need to take action to make friends.

Greetings and Introductions

Learning basic greeting and introduction skills is the best place to start. Friendships start with good body language—most important, a smile. A great greeting also includes an introduction: "Hi, I'm Sunshine. What's your name?" People *love* to hear their own name, so the next step is to respond using their name, "Nice to meet you, Morgan!" Once the pleasantries are done, the next step is a simple, nonthreatening question. Kids at camp came up with the following questions that can be used when meeting someone on the first day:

- Have you been to camp before?
- How old are you?
- Where are you from?
- What activities are you most excited about?

In a group setting, another good introduction skill kids can practice is introducing their new friend to someone else they know. This sounds like:

"Have you met Joe?"
"Morgan, this is Joe. He goes to my school."

At camp, I spend five minutes talking to the campers about these skills. I have a flip chart with the steps outlined, and then I give them time to practice introducing themselves and introducing others. It's remarkable to watch how kids of all ages are receptive both to the training and the practicing. Explaining the importance of greetings and introductions, and normalizing the practice of these skills, helps kids learn that a good greeting and introductory conversation is how most friendships begin. I've had numerous campers report back to me that they've practiced the skill and made new friends. While these steps may sound simple to adults, many kids have never had anyone explain to them the process of greeting others and introducing themselves. Like the rest of the social skills covered in this chapter, with a bit of gentle coaching from us and some guided practice, our kids can improve their skills tremendously.

Basic Conversation and Invitation Skills

> I think a great skill that I learned at camp was communication. I was a very shy person before camp and was very introverted. When I went to camp, I learned that it's not hard to say a simple hello to start a conversation.
>
> —Olivia

Once the initial introduction pleasantries are done, and the first question has been asked, that's when kids have the opportunity to practice basic conversation skills or extend a small invitation. Conversation skills include listening to responses, acknowledging similarities or differences, and asking more follow-up questions. Using the camp example above, if one child asks if the other child has been to camp before, and the second child responds, "No," an appropriate response could be, "This is my first year at camp, too!" These responses will be reviewed in more detail in the "Activities to Promote Friendship Skills" section at the end of this chapter.

Very young children—especially boys, even well into adolescence—often aren't comfortable going much deeper into the conversation than an initial question or two. An alternative is offering a small invitation, or what we call a friendship "bid." For a friendship to begin, someone has to take action. This can be one person inviting another to do something, or it can be asking to join in with what a child or group is already doing. Examples of small invitations a child can make include:

"Do you want to go on the swings?"
"Do you want to play a game of cards?"
"Let's sit next to each other at lunch!"
"Will you be my bathroom buddy?"

If your child is meeting someone who's new to your school or team, or if another child is visiting your home to play for the first time, a great thing to teach your child to do is to offer to show them around.

"Do you want me to show you where the playground is?"
"Let me show you my room."
"Here's where we get snacks and drinks."

It may seem like a no-brainer to adults, but some kids do not naturally remember to tell a friend they're hosting where things are located. This, like the other social skills, needs to be reviewed and practiced.

Understanding How to Find Good Friends and Be a Good Friend

Once your child has met another child and initiated a friendship, there are more skills to learn and practice. These skills include discerning if someone is a good friend, knowing their "tribe," sharing the spotlight, complimenting friends and celebrating their victories, developing empathy, learning to deal with difficult emotions, and conflict resolution strategies.

One of the most important social skills our kids need is the ability to discern who might be a good friend. Kids need to find other kids who accept who they are, consider them an equal, and share some of the same interests. Some kids try to join the perceived popular group only to find they are not truly welcome. Such "friendships" are lopsided and unfulfilling because they are not based on mutual liking. Often only one child considers the friendship viable and is investing in it. Rather than encouraging children to continue forcing themselves into friendships or a group where they are not wholeheartedly accepted and welcome, help them instead discover where their real tribe is, which may be just one or two other like-minded kids. When our kids experience the reciprocity of a friendship based on mutual liking, they experience the feeling of connection that is at the heart of real friendships.

A conversation I've had with many parents over the years revolves around adult friendships. A parent will call, concerned that they don't think it's a good idea for their child to be in the same cabin group with a longtime family friend's child. They don't want to hurt anyone's feelings, but they know that the kids are not a great match for one another. Based on convenience, our kids often spend a lot of time with their cousins or the children of our adult friends. While this often works well and leads to fun family get-togethers, it also can have some pitfalls. Sometimes we as parents are so excited for our kids to be friends with specific kids we neglect to notice that the kids are not a great match as friends.

When we invest too much effort into forcing our kids to be friends with certain people, we limit their ability to find their own tribes. Be aware of what you're seeing in your children's friendships—if there is intimacy, kindness, mutual liking, and reciprocity, then it's probably a good friendship. But if you see your child is not experiencing that kind of close, mutual connection, it's best to allow them more time with other children.

One of the many reasons kids make so many close friends at camp is that they are exposed to more different children. No longer are they just with the sports kids or the theater kids or the kids from the same neighborhood. Kids discover that they can be friends with kids who are older or younger, from a different religious or ethnic background or from another region or country. They discover that their tribe doesn't depend on outside appearances but on internal qualities that form the bonds of friendship. Sometimes, in order for our kids to find their tribe, we need to encourage them to get outside their current circles and meet some new people.

Besides learning to discern what makes a good friend, experiencing what a good friendship feels like, and knowing the feeling of belonging that having a tribe brings, our kids also need some other social skills to maintain their friendships. People love to talk about themselves, and asking good questions is often the entry point for building friendships. Listening to people's answers, showing interest, and asking appropriate follow-up questions are equally important.

Sharing about oneself is also an important social skill, because if done well, it can enhance friendships. When lacking or done poorly, it can serve as a social repellant. Young kids need assistance learning to share objects—toys, books, markers, and so on. As they get older, kids need to learn to share about themselves in a way that doesn't sound boastful but helps others get to know them. On a vacation last year, my family and I found ourselves in the resort's hot tub with a boy who went on and on about how he was professional at parkour. He talked about stunts he performed and how he was the best at certain maneuvers. My kids still talk about him, because his bragging was unforgettable. It's a lesson for us all. Yes, share about yourself to help others get to know you, but also ask questions and listen to what others have to say. Sharing the spotlight is an important skill. Let others be in the high beam sometimes.

Responding positively to others' triumphs is a friendship-enhancing skill that research has proven also enhances marriages and other relationships.[11] If you can truly be as happy and excited for your friend's victory as if it were your own, that's an excellent relational skill. When talking with younger kids, you could use the example of how you feel when your friend beats you in a race or gets a better grade on a test. While the natural response might be jealousy, celebrating and congratulating your friend will be great for the friendship. When we truly celebrate others' accomplishments, our connection gets stronger; hopefully, the friend reciprocates by being happy for us and our victories.

Empathy is a social skill that is difficult to teach, to explain, and to define to kids. It encompasses our ability to read others' nonverbal cues and facial expressions, sense their emotions and respond appropriately, and imagine what they may be thinking or feeling. Empathy involves demonstrating caring toward others and is an important trait necessary to form healthy relationships. Many adults struggle with empathy, so it's not a huge surprise that our kids need help in this social area, as well. Self-awareness, self-regulation, and the ability to take another's perspective are all important skills our children must develop in order to have positive, fulfilling relationships both in childhood and adulthood.

In research on which kids are most well liked by peers and which kids are disliked or rejected, difficulty handling emotions (self-regulation) appears to be the biggest repellant. Kids (and adults!) who lash out or overreact to negative situations just aren't pleasant to be around and are often disliked by peers. Therefore, it is vitally important that kids who struggle with their emotion regulation learn how to handle difficult emotions in a constructive way. Similarly, kids need to learn how to handle disagreements and conflicts without running to an adult right away. Kids who run to an adult every time they get their feelings hurt and don't know how to solve problems with their peers need assistance learning to resolve their own conflicts. They specifically need to learn how to respond to teasing, unkind comments, losing, accusations, being left out, and peer pressure. Reviewing different ways to resolve conflicts and solve problems can help kids learn important life and relationship skills.

Assess Your Child's Current Social Skills Strengths and Deficits

As you read through the above section and thought about your child, which skills came to mind as being strengths? Which social skills are areas where you could help your child? Assessing their overall social skills, and then picking just one skill to address at a time, is a great place to start your coaching. There are many social skills assessment tools available. School psychologists have detailed inventories available and are a great resource for kids who are struggling socially at school. I've developed a simple tool that you can use as a basic assessment of your child. I've used it with campers to have them think about and share their strengths as a friend and areas they can work on during camp. My "Social Skills Checklist" is in the "Resources" section at the back of the book and is also available for download at http://happycampersbook.com.

After you have assessed your child's skills, the next step is to prioritize which skill to focus on first in your coaching. If your child struggles with their ability to cope with difficult emotions, that would be a great place to start. Learning to handle strong emotions will help them be more appealing as a friend to other children.

Coaching Techniques

A good coach can change a game. A great coach can change a life.
—John Wooden

Now you're ready to start coaching, but don't worry. You don't need a whistle or a clipboard, and like I said earlier, you're already fully qualified. You can coach your child using a combination of modeling, instruction, discussion, role-playing, and debriefing.

Modeling

As with all things parenting, our kids learn more from what we do than from what we tell them to do. Let them see you being a good friend. If you are writing a note to a friend whose parent just died, or taking a meal to someone who is sick, let your child in on it. If they see you being a good friend, they'll start to understand what good friends do. Find more on modeling in the "One Simple Thing" section of this chapter.

Instruction, Discussion, and Role-Playing

As you introduce a new social skill, be positive and not condemning or critical. Say something like, "Making friends can be hard sometimes. I'd like to talk with you about something you can do that will help you make friends. How does that sound?"

For whichever skill you're working on, break the skill down into simple steps.

For example, if you're teaching about sharing the spotlight, you could follow this discussion guide:

Step 1: Ask, "Think about someone you like a lot. When they share information about themselves, how do they say it?" Discuss different ways people can share things about themselves and the words that come to mind, like *humble, proud, bragging,* and *know-it-all.*

Step 2: Ask, "What do you like to share about yourself?" Talk about hobbies, interests, and other things they're proud of and like to talk about with friends.

Step 3: Brainstorm ways to share information in a manner that doesn't sound arrogant. Talk about tone of voice and the words used.

Step 4: Role-play a discussion by asking them questions and having them share about themselves. Assess how they sound and gently coach if they come across in a negative way. You can say, "I could tell how much you like *Star Wars,* but when you insisted that I had the wrong name for the Wookie, it made me feel bad. How else could you have shared that?"

Step 5: Keep practicing!

Bringing Camp Home: Activities to Promote Friendship Skills

Friendship is the gold of childhood.

— Michael Thompson, PhD

One of the best ways to foster your child's social skills and help them form good friendships is to make sure they have plenty of free-play time—both alone and with siblings or other kids. At camp we talk about creating an environment that's a "friend-making factory." Parents can take a similar approach at home by setting up the environment to maximize their children's ability to learn and practice good friendship skills. This often means limiting screen use and having clear guidelines about screens when friends are over.

Early friendships are so important, because they are both the source of much childhood joy and the building blocks and practice for later adult relationships. For our children, their earliest relationships are with us and with their siblings or other family members. Positive relationships are what make a happy life, so let's help our kids build the social skills they need now to have strong friendships and positive relationships throughout their lives!

One Simple Thing

While researching, writing, and speaking about children and friendship skills over the past several years, I've come to realize how important friendships are for me as an adult. I know how vital it is to my well-being to nurture my friendships. With our overscheduled, busy family lifestyles, our friendships often get put on the back burner. In a recent study on the number of close adult friendships, 48 percent of respondents listed one name. On average, participants listed 2.03 confidantes, and 4 percent of those surveyed said they didn't have any close friends.[12] But regardless of whether you think you have zero, one, or more close friends, is there someone you've been missing or wanting to reconnect with? Today I challenge you to do a quick friendship activity:

- Pick up the phone and call a friend to check in.
- Send a text message to a friend saying you're thinking about them or asking how they're doing.
- Write a sticky note with words of encouragement to someone who lives in your apartment, dorm, house, or tent.
- Write a note or letter to someone who is important to you and mail it.

If you're thinking, *But I don't have any good enough friends to call, text, or write!* then reach out to a family member. They are often some of your closest friends, anyway. We are social animals who were made to connect, and we all want to connect with others, but sometimes we are our own worst enemy in forming and maintaining close relationships. We keep ourselves from connecting by our overly busy, self-focused way of living or by our desire to be seen in a positive light the way only social media—without the messiness of real life—can present us. It gets lonely.

In the past, I've found myself thinking, *It's been so long, and I don't have that much time to talk*, dissuading myself from making that call. No more. When a person pops into my head, instead of just *intending* to reach out, I'm committed to actually calling, texting, or writing them a note.

Taking just a few moments to think about another person—and then connect with them—is how we nurture and grow friendships and bring more health and contentment to ourselves. So whether it's a friend down the street, across the country, or in a different part of the world, why not reach out and connect today? That's one simple way to be a good friend and show your kids how it's done.

The Sticky Note Solution

As you've thought about your child and their social skills, I bet you've noticed many of their social strengths. Kids often demonstrate their strengths with us and with their siblings. Letting them know that you notice those things will encourage them to keep practicing good social skills.

Write them a sticky note complimenting them on a positive social action you noticed at home:

> "Thank you for giving me a hug when I was feeling sad about my sick friend."
>
> "I appreciate how you got so excited about my work promotion. It makes me feel so good when you help me celebrate good things!"
>
> "You led a great discussion at dinner last night. Thanks for thinking up good questions for us all to answer."

Make It Fun

All of family life is a training ground for social skills. Whatever your family traditions—game nights, road trips, or weekend bike rides or hikes, make sure that you have quality time to connect and communicate as a family—without screens. Find a fun game—even one that brings out everyone's worst, most competitive sides. Learning good sportsmanship and how to be a good loser is an important social skill. Designate screen-free communication time daily as well as weekly, screen-free family playtime. Let the kids pick the activity, as long as it doesn't involve a screen.

Around the Campfire

For kids with challenges making friends, learning better conversation skills has been the intervention that has the most positive outcomes. Specifically, research has shown that when kids are coached on the specific skills of self-expression (sharing), questioning, and how to give help, suggestions, and advice, they later demonstrate higher interaction rates with other children.[13] Family dinner is the ideal practice ground for having discussions about social skills and practicing those skills. Every conversation you have around the table is an opportunity for kids to learn better communication skills.

One idea is to have a "social skill of the week" discussion over family dinner. The skill could be discussed all week, or it can be introduced and discussed on a designated "friendship" night or as part of the family meeting agenda. Following are some possible topics to include:

Manners: When my son didn't get up to greet his sister, that was a manners issue. He didn't know what was the common social courtesy in that situation. There are many more common courtesies and manners our kids need to know that they may not pick up on or notice. They need to be specifically taught. These can include things like holding doors open for others rather than letting it slam in their face and helping older people—like grandparents—with their chair. Dinnertime is also a great training ground for table manners like putting their napkin in their lap, chewing with their mouth closed, and not talking with their mouth full. Each of these manners can be presented in a matter-of-fact, informative way, led with, "I don't think I've ever explained to you..." Kids will be much more receptive to learning manners when they are presented in a nonaccusatory way.

Questions and Listening: Because asking questions and listening well are important conversation skills, talk about it with your kids. Brainstorm what types of questions they might ask both new and old friends at school. Write down the ideas. If your child is old enough to write (and enjoys writing), let them be the scribe. If not, keep the list going yourself. As with any brainstorm, every idea gets on the list and no idea gets shot down. This is especially important to review if you have more than one child contributing to the brainstorm. If they have trouble coming up with questions, spur them on by offering suggestions like:

Do you play any sports?
What do you like to do after school?
What's your favorite recess game?

What's in your lunch?
How many brothers and sisters do you have?
Who's your teacher?

Practice asking and answering questions at the dinner table. You can ask each other questions, and you can also role-play being a potential friend and have your child initiate some questions. Listening to the answer and asking follow-up questions is also extremely important. At camp, we often use a talking stick at campfires to remind kids to take turns talking. If you're having trouble with interrupting and not listening, try creating a family object to use that designates whose turn it is to talk. Kids (and adults) who master initial question asking, listening, and showing interest by asking good follow-up questions, are well liked because they give people the opportunity to share about themselves.

Invitations: For a friendship to begin, one person has to take some kind of action toward the other person. This is called making a friendship bid. This can be one person inviting another to do something, or it can be simply joining in with what a child or group of children is already doing. While it seems like a basic social skill, many kids struggle with shyness, anxiety, or such a great fear of rejection that they don't feel comfortable extending even small invitations to other children. They may need practice at home or with family members or close friends. Explain the concept of invitations with your child and brainstorm simple, low-risk invitations:

- Do you want to play basketball or something else (during recess)?
- Can I sit next to you?
- Do you want to play catch?
- Would you like to come over after school?

Another way to connect is for the child to ask to join a game. It's important for the child to recognize that it's not always appropriate to ask to join, because it won't be well received if it disrupts the flow of play. Sometimes, in the middle of a game, it's difficult to include a new player. So, rather than asking to join right then, the child can assess what others are doing and say, "Hey, can I play the next game?" rather than intruding at the midway point.

Family Meeting Topic: Relationships

Relationships, as all adults have experienced, can be hard, but sometimes our kids don't know that we, too, have struggled with friendships and other relationships. By making the topic of friendship common in your home, you will help open your child's eyes both to the complexities of relationships and an understanding that there are things they can do to make friends and be a good friend.

Having regular conversations about friendship is a great way to dive deeper into social skills coaching. You can create a poster or list of the traits of a good friend by brainstorming as a family the answer to the question, "What makes a good friend?" To think about offering friendship to others, you can discuss questions like:

How can you show your friends you care about them?
What can you do this week to be a good friend?

Sharing your stories and discussing different scenarios that either have come up or may come up with friends is a great way to connect with your kids on the important topic of friendships. Many Disney movies have stories of great friendships: Timon and Pumbaa from *The Lion King*; Lilo and Stitch; Sully, Mike, and Boo from *Monsters, Inc.*; Marlin and Dory from *Finding Nemo*; Carl and Russel from *Up*; and Woody and Buzz from *Toy Story*. Consider watching (or rewatching) one of these classic movies with your kids with the intent to look for and discuss friendship qualities of the characters.

Diving Deeper

While most parents are able to serve as our kids' social skills coaches and are able to help them learn the basic skills they need to make and keep friends, there are some kids whose limitations are caused by underlying issues that simple coaching at home won't be able to address. There are underlying diagnoses, relational issues, and background situations—such as early childhood trauma, adoption, divorce, problems with stepparents or siblings—that can be the underlying cause of your child's challenges making friends. If you suspect that is the case, it is important that in addition to providing your child with gentle social skills coaching at home, you also enlist professional support. Your school psychologist or your child's pediatrician are a great place to get advice about whether or not your child needs professional support with their social challenges.

Many kids learn social skills best in an environment with other kids who are also learning new skills, rather than in one-on-one coaching situations.[14] Therefore, knowing when to seek assistance with your child for their social skills deficits is important. They may benefit from programs that are specifically geared toward teaching social skills in a supportive setting where kids can practice their skills.

Regardless of your child's age, remember that their best practice ground for positive relationships starts with you at home. Siblings, cousins, and close family friends are our kids' first "friends," and by coaching our kids through the ups and downs of those relationships, we are helping them gain important social skills that will benefit them throughout their lives. Seeing ourselves as our kids' friendship coaches reminds us that our most important job as parents is modeling and teaching our kids about how to form positive relationships. It is from parents that our children first learn how to connect with others.

Final Thoughts
The Magic of Family

Summer camp has been a source of much joy and fulfillment for me over the past three decades, and I have been energized to continue my work by the affirmative words of campers, staff, and parents who describe the "magic" I helped create. I am grateful for my role as a camp director, and I can't imagine spending my career doing anything other than connecting with thousands of kids and young adults in water ski boats, on trails, and around campfires. And while I will continue to proudly be a camp "evangelist," as I was once described,[1] I know that I have a final, important secret to share.

Many kids will never get to experience the magic of summer camp. And while summer camp is an excellent place for kids to develop important character traits and skills, kids *do not* need to attend summer camp to grow into kind, optimistic, self-reliant humans. What kids *do* need to grow into thriving adult humans is a loving parent who intentionally focuses on forming and maintaining a positive relationship with them and who creates a positive family culture. When parents create that kind of relationship and home for kids, it is a far more powerful magic than anything we create during two weeks at summer camp.

But the job of being a parent—which entails being responsible for a child's entire development into adulthood—is difficult. People often say that being a parent is their favorite or most important job. But what they don't often admit is that it's often a thankless, underappreciated, boring, and repetitive one. Parenting, especially with young kids, can be unrewarding. As a parent, we rarely get positive feedback from our kids about the job we're doing. In fact, oftentimes when we're doing something right, like assigning chores or limiting screen time, we get negative feedback from our kids. It can be tempting to work longer hours to stay away from a tantruming toddler or a surly teen, or avoid trying to get everyone together for family dinner because it's just not that pleasant. I welcomed the respite of work or a long run to have a break from my kids when they were little.

Being of middle age, having adult children, and caring for aging parents has taught me important lessons in recent years. I've developed a level of insight and wisdom that I didn't have when my kids were younger. It's the kind of wisdom that comes only retrospectively, looking at life in hindsight. Whatever our season of life— young person starting adult life, the busy family years, middle age, or senior citizen, we need to regularly stop and reflect and make sure we are living our life in a way that is authentic to us and bringing us and our loved ones great well-being. I'll share a few final thoughts in the hope that it will benefit those of you who are in what my husband and I refer to as the "red zone," those family years when life can become a swirl of homework, dinner, careers, driving, exhaustion, and chaos.

Put First Things First

Our social connections and positive relationships are what best predict a good life at any age. On our deathbeds, we will not be admiring our houses, décor, clothes, or cars. Nor will we be reflecting on an award we received, a best-selling book we wrote, or an important job we attained. Instead, if we are among the fortunate who make it to old age, on our deathbeds we will be looking into the eyes of the people who surround that bed. Who are those people? I know for me, it is my husband, sister, and a few dear friends. And my adult children. While this may be a morbid thought, it's an important consideration that should help us prioritize our time now. We need to focus our time on nurturing the relationships that are most important to us.

Be assured that those minutes you spend snuggling with your two-year-old reading stories will develop later into pillow talks with your teen after a heart-wrenching breakup. Later still, your adult child will text, call, or visit you to talk about the struggles and victories from their life. That toddler will grow into one of the adults whom you will want to stay closely connected with through life's ordinary and most important moments. Prioritize your connection and relationship with your child for both their well-being and your own.

Focus on the Little Things

As a high-achieving, perfectionist type, I always wanted to do everything right. Whether in my role as a camp director or mom, I wanted to do well. But I have learned that like most parents, I did not always live up to my own expectations. In fact, on some recent mornings, even after reminding myself about the importance of pointing out something positive, I instead found myself nagging my teenage son about how Cup Noodles does not qualify as lunch. But I've learned to forgive myself for my shortcomings, just as I forgive my kids for theirs.

And I've also come to realize that a happy childhood is not made up of a series of perfect moments or years, orchestrated by always-calm, patient, positive parents. Instead, a happy childhood is made up of a bunch of little moments—nightly reading time, daily hugs, family dinners, music, and laughing together over YouTube videos. While vacations and big events are fun, they are not what our kids will remember most from their childhood. It's the little, ordinary parts of our family life that our kids will remember. The feeling of what it was like to be home and to belong.

When we create a home where our kids feel a deep sense of

connection, acceptance, and belonging, we have given our children the best chance possible at a good life. This book, in which I've shared the simple strategies I learned at camp and brought home to my own family, has been a labor of love. My hope is that by implementing some of these ideas and strategies, you, your children, and your family will thrive.

Acknowledgments

None of life's best endeavors are ever accomplished alone, and *Happy Campers* is no exception. I am grateful for the encouragement, guidance, and support from my large and loving tribe and my trusted advisors.

What an honor it has been to watch two generations of campers and staff grow up at Gold Arrow Camp! My sincere thanks for allowing me to be part of your lives, trusting me with your stories, and being part of what I now consider my large, extended family. Thank you also to the year-round camp office team, whose support over the past decade has allowed me to pursue my writing and speaking while still being part of our magical camp. For keeping the fun, friends, and growth going all year long, my sincere gratitude goes to Chelsea "Chelster" Rowe, Amy "Glitter" Bolton, Andy "Soy" Moeschberger, and Brittany "Delta" Grissett.

Every time one of my loyal Sunshine Parenting readers sent me a WOW via a comment, an email, or an in-person compliment, I was encouraged to keep on writing and sharing. Thank you for reading my words and supporting and sharing my message.

The camp industry is such a unique and amazing one. Although technically we are business competitors in the same industry, we work together toward the common purpose of making this world a better place. My gratitude goes to the camp colleagues I've met through the American Camp Association (ACA), and especially those in WAIC (the Western Association of Independent Camps), a tightknit group of camp professionals with whom I have a deep kinship and who have become close friends and mentors over the past decades. From the beginning of my camp career, I have been blessed with mentors willing to share ideas freely and who have helped me become a better camp director. For my early mentors, Ken Baker, Greg Schneider, and Carole Cheley, I am grateful. I am also indebted to each of the camp owners and directors who trusted me with confidential data for my research project, joined me for a podcast interview, or shared quotes and ideas for this book. Because of you, this book includes the story not just of my camp but of numerous accredited, life-changing camp programs throughout the United States. My sincere thanks for their sharing and support go to Sara and Steve Kuljis (Yosemite Sierra Summer Camp and Emerald Cove Day Camp), Jeff Cheley and Brooke Cheley Klebe (Cheley Colorado Camps), Tom and Maria Horner (Catalina Island Camps), Steve Proulx and Susan Reeder (Carmel Valley Tennis Camp), Daniella Garran and Stephen Gray Wallace (Cape Code Sea Camp), Don, Scott, and Sally Whipple (Mountain Camp), Tom Holland (Wilderness Adventures), Steve and Susan Baskin and Kate Hutson (Camp Champions), Kevin Nissen (Friendly Pines), Emma Bundy and Gretchen Collard (Mountain Meadow), Clay Colvig (Colvig Silver Camps), Erica Jameson (Jameson Ranch Camp), Guy and Sarah Fish (Tom Sawyer Day Camp), and Ross and Kristi Turner (Catalina Sea Camp and Astro Camp).

The camp world was a comfortable and safe one for me, but the writing world was not. Filling out an inquiry form on Jennie Nash's website will continue to go down in my life's history as one of my best decisions. Thank you for being more than a fabulous book coach. Your words and guidance gave me the confidence to get this book out into the world.

In my agent Laurie Abkemeier's first email response to my book proposal, she gushed about how much her daughter, an eight-year camper at Camp Oneka, counts down the days to camp. Laurie knew firsthand the value of camp experiences and that camp professionals like me have important lessons to share with parents. Thank you for guiding me and *Happy Campers* through this process with your direct, no-nonsense approach and for answering my rookie questions with patience.

From our first conversation, I knew I wanted to work with Virginia Bhashkar, my editor at Center Street. Your thoughtful suggestions and edits, delivered with a calming southern lilt, as well as your encouragement to share more of my own stories and insights and less of what I've learned elsewhere, helped me find more of my own strong voice.

To my dear friends and earliest readers of *Happy Campers*, Karen "Tahoe" Radke and Alison "Bean" Moeschberger, your feedback and enthusiasm were more valuable than a hundred critics' reviews. Thank you for your honesty, friendship, and for cheering me on through this project and everything else I do.

To my favorite book store owner, Anne Driscoll (Branches Books and Gifts in Oakhurst, California), I love meeting you for cycle class and coffee and talking books and life. Let's sell some books!

To Chuck "Woody" Radke—without your editing help over the past decade, I would never have gotten so many words out into the world in blog posts and articles. Thank you for not only fixing my grammar mistakes but for knowing my voice and keeping me on track with my positive message.

My parents, Bonnie and Peter Kremer, provided an idyllic childhood. I took love, connection, and fun for granted, and I know now how very blessed I was to be born into your family. Without your modeling, encouragement, and support, I would not have the work ethic, education, and courage to pursue my dreams.

To Leslie, our extra-long phone calls talking about crazy teenagers, menopausal moments, and aging parents are a near-daily comfort for me. Thank you for the encouraging words and laughs during these challenging years and for being proud of your little sister.

I knew I'd love being a mom to little kids, because I've always loved snuggling babies, but I didn't realize how fun it would be to parent teens and young adults. To Gretchen, Meredith, Charlotte, John, and Owen: Being your mom has been my greatest joy, and time with each of you is what I look forward to most.

Finally, my love and thanks to my husband Steve ("Monkey"),

the big brain and support behind camp, our family, and everything I've accomplished as an adult. I am so thankful I found you. Every chaotic-minded, idea dreamer-upper needs a steady, clear-headed, focused companion. You are mine. Thank you for joining me on all of my life's best adventures—summer camp, parenting, running, adoption, writing, and marriage. You've made me a happy camper.

RESOURCES

Note: PDF versions of each of these resources are available at
http://happycampersbook.com.

Bringing Camp Home Activities

Secret	One Simple Thing	The Sticky Note Solution	Make It Fun	Around the Campfire	Family Meeting Topic	Diving Deeper
#1 Connection 10	One-on-One Chat 27	A Note of Appreciation 28	Home Movies/ Pictures; 100 Memories; Outdoor Fun 29	Questions for Connection 30	Screen Usage 31	Create a Family Contract 34
#2 Positive Behavior 37	Brainstorm "Skills to Build" List 56	"I noticed…" 58	Finding Family Flow 58	What Went Well Today? 60	Family Values and Rules 61	Evaluate Your Parenting 63
#3 Optimism 65	Four Smiles 78	Inspirational Quote 78	Sing or Dance (or Both) 78	Three Good Things; WOWs 79	Optimism vs. Pessimism; Optimism Quiz 80	No Complaining for 24 Hours 80
#4 Independence 82	Let Them Go 98	"What Are You Going to Do?" 98	"Be the Adult" Game 99	Biggest Independence Challenge 99	Responsibility and Freedom 100	Acknowledge Ambivalence About Kids' Independence 101
#5 Grit 102	Personal Goals 122	"Yet." 123	Gritty Movies and Books 123	Courage Box 125	Family Goals 125	Comfort Zones 127
#6 Responsibility 129	Chore Audit 143	Saturday Sticky 143	Make Chores More Fun 144	Delayed Gratification 145	Sharing Household Duties 146	Raise Future Adults 147
#7 Structure 153	Hot Spots and Routines 165	What's Happening Today 167	Unplugged Family Time 167	How We Relax 168	The "Why" Behind the Rules 169	Family Culture 170
#8 Kindness 173	Stay Calm 188	Acts of Kindness 189	Notes and Gifts 190	Kindness Brainstorm 191	Donating 192	Kindness Challenge 193
#9 Making Friends 195	Model Friendship 210	Compliment on Social Skill 211	Play a Game 212	Social Skill of the Week 212	What Makes a Good Friend? 215	Seek Support 215

Camp Secrets Recap

Camp Secret #1: Connection Comes First

- Creating a close and connected family culture that promotes positive, lifelong relationships is the most important thing we can do for our children.
- Social connections, more than athletic or academic accomplishments, predict happiness and success.
- Forming a positive, nurturing relationship with your child will help ensure your child's future happiness and success in all areas of life.
- Feeling appreciated and accepted for who they are, and knowing that parental love is not conditional on performance, is critical to your child's well-being.
- Our kids need to clearly get the message of belonging at home: "You are valued and needed here."
- To foster closer connections and better relationship skills, parents and kids need to unplug and spend time connecting face-to-face.

Camp Secret #2: Catch Them Doing Something Right

- Punitive, negative parenting methods don't work to produce lasting behavioral changes.
- Kids make better choices and behave better when guided by a caring, trusted adult.
- We cannot talk logically to our kids when either of us is upset or emotions are running high. Let the calm begin with you!
- Kids need connection before correction.
- Identify and focus on strengths.

- Clearly articulate the desired behaviors you want from your child.
- Focus on privileges, not punishments.
- Say yes as often as you can.
- Catch kids doing something right.
- Remember to keep conversations about the issue (specific behavior) not the child.
- Use the 80-20 Rule in conversations: The child speaks 80 percent of the time.
- Find your child's (and your) prime time.

Camp Secret #3: Positive Practices Produce Optimistic Kids

- An optimistic outlook predicts success in the areas of health, happiness, and relationships.
- Optimism leads to more resilience in the face of inevitable setbacks.
- Optimism can be encouraged in a positive culture.
- Compliments are an optimism-producing practice.
- Practice what positive people do and say, and you'll be more positive.
- Take fun seriously.
- Simple daily practices can create more positive thinking, words, and actions.
- Going outside is a positivity practice.

Camp Secret #4: All Kids Can Be More Independent (Even Clingy Homebodies!)

- Kids need to separate from us and become independent.
- Homesickness can be challenging.
- Letting our kids go can be hard.
- Kids need to learn to communicate with strangers.
- Ask "What are you going to do?" to teach problem-solving and decision-making.

Camp Secret #5: Grit Is Grown Outside the Comfort Zone

- Discomfort is necessary for growth.
- Everyone has comfort, growth, and blackout zones.
- What kids say isn't always what they feel.
- Five Ways to Grow Grit
  1. Learn self-reliance and responsibility.
  2. Experience mistakes and failures.
  3. Talk about, set, and reach goals.
  4. Face new challenges.
  5. Feel discomfort.
- Three Things to Get Kids out of Their Comfort Zone
  1. Let them do it alone.
  2. Practice "baby steps."
  3. Remember the "blessing" of the least favorite activity.
- Embrace hard emotions and teach a growth mindset.
- Young adults still need to grow their grit.

Camp Secret #6: Kids Are More Capable Than Parents Think They Are

- Kids learn to do things only when we let them learn how.
- Mistakes and natural consequences are great teachers.
- Kids need to do chores.
- Being able to delay gratification is an important life skill.
- Teach kids to ask, "What else can I do?" so that they are finishers.

Camp Secret #7: Kids Thrive with Structure

- Kids thrive with structure, routines, and clear expectations.
- Evaluate your family's pace of life and if your activities reflect your values.
- Communicate your values to your kids.

Camp Secret #8: Make It Cool to Be Kind

- We need to focus on raising kinder humans.
- Kindness makes us happier, healthier, better people.

- Kids who feel loved, valued, and appreciated don't feel the need to put others down.
- Distinguish between behaviors that are rude, mean, or actual bullying.
- Kindness is undervalued. We need to make it "cool to be kind."
- Make kindness part of your family life.

Camp Secret #9: Coach Kids to Better Friendships

- Social skills do not come naturally to all kids. They need to be taught.
- Children's friendships are vitally important to their well-being.
- You can be your child's "friendship coach."
- Skills needed to make friends:
  Greetings and introductions
  Basic conversation and invitation skills
  How to find friends and be a good friend
  Understanding friendship reciprocity
  Celebrating each other's victories
- Assess your child's social skills strengths and deficits.
- Coaching Techniques:
  Modeling
  Instruction, Discussion, Role-Playing

Family Meetings

Strengthening the family bond can prove to be challenging even for the most dedicated parents. One of the best tools to achieve this goal is holding a Weekly Family Meeting.

—Barton Goldsmith, PhD[1]

At camp, we always start the session with what we call our "First Night Campfire." The counselor has a specific printed agenda for the campfire, which includes all the kids getting to know each other, sharing a goal they have for camp, and talking about the guidelines they want to live by during their two-week stay.

Families can do a similar checking in with each other at a weekly family meeting, which can be part of your dinner conversation one evening per week.

You don't have to get fancy with your agenda. We keep ours on a legal pad, and we take turns being the chair of the meeting. Leading the meeting is good communication practice for kids.

Ideas for items to have on your family meeting agenda:

- What's going on this week?

    Talk about the schedule for the coming week, including any school or work projects, assignments, tests, and upcoming events. I love finding out about the poster board that's needed for a school project early! Are parents or kids going anywhere this week? Any special travel or driving needs? This is a great time to lock down everyone's schedule for the week.

- Goal for the week.

    Each person shares a goal for the week (something they'd like to get done, do better at, etc.).
- A value or social skill.

    If there is a value you are trying to instill in your kids, such as kindness, the weekly meeting could be a great time to check in and have everyone answer the same question. For example, "What kind thing did you do for someone this past week?"
- Problems or issues that need to be resolved.

    This is when you can discuss any challenges family members are having, offer support, and discuss ideas. This can also be a time to talk about any ongoing family conflicts.
- WOWs.

    Take a few minutes to compliment one another on good things you witnessed this past week.
- Questions/comments about anything else any family member wants or needs to talk about.
- End the meeting with a fun game or family event.

    Playing a board game or watching your favorite TV show together could be a reward for having the meeting!

Questions for Connection

1. What is your favorite color?
2. What is your favorite hobby or sport?
3. What is your favorite fruit?
4. What is your favorite TV show?
5. What is your favorite food?
6. What is your favorite article of clothing?
7. What is your favorite game?
8. What is your favorite snack?
9. What is your favorite animal?
10. What is your favorite musical artist or song?
11. What is your favorite book?
12. What is your favorite movie?
13. Who is your best friend?
14. What is your favorite cereal?
15. What is your favorite thing to do outside?
16. What is your favorite drink?
17. What is your favorite holiday?
18. What do you like to eat for breakfast?
19. What do you request for dinner on your birthday?
20. How do you want to change the world?
21. What was your favorite part of today ("high")?
22. What was the most challenging or worst part of your day ("low")?
23. If you had a million dollars to do anything you wanted, what would you do?
24. How would you describe your dream vacation?
25. What qualities make a great friend?
26. What one word best describes you?

27. What would a movie about your life be called?
28. If you had to give everything you own away, who would you give it to and why?
29. What is your favorite word?
30. What is the funniest joke you know?
31. If you could change one thing in the world, what would you change?
32. Where is your favorite place to be?
33. What are you good at?
34. What's the nicest thing anyone has ever said to you?
35. What makes you sad?
36. What are you scared of?
37. What is your favorite memory?
38. If you could be any animal, what animal would you be and why?
39. Who is your hero?
40. If you had a superpower, what would it be?
41. Do you have a lucky number? Why is it lucky to you?
42. Who is someone in history you'd like to meet?
43. What is a dream you've had recently that you remember? What do you think it means?
44. What's something you'd like to learn how to do?
45. What is something that you're thankful for?
46. What is something you want to get better at?
47. What three words would your friends use to describe you?
48. What's the hardest thing you've ever had to do?
49. How would you describe your perfect day?
50. What's the greatest thing about being you?

Undesired Behaviors and Skills to Build

On the left, make a list of your child's undesired behaviors.

On the right, reword that behavior as a skill your child needs to build.

Undesired Behavior	Skill to Build
Forgetting homework.	Managing belongings.

VIA Character Strengths

Wisdom:

Creativity
Curiosity
Judgment
Love of Learning
Perspective

Courage:

Bravery
Honesty
Perseverance
Zest

Humanity:

Kindness
Love
Social Intelligence

Justice:

Fairness
Leadership
Teamwork

Temperance:

Forgiveness
Humility
Prudence
Self-Regulation

Transcendence:

Appreciation of Beauty
    and Excellence
Gratitude
Hope
Humor
Spirituality

Household Task Audit

Use this checklist (or create your own) to assess which tasks you are currently doing for your kids that they can learn to do for themselves.

Task	Who is currently doing?	Who needs to learn/start doing?	By when?
Wash dishes			
Clean counters			
Clean bathroom			
Change sheets/bedding			
Vacuum			
Dust			
Sweep			
Wash windows			
Prepare breakfast			
Pack lunch			
Shop for food			
Make dinner			
Trim fingernails and toenails			
Care for pets			
Laundry			
Iron clothing			
Sew buttons			
Pack for trips			
Wake up in morning			
Pack backpack for school			

Ready for Adulthood Checklist

Hi, kids! Here's a checklist for you to assess what adult skills you already have and what skills you still need to learn. Use this checklist to congratulate yourself as you gain new skills that will help you launch into an independent, successful adult life (without your parents reminding you about *anything*!).

Interpersonal Skills

- ☐ How to talk to strangers
- ☐ Appropriate greeting/body language for meeting new people
- ☐ Making conversation
- ☐ Nonverbal communication skills
- ☐ How to be a good friend
- ☐ How to resolve conflicts
- ☐ Table manners
- ☐ Other manners (holding door open, what to say when you bump into someone, etc.)
- ☐ When and how to write thank-you notes (and how to address an envelope!)
- ☐ Gift-giving skills
- ☐ How to positively represent yourself on social media
- ☐ What not to put in texts or emails (naked photos, mean comments, angry outbursts)
- ☐ How to take care of a child
- ☐ How to take care of an elderly person

Nutrition/Food Planning and Preparation

- ☐ Prepare breakfast foods (eggs, pancakes, bacon, etc.)
- ☐ Prepare and pack a well-balanced lunch
- ☐ Shop for and cook 8–10 well-balanced dinners
- ☐ Select well-balanced meals (that include fruits and vegetables)
- ☐ Make a salad
- ☐ How to read and interpret nutrition labels
- ☐ How to prepare, serve, and store foods to avoid spoilage (including meats and other perishables)
- ☐ How to clean counters and cutting boards
- ☐ How and when to use different appliances: can opener, microwave, oven, stove, blender, Crock-Pot
- ☐ How to start and use a barbeque

Health and Hygiene

- ☐ How to make appointments (doctor, dentist, hair, car servicing, etc.)
- ☐ How to keep yourself clean and pleasant smelling
- ☐ How to care for someone who's ill
- ☐ How to take care of yourself when you're ill (including when to call a doctor)
- ☐ How to trim your fingernails and toenails
- ☐ Perform basic first aid (removing splinters, cleaning and treating small wounds and burns)
- ☐ When and how to seek help for medical or mental health issues

Clothing

- ☐ Do laundry (including stain treatment, washing by hand, reading labels, ironing, folding, and putting away)
- ☐ Sew a button on
- ☐ Pack for a trip
- ☐ How to select appropriate attire depending on the occasion

Time and Life Management

□ Keep a calendar up-to-date with appointments, due dates, etc.

□ Time management system (to-do list, daily priorities, or whatever works)

□ How to set and reach goals

□ Wake self up in the morning

□ The cost and time involved in owning a pet

□ Keep important documents/papers organized (immunizations, health records, academic records, tax documents)

Citizenship

□ How to register to vote

□ How to vote

□ How jury duty (and summons) work

Managing Money

□ Open and use a bank account, including ATM

□ How to balance your bank account

□ How to budget (weekly, monthly, yearly, retirement planning)

□ Saving

□ Giving to charity

□ Keep track of important papers (receipts that need to be turned in, W-2 forms, etc.)

□ Prepare and file tax returns

□ Understand what a mortgage is

□ Understand debt, interest, and penalties (credit cards, car loans, etc.)

□ How to research, purchase, and return items

□ How much to tip people (servers, valets, drivers, hairstylists)

Home/Apartment Skills

□ Do dishes (hand washing and loading/unloading dishwasher)

□ Clean bathroom (toilet, sink, shower, counter, floor, mirror)

□ How to fix a running toilet

☐ How to plunge a toilet

☐ Wash sheets and towels weekly

☐ Vacuum

☐ Dust

☐ Wash windows

☐ When/where to check for a tripped breaker

☐ How to shut off gas

☐ How to shut off water

☐ How to use a fire extinguisher

Navigation and Car Skills

☐ Map reading—how to read a real map, including city streets, public transit, mall directory, etc.

☐ How to use public transportation in your area

☐ How to drive a car

☐ Put gas in the car

☐ Add air to tires

☐ Check oil level manually

☐ Arrange routine car maintenance (oil changes, other service needs)

☐ Drive through a car wash

☐ Wash car yourself

☐ Steps to take if you're in a car accident

☐ Dealing with a ticket

☐ Maintaining car insurance, how it works

☐ How to jump-start a car

☐ How to change a tire

Safety and Judgment

☐ Know when to use the buddy system, safe and unsafe places in your area

☐ Know when you're too tired to drive

☐ Know what to do if your driver has been drinking

☐ Self-control to drive without texting or looking at phone

- [ ] How to respond in different emergency situations
- [ ] When to seek guidance/professional support (suicidal friend, mental health issues, eating disorder)
- [ ] Checklist for when you're leaving your dorm room, apartment, or house (appliances off, lights off, thermostat adjusted, doors and windows locked, alarm turned on)
- [ ] Behave in a sexually responsible way
- [ ] Be aware of dangers of drug and alcohol use

Education and Job Skills

- [ ] Manage assignments and deadlines
- [ ] How to take notes and study for a test
- [ ] How to get extra help (tutoring, etc.)
- [ ] How to write an essay
- [ ] Where to look for a job
- [ ] What to put on a job application
- [ ] How to interview
- [ ] How to proofread
- [ ] How to write a professional email to a professor or potential employer

Self-Knowledge

- [ ] Appropriate confidence/know what qualities you like in yourself
- [ ] Qualities you like in other people/good potential friends (i.e., finding your "tribe")
- [ ] Know how much sleep you need and self-regulate to get enough
- [ ] Know good coping mechanisms for when you're feeling stressed/healthy ways to relax
- [ ] Know what activities recharge you

Social Skills Checklist

Circle 1 if you are NEVER good at using the skill.
Circle 2 if you are HARDLY EVER good at using the skill.
Circle 3 if you are SOMETIMES good at using the skill.
Circle 4 if you are ALMOST ALWAYS good at using the skill.
Circle 5 if you are ALWAYS good at using the skill.

Joining into conversations with other people	1	2	3	4	5
Extending invitations to other people	1	2	3	4	5
Asking questions to get to know others	1	2	3	4	5
Listening well/not interrupting	1	2	3	4	5
Sharing about yourself without bragging	1	2	3	4	5
Being trustworthy (no gossip, good at keeping a secret)	1	2	3	4	5
Including others	1	2	3	4	5
Introducing yourself to new people	1	2	3	4	5
Introducing your friends to each other	1	2	3	4	5
Forming equal friendships (mutual)	1	2	3	4	5
Smiling and other nonverbal social skills	1	2	3	4	5
Staying calm when angry	1	2	3	4	5
Managing conflicts independently	1	2	3	4	5
Being kind	1	2	3	4	5
Celebrating others' victories	1	2	3	4	5

Notes

Introduction

1. The following camps participated in my 2014 thesis research project: Mountain Camp, Cheley Colorado Camps, Yosemite Sierra Summer Camp, Colvig Silver Camp, Mountain Meadow Ranch Camp, Friendly Pines Camp, and Gold Arrow Camp.
2. Audrey Monke, "The Perceived Impact of Camp Experiences on Youth Social Skills and Subjective Well-Being" (MA thesis, California State University, Fresno, 2015), https://digitized.library.fresnostate.edu/digital/collection/thes/id/129326.
3. "Mental Health in America—Youth Data," Mental Health America, http://www.mentalhealthamerica.net/issues/mental-health-america-youth-data.
4. "Facts & Statistics," Anxiety and Depression Association of America, https://adaa.org/about-adaa/press-room/facts-statistics.
5. "Suicide in Children and Teens," American Academy of Child & Adolescent Psychiatry, https://www.aacap.org/aacap/families_and_youth/facts_for_families/FFF-Guide/Teen-Suicide-010.aspx.
6. Anya Kamenetz, "The 'Over-Parenting Crisis' in School and at Home," 89.3 KPCC, July 24, 2018, https://www.scpr.org/news/2018/07/24/84940/the-over-parenting-crisis-in-school-and-at-home/; Juliann Garey, "Teens and Sleep: The Cost of Sleep Deprivation," Child Mind Institute, https://childmind.org/article/happens-teenagers-dont-get-enough-sleep/; Nicole Beurkens, "Screen Time Can Be Dangerous for Kids' Mental & Physical Health," Dr. Nicole Beurkens, November 18, 2017, https://www.drbeurkens.com/dangers-overexposure-electronics-kids-mental-physical-health/.

The "Magic" of Summer Camp

1. Kim Davis, "The Value of Movement Activities for Young Children," Indiana University Bloomington, https://www.iidc.indiana.edu/pages/The-Value-of-Movement-Activities-for-Young-Children.

Camp Secret #1: Connection Comes First

1. "Parenting," Mental Health America, http://www.mentalhealthamerica.net/parenting.
2. Martin E. P. Seligman, *Flourish: A Visionary New Understanding of Happiness and Well-Being*, New York: Free Press, 2011.

3. Liz Mineo, "Good Genes Are Nice, But Joy Is Better," *Harvard Gazette*, Harvard University, April 11, 2017, https://news.harvard.edu/gazette/story/2017/04/over-nearly-80-years-harvard-study-has-been-showing-how-to-live-a-healthy-and-happy-life/.

4. Shawn Achor, *The Happiness Advantage: The Seven Principles of Positive Psychology That Fuel Success and Performance at Work*, Danvers, MA: Crown Publishing Group, 2010.

5. Jean Twenge, *iGen: Why Today's Super-Connected Kids Are Growing Up Less Rebellious, More Tolerant, Less Happy—and Completely Unprepared for Adulthood—and What That Means for the Rest of Us*, New York: Atria Books, 2017.

6. "The Impact of Media Use and Screen Time on Children, Adolescents, and Families," American College of Pediatricians, November 2016, https://www.acpeds.org/the-college-speaks/position-statements/parenting-issues/the-impact-of-media-use-and-screen-time-on-children-adolescents-and-families.

7. Jessica Joëlle Alexander and Iben Sandahl, *The Danish Way of Parenting: What the Happiest People in the World Know About Raising Confident, Capable Kids*, New York: TarcherPerigee / Penguin Random House, 2016; "Ep. 24: The Danish Way of Parenting with Jessica Alexander," *Sunshine Parenting with Audrey Monke* (podcast), http://sunshine-parenting.com/2018/02/16/ep-24-danish-way-parenting-jessica-alexander/.

8. Daniel J. Siegel and Tina Payne Bryson, *The Whole-Brain Child: 12 Revolutionary Strategies to Nurture Your Child's Developing Mind*, New York: Random House, 2011.

9. Table Topics conversation starters: https://www.tabletopics.com/.

10. Sylvie Naar-King and Mariann Suarez, *Motivational Interviewing with Adolescents and Young Adults*, New York: Guilford Publications, 2011.

11. Daniel J. Siegel and Tina Payne Bryson, *No-Drama Discipline: The Whole-Brain Way to Calm the Chaos and Nurture Your Child's Developing Mind*, New York: Bantam Books / Random House, 2014.

Camp Secret #2: Catch Them Doing Something Right

1. Daniel J. Siegel and Tina Payne Bryson, *No-Drama Discipline: The Whole-Brain Way to Calm the Chaos and Nurture Your Child's Developing Mind*, New York: Bantam Books / Random House, 2014.

2. Foster Cline and Jim Fay, *Parenting with Love and Logic*, Colorado Springs, CO: NavPress, 2006.

3. "Signature Strengths," VIA Institute on Character, https://www.viacharacter.org/www/Research/What-the-Research-Says-About-Character-Strengths-Signature-Strengths.

4. Mihaly Csikszentmihalyi, *Flow: The Psychology of Optimal Experience*, New York: Harper and Row, 1990.

5. "Ninja" game: http://www.ninjaslap.com/.

6. "Motivating Learning in Young Children," National Mental Health and Education Center, http://www.naspcenter.org/parents/earlychildmotiv_ho.html.

7. "80-20 Rule of Communication," Brilliant Leader, December 22, 2011, http://brilliantleader.blogspot.com/2011/12/8020-rule-of-communication.html.

8. Chris Thurber, "Stop Yelling, Get the HINT: Seven Simple Ways to Engage Cooperation," Thurber, C. A. (2018).

9. Western Association of Independent Camps (WAIC) Annual Conference Keynote, November 2017.

10. Csikszentmihalyi, *Flow: The Psychology of Optimal Experience*.

11. "Why Do I Need to Know My Character Strengths?" VIA Institute on Character, http://www.viacharacter.org/www/Character-Strengths.

12. The Gordie Center, University of Virginia, http://gordie.studenthealth.virginia.edu/.

Camp Secret #3: Positive Practices Produce Optimistic Kids

1. Paul Tough, *How Children Succeed: Grit, Curiosity, and the Hidden Power of Character*, Boston: Mariner Books / Houghton Mifflin Harcourt, 2013.

2. Steve Baskin, "How to Teach Kids Optimism: The 5 Tips to Raise an Optimistic Child," *Camp Champions Blog*, Camp Champions, December 16, 2013, http://blog.campchampions.com/blog/how-to-teach-kids-optimism.

3. "The Mirror Neuron Revolution: Explaining What Makes Humans Social," *Scientific American*, https://www.scientificamerican.com/article/the-mirror-neuron-revolut/.

4. Sho K. Sugawara et al., "Social Rewards Enhance Offline Improvements in Motor Skill," *PLoS ONE* 7, no. 11 (2012): e48174, https://doi.org/10.1371/journal.pone.0048174.

5. Shawn Achor, *The Happiness Advantage: The Seven Principles of Positive Psychology That Fuel Success and Performance at Work*, Danvers, MA: Crown Publishing Group, 2010.

6. Children and Nature Network, https://www.childrenandnature.org.

Camp Secret #4: All Kids Can Be More Independent (Even Clingy Homebodies!)

1. Peter Blos, *The Adolescent Passage: Developmental Issues*, New York: Intl Universities Press, Inc., 1979.

2. Andrew Averill, "Helicopter Parenting College Students: Study Shows Ill Effects," *Christian Science Monitor*, February 20, 2013.

3. Jessica Lahey, *The Gift of Failure: How the Best Parents Learn to Let Go So Their Children Can Succeed*, New York: HarperCollins, 2015; Julie Lythcott-Haims, *How to Raise an Adult: Break Free of the Overparenting Trap and Prepare Your Kid for Success*, New York: St. Martin's Griffin, 2016.

Camp Secret #5: Grit Is Grown Outside the Comfort Zone

1. "Poisoned Halloween Candy," Snopes, November 2, 2000, https://www.snopes.com/fact-check/halloween-non-poisonings/.

2. Jean M. Twenge and Stacy M. Campbell, "Generational Differences in Psychological Traits and Their Impact on the Workplace," *Journal of Managerial*

Psychology 23, no. 8 (2008): 862–877, https://www.emeraldinsight.com/doi/abs/10.1108/02683940810904367.

3. Amanda MacMillan, "5 Weird Ways Stress Can Actually Be Good for You," Health, August 18, 2014, https://www.health.com/stress/5-weird-ways-stress-can-actually-be-good-for-you.

4. Paul Tough, *How Children Succeed: Grit, Curiosity, and the Hidden Power of Character*, Boston: Mariner Books / Houghton Mifflin Harcourt, 2013.

5. Angela Duckworth, *Grit: The Power of Passion and Perseverance*, New York: Scribner, 2016.

6. Wendy Mogel, *The Blessing of a Skinned Knee: Using Jewish Teachings to Raise Self-Reliant Children*, New York: Penguin Books, 2001.

7. "18 Facts About Goals and Their Achievement," GoalBand, http://www.goalband.co.uk/goal-achievement-facts.html.

8. Daniel Siegel, *The Yes Brain: How to Cultivate Courage, Curiosity, and Resilience in Your Child*, New York: Bantam Books, 2018.

9. Ibid.

Camp Secret #6: Kids Are More Capable Than Parents Think They Are

1. The Center for Parenting Education, "Part 1—The Big Picture: Teaching Responsibility to Your Children," https://centerforparentingeducation.org/library-of-articles/responsibility-and-chores/developing-responsibility-in-your-children.

2. Ibid.

3. James Clear, "40 Years of Stanford Research Found That People with This One Quality Are More Likely to Succeed," James Clear (author's website), http://jamesclear.com/delayed-gratification.

4. https://askdoctorg.com.

5. Foster Cline and Jim Fay, *Parenting with Love and Logic*, Colorado Springs, CO: NavPress, 2006.

6. K. J. Dell'Antonia, *How to Be a Happier Parent: Raising a Family, Having a Life, and Loving (Almost) Every Minute*, New York: Penguin Random House, 2018.

7. Ron Lieber, *The Opposite of Spoiled: Raising Kids Who Are Grounded, Generous, And Smart About Money*, New York: Harper Paperbacks, 2016.

8. Julie Lythcott-Haims, *How to Raise an Adult: Break Free of the Overparenting Trap and Prepare Your Kid for Success*, New York: St. Martin's Griffin, 2016.

9. Lieber, *The Opposite of Spoiled*.

Camp Secret #7: Kids Thrive with Structure

1. Stephen King, *On Writing: A Memoir of the Craft*, New York: Scribner, 2010; #AmWriting with Jess & KJ: https://kjdellantonia.com/amwriting/.

2. Gwen Dewar, "The Authoritative Parenting Style: Warmth, Rationality, and High Standards," Parenting Science, http://www.parentingscience.com/authoritative-parenting-style.html.

3. "Episode 35: Unplugging Your Family with Jill Stribling," *Sunshine Parenting with Audrey Monke* (podcast), http://sunshine-parenting.com/2018/05/04/ep-35/.

4. Laura Markham, *Peaceful Parent, Happy Kids: How to Stop Yelling and Start Connecting*, London: Perigee Book / Penguin, 2012.

5. Anne Fishel, "The Most Important Thing You Can Do with Your Kids? Eat Dinner with Them," *Washington Post*, January 12, 2015, https://www.washing tonpost.com/posteverything/wp/2015/01/12/the-most-important-thing-you -can-do-with-your-kids-eat-dinner-with-them/?utm_term=.f3d48a896b89.

6. "The Healthy Mind Platter," Dr. Dan Siegel (website), http://www.drdansiegel .com/resources/healthy_mind_platter/.

Camp Secret #8: Make It Cool to Be Kind

1. Amy Joyce, "Are You Raising Nice Kids? A Harvard Psychologist Gives 5 Ways to Raise Them to Be Kind," *Washington Post*, July 28, 2014, https://www .washingtonpost.com/news/parenting/wp/2014/07/18/are-you-raising-nice -kids-a-harvard-psychologist-gives-5-ways-to-raise-them-to-be-kind/?utm _term=.41709e1781a1.

2. Stephanie Watson, "Volunteering May Be Good for Body and Mind," *Harvard Health Blog* (blog), Harvard Medical School, June 26, 2013, https://www .health.harvard.edu/blog/volunteering-may-be-good-for-body-and-mind -201306266428.

3. Jun Yan, "Percentage of Americans Taking Antidepressants Climbs," *Psychiatric News*, American Psychiatric Association, September 15, 2017, https://psychnews .psychiatryonline.org/doi/full/10.1176/appi.pn.2017.pp9b2.

4. "Kindness Health Facts," Wellness at Dartmouth, https://www.dartmouth.edu /wellness/emotional/rakhealthfacts.pdf.

5. "4 Reasons Doing Good Is Good for Your Brain," The Best Brain Possible with Debbie Hampton, June 18, 2017, https://www.thebestbrainpossible.com/four -reasons-kindness-is-good-for-your-brain/.

6. Signe Whitson, "Rude vs. Mean vs. Bullying: Defining the Differences," *Life* (blog), *HuffPost*, November 26, 2012, https://www.huffpost.com/entry /bullying_b_2188819?comm_ref=false%5B%2Fembed%5D+&src=sp&utm_hp _ref=fb; "The Author," Trudy Ludwig (author's website), http://www.trudylud wig.com/author.html.

7. Carol McCloud, *Have You Filled a Bucket Today? A Guide to Daily Happiness for Kids*, Northville, MI: Ferne Press, 2006.

8. Random Acts of Kindness, https://www.randomactsofkindness.org.

9. R. J. Palacio, *Wonder*, New York: Random House, 2012.

Camp Secret #9: Coach Kids to Better Friendships

1. R. Crosnoe, "Friendships in Childhood and Adolescence: The Life Course and New Directions," *Social Psychology Quarterly* 63, no. 4 (2000): 377–391, https:// dx.doi.org/10.2307/2695847.

2. E. Oberle, K. Schonert-Reichl, and K. Thomson, "Understanding the Link Between Social and Emotional Well-Being and Peer Relations in Early Adolescence:

Gender-Specific Predictors of Peer Acceptance," *Journal of Youth and Adolescence* 39, no. 11 (2010): 1330–1342, https://doi.org/10.1007/s10964-009-9486-9.

3. Crosnoe, "Friendships in Childhood and Adolescence."

4. A. Sherman, B. de Vries, and J. Lansford, "Friendship in Childhood and Adulthood: Lessons Across the Life Span," *International Journal of Aging and Human Development* 51, no. 1 (2000): 31–51, https://doi.org/10.2190/4QFV-D52D-TPYP-RLM6.

5. M. von Salisch et al., "Prospective Relations Between Adolescents' Social-Emotional Competencies and Their Friendships," *Social Development* 23, no. 4 (2014): 684–701, https://dx.doi.org/10.1111/sode.12064.

6. Thomas H. Ollendick et al., "Sociometric Status and Academic, Behavioral, and Psychological Adjustment: A Five-Year Longitudinal Study," *Journal of Consulting and Clinical Psychology* 60, no. 1 (1992): 80–87, http://psycnet.apa.org/buy/1992-23086-001.

7. N. Park, "The Role of Subjective Well-Being in Positive Youth Development," *Annals of the American Academy of Political and Social Science* 591, no. 1 (2004): 25–39, https://doi.org/10.1177/0002716203260078.

8. Elizabeth Landau, "Rejection, bullying are risk factors among shooters," CNN, https://www.cnn.com/2012/12/18/health/ct-shooting-mental-illness/index.html.

9. Debra J. Pepler, Wendy Craig, and William L. Roberts, "Social Skills Training and Aggression in the Peer Group," Thompson Rivers University, http://faculty.tru.ca/wlroberts/social_skills_training.pdf.

10. Carol S. Dweck, *Mindset*, New York: Random House, 2006.

11. Kyle Benson, "The One Daily Talk That Will Benefit Your Marriage," *The Gottman Relationship Blog* (blog), The Gottman Institute, November 30, 2016, https://www.gottman.com/blog/the-one-daily-talk-that-will-benefit-your-marriage/.

12. Jeanna Bryner, "Close Friends Less Common Today, Study Finds," Live Science, November 4, 2011, https://www.livescience.com/16879-close-friends-decrease-today.html.

13. J. A. Kelly et al., "Teaching Conversational Skills to Retarded Adolescents," *Child Behavior Therapy* 1, no. 1 (1979): 85–97, http://dx.doi.org/10.1300/J473v01n01_09.

14. Ibid.

Final Thoughts: The Magic of Family

1. Sarah Kidwell, "Making Summer Last," *Cate Bulletin*, Fall 2014, https://issuu.com/cateschool/docs/131070_cate-2014bulletin_web_r1.

Resources

1. Barton Goldsmith, "10 Tips for Holding a Family Meeting," *Psychology Today*, September 5, 2012, https://www.psychologytoday.com/blog/emotional-fitness/201209/10-tips-holding-family-meeting.